Standing Up Country
The Canyon Lands of
Utah and Arizona

STANDING UP COUNTRY
THE CANYON LANDS
OF UTAH AND ARIZONA
C. Gregory Crampton

Gibbs M. Smith, Inc.
Peregrine Smith Books
Salt Lake City
1983

This is a Peregrine Smith Book,
published by
Gibbs M. Smith, Inc.
Peregrine Smith Books
P.O. Box 667
Layton, UT 84041

Library of Congress Cataloging in Publication Data
Crampton, C. Gregory (Charles Gregory), 1911-
    Standing up country.

    Reprint. Originally published: New York: A.A. Knopf,
1964.
    Bibliography: p. 181.
    Includes index.
    1. Colorado River Valley (Colo.-Mexico)—Description
and travel. 2. Colorado River Valley (Colo.-Mexico)—
History. 3. Canyons—Utah. 4. Canyons—Arizona.
I. Title.
F788.C79   1983   979.1'3   83-18750
ISBN 0-87905-081-0

TO THE MEMORY OF MY PARENTS

Who taught me not to look but to see

Preface

This book is a biography of a region that stretches from the Book Cliffs in Utah south to White Mesa in the Navajo country of Arizona, and from Bryce Canyon National Park eastward to where Utah, Arizona, New Mexico, and Colorado come together. Sandstone country, elaborately carved by the Colorado River, until about 1922 its history was as romantic as the landscape. Its recorded history—dating from 1776—is as old as the United States, yet the region was little known to the general public until the beginning of the twentieth century. Within the next twenty years, however, men began to see something in it besides economic potential, but as they began to see and appreciate the landscape, their focus was on the part, the segment, and not the whole. One reason for this was that no history of the entire region had ever been written; thus the popular image was a partial view.

Until recently, the public has generally believed that the gorges of the Colorado River begin and end in Grand Canyon. How many of the millions who have visited that national park have ever asked: "Is this the only canyon? Are there others? What is the country upstream like? What men have passed through there?" I have attempted to answer these questions here, and I have also tried to show what those who passed that way felt about their experience.

My own acquaintance with this sculptured land dates back to 1941 when I drove the late Herbert E. Bolton on a trip from Berkeley to Mexican Hat, Utah. Bolton believed that historians could improve the quality of their writing by being acquainted with the places they wrote about. We reached Mexican Hat by way of Cameron, Tuba City, and Kayenta; we spent one night at Kayenta and were entertained with stories of the big sandstone country by Louisa Wade Wetherill. Glimpses of the mouth of the Segi, of Comb Ridge, Agathla, Hoskininni Mesa, Monument Valley, Alhambra Rock, Mexican Hat, and that stark and beautiful stream, the San Juan River, convinced me that I had to see more of this land. With Norman Nevills, Bolton went through the San Juan Canyon and stopped in Glen Canyon to make a reconnaissance of the Crossing of the Fathers before going on to Lee's Ferry. The data were incorporated in Bolton's edition of the Escalante diary published as *Pageant in the Wilderness* (1950).

In 1945, I joined the staff of the Department of History, University of Utah, and thus came within close range of the canyon country. There followed trips to it with family and colleagues. Two years in a row I rafted through Glen Canyon. There were hours spent in the libraries and with people who were familiar with the canyon lands. I found that the region had a history as rich as its matchless landscape, but no one had written about it in any comprehensive way. This was true up to 1956 when the Colorado River Storage Project Act became law. That huge reclamation program was a culmination of forces that had taken shape by 1922 when the Colorado River Compact was signed. The construction of Glen Canyon Dam, one of the basic units of the project, would destroy valuable historical values in the canyon. When the National Park Service began to formulate plans for undertaking salvage studies in the area of the projected reservoir—to be called Lake Powell—I urged that adequate study be made of the historical remains jeopardized by this construction. I was indeed happy to accept responsibility for the supervision of the salvage studies in history, a pleasant and exciting task, undertaken through formal arrangements between the National Park Service and the University of Utah and completed in 1963. This was part of a comprehensive and thorough-going program of salvage which included archeology, ecology, and geology carried out by the University of Utah and the Museum of Northern Arizona.

In large measure, this book is an outgrowth of the historical field work undertaken in the Glen Canyon region. During the course of these salvage studies I traveled through the canyons, through some of them several times, and became intimately familiar with much of the canyon country and generally acquainted with parts of it I had not known before. As these studies progressed, I drew plans for this work, one that would entirely encompass the great sculptured land, a land that is given a historical and geographical unity by the canyons and by the river that made them.

So many individuals and institutions contributed to the making of this book that I feel it is only partly mine. They are acknowledged in the original 1964 edition, published jointly by Alfred A. Knopf and the University of Utah Press, in association with the Amon Carter Museum of Western Art at Fort Worth.

National awareness of the scenic beauty of the entire canyon country, practically non-existent before 1956, greatly accelerated as the dam took shape. Where hundreds had traveled before, thousands now boated through Glen Canyon to see some of the spectacular landscape before it was drowned by the impounded waters of Lake Powell. The governors of Utah and Arizona joined in. In a well-publicized trip in May 1962, they spent three days on the water in what was described as the "Governors' Farewell to Glen Canyon."

In 1963, after the gates had closed and the reservoir had begun to fill, the Sierra Club published a handsome folio volume, *The Place No One Knew, Glen Canyon on the Colorado*, containing seventy-two brilliant photographs in color and an essay on "The Living Canyon" by Eliot Porter. The book is an eloquent admission by one of our strongest conservation organizations that Glen Canyon and much of the red rock country on either side of it were all but unknown to those dedicated to the protection of the earth's natural scenic resources. Thus, when opposition to the dam builders might have been successful, few voices were heard.

Of course the canyon lands were known—and intimately by some—to pre-Columbian and modern Indians, Spanish friars, Mexican traders, American trappers, Mormon scouts and settlers, government explorers, stockmen, miners, surveyors, river runners, archeologists, nature lovers, and dam builders, all of whose activities were detailed in *Standing Up Country*, published in 1964.

Since then public appreciation of the canyon lands has risen rapidly, boosted along by a number of books, among them two more by the Sierra Club: *Navajo Wildlands* (1967) by Stephen C. Jett with photographs by Philip Hyde; and *Slickrock, the Canyon Country of Southeast Utah* (1971) by Edward Abbey with commentary and photographs by Philip Hyde. More boosters include Edward Abbey's *Desert Solitaire* (new ed. 1981); T. H. Watkins and others' *The Grand Colorado*; and Eliot Porter's photographs and epilogue in *Down the Colorado* (1969), a reproduction of John Wesley Powell's diary of the first trip through the canyons in 1869. Articles by the dozen, making full use of color photography, have appeared in diverse magazines.

The formation of Canyonlands National Park (1964) and the Glen Canyon National Recreation Area (1965) has sharpened the public focus, as has the upgrading of Arches and Capitol Reef from national monuments to national parks. It is good to feel that the public is finally beginning to recognize that the whole sweep of country between the Book Cliffs in Utah and White Mesa in Arizona, and between Bryce Canyon and the Four Corners is rich in history and is one of unparalleled grandeur—that it is indeed one of the earth's great places.

A word about spellings of Indian proper names. The Navajo Tribe spells the name with a "j"; I see no reason to use the "h," long advocated by some anthropologists. I have used the spelling "Paiute" except where established usage of place-name nomenclature calls for "Piute," as in Mesa, or Creek. Hoskininni is the Navajo Chief, but it is the Hoskaninni Company.

"Utah 1962" found on some of the picture captions means that the photograph was made before January 1963, when Lake Powell began to form. Portions of the area shown in these pictures have been altered in appearance by the reservoir.

Those national parks which were national monuments in 1964 are still referred to as national monuments in the text and index. Canyonlands National Park and Glen Canyon National Recreation Area, created after the book's 1964 publication, do not appear in the text or index.

My thanks go to Gibbs M. Smith and company, long interested in the history of man and his environment, for their enthusiastic interest in the book and for putting it back into print.

C. Gregory Crampton
St. George, Utah
June, 1983

Contents

1 / Names on the Land 3

2 / Standing Up Country
    Slick-Rock Wilderness 15
    West Side 16
    East Side 24
    The River and the Canyons 34

3 / The Mythical River
    The Crossing of the Fathers 43
    The San Buenaventura 45
    Caravans and Furs 48

4 / Topographical Engineers
    The Road to Cathay 55
    A Land of Wonder 59

5 / The Scientists
    The Man with One Arm 65
    Wheeler and Hayden 71

6 / Canyon Country Primeval
    The Conditions of Life 79
    The Ancient Ones 85

7 / Mormon Frontier

Mission to the Hopis	89
War with the Navajos	92
Lee's Ferry	95

8 / Hole-in-the-Rock

Villagers Under the Rim	101
Hole-in-the-Rock	103

9 / The Rock Jungle

Twisting the Mule	111
The Rock Jungle	114
The Canyons of The People	116

10 / El Dorado

Sierra Azul	120
Pish-la-ki	121
Gold in Glen Canyon	124

11 / Canyon Conquest

Ho! For the San Juan	131
Boom Times in the Canyons	134
Robert B. Stanton's Gold Dredge	138
The Zahns and Spencer	141
The Conquest	144

12 / Symphony in Sandstone

Blank Verse	149
"Holes, Hills and Hollows"	150
Bridges of Stone	153
Crescendo	158

NOTES	169
BIBLIOGRAPHY	181
INDEX	*follows page* 191

Color Plates

FACING PAGE 14

Clear Creek. *Canyon tributary of the Escalante River.*
   Utah 1962.

Prehistoric Town of Betatakin. *Segi Canyon, Navajo National*
   Monument, Arizona.

Grand Gulch. *Utah.*

Delicate Arch. *Arches National Monument, Utah.*

Prehistoric Pictographs. *Horseshoe Canyon, Utah.*

Junction Butte from The Silver Stairs. *The Needles country, Utah.*

Evening Glen Canyon. *Mile 44. Utah. 1962.*

Totem Pole and Yei-Bichei. *Monument Valley, Arizona.*

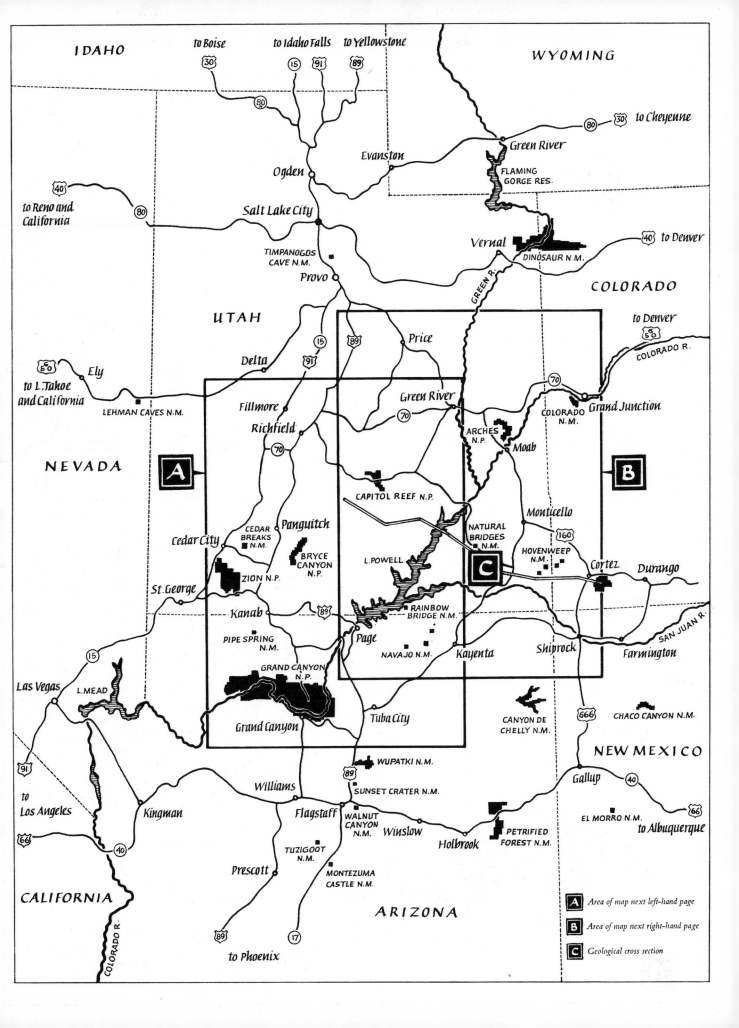

Standing Up Country

THE CANYON LANDS OF UTAH AND ARIZONA

COMPILED BY C. GREGORY CRAMPTON

Denotes a feature flooded by Lake Powell

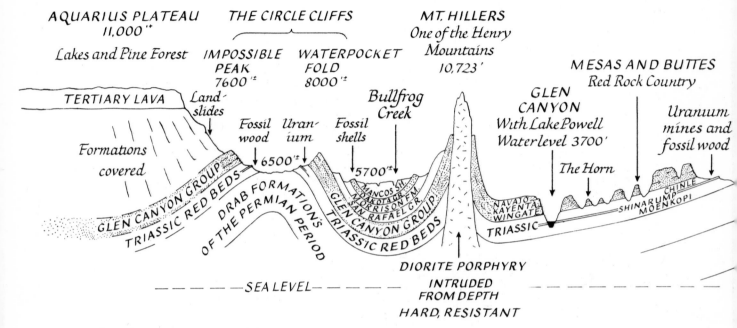

AQUARIUS PLATEAU
11,000'⁺

THE CIRCLE CLIFFS

MT. HILLERS
One of the Henry
Mountains
10,723'

Lakes and Pine Forest

IMPOSSIBLE
PEAK
7600'⁺

WATERPOCKET
FOLD
8000'⁺

MESAS AND BUTTES
Red Rock Country

TERTIARY LAVA

Land-
slides

Fossil
wood

Uran-
ium

Fossil
shells

Bullfrog
Creek

GLEN
CANYON
With Lake Powell
Waterlevel 3700'

Uranum
mines and
fossil wood

Formations
covered

6500'⁺

5700'⁺

The Horn

GLEN CANYON GROUP

TRIASSIC RED BEDS

DRAB FORMATIONS
OF THE PERMIAN PERIOD

GLEN CANYON GROUP

TRIASSIC RED BEDS

MANCOS SH.
DAKOTA SS.
MORRISON FM.
SAN RAFAEL GR.

NAVAJO
KAYENTA
WINGATE

TRIASSIC

SHINARUMP
CHINLE
MOENKOPI

DIORITE PORPHYRY
INTRUDED
FROM DEPTH
HARD, RESISTANT

— — — SEA LEVEL — — —

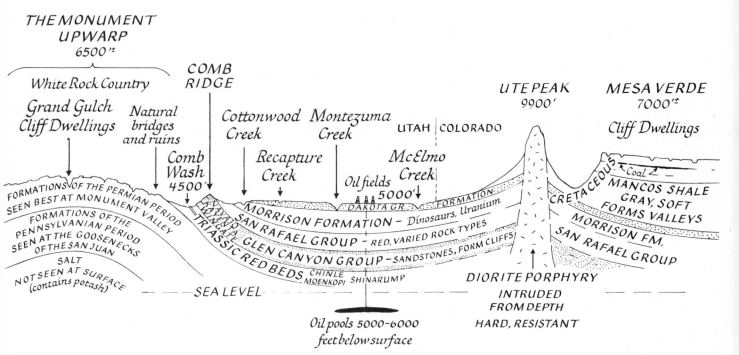

THE MONUMENT
UPWARP
6500'±

COMB
RIDGE

UTE PEAK
9900'

MESA VERDE
7000'±

White Rock Country

Grand Gulch
Cliff Dwellings

Natural
bridges
and ruins

Comb
Wash
4500'

Cottonwood
Creek

Recapture
Creek

Montezuma
Creek

UTAH | COLORADO

McElmo
Creek

Oil fields
5000'

Cliff Dwellings

FORMATIONS OF THE PERMIAN PERIOD
SEEN BEST AT MONUMENT VALLEY

FORMATIONS OF THE
PENNSYLVANIAN PERIOD
SEEN AT THE GOOSENECKS
OF THE SAN JUAN

SALT
NOT SEEN AT SURFACE
(contains potash)

DAKOTA GR.   FORMATION

MORRISON FORMATION – Dinosaurs, Uranium

SAN RAFAEL GROUP – RED, VARIED ROCK TYPES

TRIASSIC RED BEDS   GLEN CANYON GROUP – SANDSTONES, FORM CLIFFS

CHINLE
MOENKOPI SHINARUMP

SEA LEVEL

CRETACEOUS

MANCOS SHALE
GRAY, SOFT
FORMS VALLEYS

Coal

MORRISON FM.

SAN RAFAEL GROUP

DIORITE PORPHYRY

INTRUDED
FROM DEPTH

HARD, RESISTANT

Oil pools 5000-6000
feet below surface

Geological Cross Section of the Standing Up Country

COMPILED BY WILLIAM LEE STOKES

STANDING UP COUNTRY

THE CANYON LANDS OF

UTAH AND ARIZONA

1 / Names on the Land

Hoskininni, the crossing of the fathers, Hole-in-the-Rock, Klondike Bar, Robber's Roost. The names and the land go together. Parts of it may be familiar to you. Some of you will remember the rim at Bryce Canyon or the drive along the Fremont River in Capitol Reef. The Book Cliffs were never out of your sight between Castle Gate, Utah, and Grand Junction, Colorado, a distance of over a hundred and eighty miles. On the Colorado River and at the foot of the La Sal Mountains, the town of Moab seemed to you to be surrounded on all sides by red rocks. Nearby, you found Arches National Monument, Natural Bridges National Monument, and Dead Horse Point. In one place you stood on Utah, Colorado, New Mexico, and Arizona at the Four Corners Monument. You saw the towering buttes in Monument Valley, traveled the Navajo Reservation to Page, Arizona. There you gasped as you drove across the Colorado River on a prize-winning bridge. You parked and walked back to look at Glen Canyon Dam, gasping again as you contemplated this colossal work of man, while you listened over the loudspeaker to the recorded voice of one who filled you in on the details.

These are some of the familiar landmarks. What of the rest of it? Pick up a map and connect these points. Draw a line clockwise connecting Bryce, Capitol Reef, Castle Gate, near Price, the town of Green River, Arches National Monument, the Four

Monolith. *Atop the eastern cliff of White Mesa, Arizona.* [*William C. Miller, Pasadena*]

Corners, the town of Kayenta on the Navajo Reservation, Page, and back to Bryce again. This book is about the country enclosed within the circle. It's big. The airline distance from Green River to Page, Arizona, is about one hundred sixty miles, and from Bryce Canyon to the Four Corners, one hundred eighty miles. It's the heart of the Colorado Plateau, a region encompassing southeastern Utah and northeastern Arizona.

If the map you used was published before 1956, the town of Page won't appear on it, but Lee's Ferry, a few miles downstream, will be there. If your map was dated before 1873, the entire area would be nearly blank. Even on recent maps there is a lot of white space. You don't see many roads. Only one railroad, the Denver & Rio Grande Western, traveling between Salt Lake and Denver, crosses the northern extremity through Price, Green River, and Grand Junction.

Don't let those blank spaces on the map fool you. The twentieth-century dam builders are the Johnnies-come-lately. People have been looking into this country for a long time, loving it, cursing it, gutting it, changing it, enduring it. Not all have found it to be beautiful. Many have come to know parts of it very well; few have come to know all of it. There is good reason for this. Individual parts are easily reached; from the peripheral areas—those connected by the lines on your map—you can travel in toward the center, but it is difficult to go by land clear across the circle or from one segment to another. Throughout the entire area, there is only one road on the diameter and that is Utah State Route

3

95. There are not likely to be many others. This is segmented land, the segments separated by canyons draining into the master stream.

The whole is a grand masterpiece of erosion, the work of the Colorado River. The waters of this great stream and its tributaries have cut out gorges, canyons, defiles in thick beds of sandstone, leaving segmented remnants in the form of plateaus, benches, mesas, buttes, and monuments between the water courses. The closer one gets to the master stream and its major tributaries, the deeper the downward departures become. The canyon predominates. Not one canyon, but a thousand: big, little, long, short, narrow, wide, deep, shallow, all in color, mostly in shades of the red that gives the Colorado its name.

For centuries men have been working their way through this great country, taking its measure, being marked by it, and leaving their mark upon it. Look at the names on the land if you want an index to history. The four states—Utah, Colorado, New Mexico, Arizona—were named by the sons of Spain who also gave us the Colorado River. It has long been forgotten that the original name of the Green River was the San Buenaventura, given by Domínguez and Escalante in 1776. The tributaries of the Colorado and the Green bear witness to Spanish discovery: the San Juan and the San Rafael. Spain named the mountains: Abajo, La Sal, Sierra Azul, and Mesa Verde.

Later arrivals were remembering the Spanish pioneers when they put down Escalante, the Crossing of the Fathers, Spanish Trail, Spanish Bottom, Spanish Valley, as well as Orejas del Oso, Casa Colorada, and Mexican Water.

The government explorers of the United States studied the region. The earliest—Simpson, Gunnison, Frémont, Macomb—were looking for a satisfactory route through a canyon wilderness. After them came Powell, Thompson, Dellenbaugh, Gilbert, Dutton, Wheeler, Hayden, Jackson, who were more interested in science and survey. Recently their attention has been focused on geology and reclamation. All of them, as they worked their way through the intricate, bewildering canyon country, or navigated its rivers or surveyed it for technical purposes, sprinkled names over it as they went.

In their choice of names the government people often remembered each other, refreshingly forgetting contemporary political figures. Happily, there appears to have been no impulse to import from Europe and Asia any of the religious and mythological names that have been fastened upon some of the spectacular formations in Grand Canyon. The explorers kept alive and commemorated the Spanish background, and for variety they used words like Echo Cliffs, Glen Canyon, Music Temple, Waterpocket Fold, and Dirty Devil. They gave us color in the Orange, Pink, White, and Vermilion cliffs. They fixed Indian names on prominent features like the Paunsaugunt, Kaiparowits, and Tavaputs plateaus, and those of the Indian tribes—Navajos, Paiutes, and Moquis—were liberally scattered throughout.

The prehistory of the canyon country, written in terms of hundreds of ruined buildings, pottery and artifacts, petroglyphic and petrographic art, is centuries old, but most of the names used by the illiterate inhabitants have been lost. When the white men saw these ruins and artifacts, some of them were reminded of the great Nahua civilization in Mexico, so it was easy to conclude that here had been the homes of Aztecs. Thus their name is found in the canyon country and also abundantly across the Southwest, as is Montezuma. Even Cortez is brought into the picture—his name was used for the capital of Colorado's southwesternmost Montezuma County.

Indian names of diverse origin like Wahweap, Skutumpah, Ticaboo, Owachomo, Hovenweep, and Ute, appear here and there in the canyon country of southeastern Utah and in the neighboring states of Colorado, New Mexico, and Arizona. Some of them—Mancos, Mike, Nasja, and Hoskininni—commemorate both respected chiefs and troublesome renegades. Even a rank outsider, Hiawatha, sneaks in. The names on the land in the Navajo country are predominantly Indian. Between Page and Four Corners and north of Marsh Pass, place-names like these appear: Segi, Betatakin, Keet Seel, Kayenta, Agathla, Oljeto, Todecheenie, Leche-e, Gishi, Kaibito, Nakai, and Cha.

PREHISTORIC RUINS. *Hovenweep National Monument, Utah.* [*Parker Hamilton, Flagstaff*]

Mormon pioneer explorers, farmers, and stockmen left a great variety of names on the canyon lands: Brigham Plains, Hole-in-the-Rock, Clay Hill Pass, Muley Twist Canyon, and Potato Valley. Cannonville, Henrieville, Adairville, Caineville, Hanksville, and Georgetown document locations of the distinctive Mormon village. There were others: Paria, Orangeville, Castle Dale, Blanding, Monticello, and Bluff.

And here is the roaring West: Buckskin Gulch, Slickhorn Gulch, Klondike Bar, Six Shooter Peaks, Gunsight Pass, Hardscrabble Bottom, Hell Roaring Canyon, and Whiskey Flat. Red Canyon, White Canyon, and Blue Notch are near Dandy Crossing, Cape Horn, Good Hope, and Smith Fork. Placer mining camps in Glen Canyon were Trachyte Bar, Grubstake Bar, California, Burro Bar, and Narrow Gauge Flat. Eagle City, Bromide Basin, Jackson Ridge, and Gold Queen Gulch, were mining locations in the Henry and Abajo mountains.

Outlaws found protection in this canyon country and they are remembered in The Hideout, Robber's Roost, Rustler Canyon, and Horsethief Spring. Hell and Devil often pop up, too, but Angel Cove is found in the canyon of the Dirty Devil River, and elsewhere we find Salvation Knoll, Moroni Slopes, Paradise Valley, Solomon Creek, Moses Rock, Babylon Pasture, Moab, and Canaan.

In a barren landscape, where eroded and fantastic rock formations are so commonly visible, the American imagination going to work gave us these: Goblet of Venus, Turk's Head, Bagpipe Butte, Cleopatra's Chair, Druid Arch, Little Egypt, Sphinx Rock, Setting Hen Rock, Rooster Rock, The Sewing Machine, Baking Skillet Knoll, Coffee Pot Rock, Teapot Rock, Goblin Valley, Joe and His Dog, Hook and Ladder Gulch, Comb Ridge, Jessie's Twist, and Mollie's Nipple. Some of the formations suggested names the map makers won't print. There's less fantasy—and less humor—in Gothic Mesas, Temple Mountain, Castle Valley, Capitol Reef, Cathedral Valley, The Tabernacle, The Hondo, The Goosenecks, Bowknot Bend, Mule Ear, Mexican Hat, Shiprock, and Tapestry Wall.

MONUMENT VALLEY. *Arizona-Utah.* [*Tad Nichols, Tucson*]

And now an alphabetical potpourri: Alhambra Rock, Blue John Spring, Cohabitation Canyon, Dance Hall Rock, Egg Nog, Fiddler Butte, Ghost Rock, Hang Dog, Ibex Point, Jahu Flat, Kigalia Canyon, Lone Parson Hole, Musentuchit, No Man's Mesa, One Toe Ridge, Pinhook, Queen Anne Bottom, Raggy Canyon, Sweet Alice Hills, Tropic, Upheaval Dome, Verdure, Woodenshoe Buttes, Yazzie Mesa, and Zahn's Camp.[1]

These names, and many more like them, envelop the canyon lands in a bright tapestry of many strands, rich in human values. *Only local history, local interest, local color,* some would say. But look again, who are the weavers of this piece?

It was begun by the first explorers, friars of the Franciscan Order who were often lost. This they said was God's punishment for their sins. But it was they who discovered this canyon country. They got through it and left a string of saints' names behind them, and reported their adventures to the Bishop of Durango, to the Viceroy in Mexico, and finally to the King himself in Spain. Those who followed, the Mexicans driving horses from California to Santa Fe and the slavers from New Mexico buying Indians, left few records, as did the beaver hunters from Taos, Santa Fe, and St. Louis.

The canyon country drew its share of the distinguished officers of the Corps of Topographical Engineers of the United States Army, men who before the Civil War mapped and scientifically explored the entire West. No matter that they left a conspicuous white spot on the map of southeastern Utah. After the war John Wesley Powell and his survey filled in the blank before he went to Washington to build a distinguished career in government science.

The Mormons came to expand the Kingdom of God; they planted villages, found timber on the high plateaus, ranged cattle in the rock jungles of the canyon wilderness, and sent missions to the Indians. Some of them found the remote canyons a good place to live according to conscience when pursued by United States marshals bent upon stamping out polygamy. The rustlers, train-robbers, later the moonshiners, and many others for their own reasons also found security in the canyons. While some men fled the law, others came and created it. The miners from nearby Colorado and other more distant states who rushed in for gold set up mining districts governed in part by laws of their own making.

Here was land big enough even for the dreamer after an empire in the Gilded Age. A railroad between Denver and Salt Lake was built skirting the canyon country on the north and tapping the coal fields of the Wasatch and Tavaputs plateaus. Robert Brewster Stanton surveyed and demonstrated the feasibility of building another railroad from Colorado to California down through the canyons of the Colorado River. There was a canyon-country copper boom, then oil, then uranium, and now it is oil again.

The West, the arid West of open spaces, fills with people and people need water. Seven states divide the Colorado at Lee's Ferry; reclamation is under way. With Hoover, the first dam up, the reclamationists boast that the Colorado, often a menace, is now becoming a national resource. As for being a "resource," one way or another it has been that ever since prehistoric man roamed the canyons, building his houses against the cliffs, growing a few ears of corn in the wet bed of a wash. The dam builders have made the first really radical changes in the appearance of the canyon country since prehistoric times. The dam, the reservoir, the towns, the highways, the power lines, have brought civilization to the wilderness in a hurry.

What has man thought of this wilderness? Of the canyons of the Colorado system, the Grand Canyon in Arizona in the popular mind has long outshone the rest. Difficult as it is to imagine and to appreciate, Grand is, nonetheless, more manageable than the canyon country upstream from it in Utah. From one rim of Grand Canyon, you can easily see the opposite rim eight to ten miles away. Standing on the edge of the canyon country in Utah, you would be one hundred miles away from the opposite side—a hundred miles of canyons,

THE SAN JUAN AND THE COLORADO. *The San Juan River (lower left) joins the Colorado River in Glen Canyon. Utah 1962.* [*A. E. Turner, Bureau of Reclamation*]

GUNSIGHT PASS. *Between Gunsight Canyon and Padre Canyon, Utah.* [*A. E. Turner, Bureau of Reclamation*]

DRUID ARCH. *In a wilderness of bare rock, The Needles country, Utah.* [*Josef Muench, Santa Barbara*]

mesas, buttes, reefs, and only here and there a fairly level space. It's easier to get around in Utah's canyon country than it is in Grand, but who could get hold of an area so vast and reduce it to canvas, to paper, or to film? There is too much of it. The painters, the writers, and the photographers could only handle segments and these were usually on the periphery of the canyon country. But they helped to popularize these segments, some of which were brought into the National Parks system. Now in this mobile age, throngs from all over the world visit Bryce Canyon National Park, Capitol Reef National Monument, Arches National Monument, Natural Bridges National Monument, and Rainbow Bridge National Monument; yet they seldom see the whole of which these are a part, the incomparable wilderness of eroded sandstone.

It has generally been thus in the canyon country of southeastern Utah and its neighboring states. In the slower-moving saddle-horse days, when most of the names were being put on the map, men got very well acquainted with a specific area rather than with the general region. The eroded formations, the canyons, the buttes, mesas, and monuments done on so enormous a scale could not be ignored; nor were they. The profusion of local names tells us that; a good many of them are, in themselves, vignettes, a report of things seen and experienced, the titles to pictures.

As a result of the focus upon the segment, the minute, and the narrow, no popular image of the whole Utah-Arizona canyon country exists. When the region is mentioned, places like Capitol Reef, Rainbow Bridge, and Dead Horse Point leap to mind, not the elaborate and intricate and beautiful country over a hundred miles square.

WAGON AND OIL DRILLING EQUIPMENT. *On the San Juan River at Slickhorn Gulch, Utah.*
[*C. Gregory Crampton*]

SLICK-ROCK TRAIL IN ANASAZI CANYON. *Navajo Mountain, Utah.*
[*Christy G. Turner II, Museum of Northern Arizona*]

CUMMINGS MESA. *A classic tabular landscape, Utah.* [*Philip M. Hobler, Museum of Northern Arizona*]

CLEAR CREEK. *Canyon tributary of the Escalante River. Utah 1962.* [*Nelson Wadsworth, Salt Lake City*]→

PREHISTORIC TOWN OF BETATAKIN. *Segi Canyon, Navajo National Monument, Arizona.*
[*William C. Miller, Pasadena*]

GRAND GULCH. *Utah.* [*Norman Van Pelt*]——————→

DELICATE ARCH. *Arches National Monument, Utah.* [*Joseph L. Dudziak, Richmond, California*]

PREHISTORIC PICTOGRAPHS. *Horseshoe Canyon, Utah.* [*Hildegard Hamilton, Flagstaff*]

JUNCTION BUTTE FROM THE SILVER STAIRS. *The Needles country, Utah.* [*Parker Hamilton, Flagstaff*]

EVENING GLEN CANYON. *Mile 44. Utah 1962.* [*C. Gregory Crampton*]

TOTEM POLE AND YEI-BICHEI. *Monument Valley, Arizona.* [*Joseph L. Dudziak, Richmond, California*]

2/Standing Up Country

Slick-Rock Wilderness

IF YOU FOLLOW THE MAIN-TRAVELED ROADS through southeastern Utah and northeastern Arizona, you will be deceived. You will see places of great interest, but from the highways you will miss much of the wild and rugged scenery. You will scarcely become aware of the immensity of the canyon country or even that canyons and cliffs are its dominant topographical features. Much of the country looks flat and uninteresting, since the highways for the most part head the canyons, staying in the open reaches whenever possible. Dramatic landscapes like Capitol Reef, the Moab Valley, Comb Ridge, Monument Valley, Echo Cliffs, and Bryce Canyon are easily reached, but as you speed along on hard surface you may be missing far more than you see.

On your map you have circled the heart of the great Colorado Plateau. The name is right, for this is rim rock country; its general surface is flat—a tableland. Approach from any direction and you will soon find yourself on a rim looking *down into* rather than *up at*. You can see for great distances. The skyline from nearly any vantage point is horizontal or nearly so. It may appear as a long, continuous line extending for many miles until it is lost in the distant haze. If you were to move toward the center you would observe, however, that the plateau in many places consists of a giant staircase descending from the edges toward the middle. There are several levels, each a platform or terrace of irregular width, sometimes extending for many miles. The platforms commonly rise above one another in precipitous steps, in some places hundreds and even thousands of feet in height. The façade of cliffs, separating the terrace levels, appear as grand majestic walls, murals, pilasters, and columns or as skirts and buttresses forming one of the most dramatic features in a dramatic landscape.

Water has thoroughly dissected the stupendous staircase, leaving separated segments of the terraces in the form of mesas, some of them many square miles in extent. Smaller remnants are detached and sculptured buttes, monuments, pinnacles, minarets, and standing rocks, in infinite variety. Very often the eroded remnants between water courses may be rounded forms covering sometimes square miles of surface. They may appear as knobs or as elongated hummocks in the close formation called "fins." They may be lumpy, bumpy forms like the grotesque figures in Goblin Valley. They may rise in beautifully proportioned spires, usually in clusters, best seen in The Needles and the Land of Standing Rocks.

The water courses are frequently broad washes but more often they are steep-walled, narrow canyons, sunken valleys whose beds are far below the level of the general surface. The Green and Colorado rivers flow through canyons; Cataract Canyon is over two thousand feet deep. Tributaries with few exceptions, enter the master stream at grade level and this is also true of their branches. The result is a country where the canyon, its "banks" surmounted by terraces, mesas, and buttes, or bare and knobby sandstone, is the dominant surface feature.

The intricacy of the canyons increases as you approach the rivers which drain the entire region, though this is not apparent from a distance. The angular character of the general topography tends to run together in horizontal lines. There are few of the broad, graceful, rounded contours of mountains and valleys commonly seen in humid climates. A mountain pass in the canyon country may be called a "gate," suggesting sharp rather than smooth lines. Curves are replaced by angles and from a distance the canyons, as H. E. Gregory says, "are lost in the general levelness." The intricately sculptured country looks like a tableland, but unless you know your way don't try to cross it. Many have discovered as they tried to do so that the table can quickly become a wall. Move toward the center of the canyon country from any direction. Soon you may find yourself standing on top of a wall, that is, the edge of a mesa or the rim of a canyon which is dropping away below you a hundred feet, a thousand feet or more. You can go no further; you have been "rimrocked" to use a good canyon-country verb. You are on the edge of the world and you probably have spread out before you a natural spectacle of surpassing magnificence. As someone expressed it years ago: "There is as much country standing up as there is laying down."[1]

Not all of the canyon country looks flat. Spectacular deviations break the horizontal plane in a number of places. Here and there the surface has been broadly warped, buckled, or folded to produce either gentle undulations in the surface or sharply plunging slopes, all of which have complicated the drainage pattern and influenced the formation of canyons.

The most dramatic departures are the huge laccolithic domes made of volcanic masses of rock that pushed up overlying sedimentary strata to great heights but never broke through them. The resultant steep surfaces eroded to form mountains of traditional appearance standing singly or in groups on top of the level platform of the plateau. Appropriately named the "island mountains," they seem alone and out of place.

Wherever you stand in the canyon country appearances are deceptive: at low elevations you are shut in by rock walls; at the upper levels you find that distant views, except for the laccolithic mountains, tend to flatten out. Only birds see the true face of the earth. The best introduction to the canyon country is to fly over it. A world unsuspected by the surface traveler comes into view: a marvelous, intricately carved and sculptured wilderness done in sandstone.

From the air you see the vertical dimension. Canyons cut deep in the bare slick rock seem to be everywhere below. The deep, narrow ones carved by the rivers, meander gracefully in sweeping curves, undercutting the walls and forming niches, alcoves, caves, grottos, glens, and amphitheaters. Occasionally a stream will break through a loop in an entrenched meander and leave a bridge or an arch of rock. A window may appear as a thinning wall of stone erodes from either side.

The panorama is done in color. There is scant vegetation except at the higher levels. Instead the bare slick rock itself gives color to the landscape—red, orange, pink, chocolate, brown, purple, yellow, white, blue, green, and gray. Shades of red predominate. It colors the land, it reflects on and tints the clouds above, and it stains the water of the river that drains the land. The Spaniards had just the right name for the stream. They called it Colorado.

West Side

ON THE WEST THE CANYON COUNTRY is sharply bounded by the lofty escarpments of the High Plateaus, which, from Bryce Canyon on the south, extend 175 miles to the Price River on the north. This great line of plateaus, ranging from eight thousand to over eleven thousand feet in altitude, forms the divide between the Great Basin and the Colorado River. Bryce Canyon National Park occupies a segment of the rim of the Paunsaugunt Plateau, a huge uplifted block running up over nine thousand feet above the sea.

The view from Bryce in essential ways is typical of the canyon country. You probably have reached the park by automobile, driving over the flat surface of the plateau. Without much warning, you suddenly arrive at the sharp angular edge of the rim and look down into a forest of pinnacles, min-

FREMONT RIVER. *At Hanksville, Utah.* [*C. Gregory Crampton*]

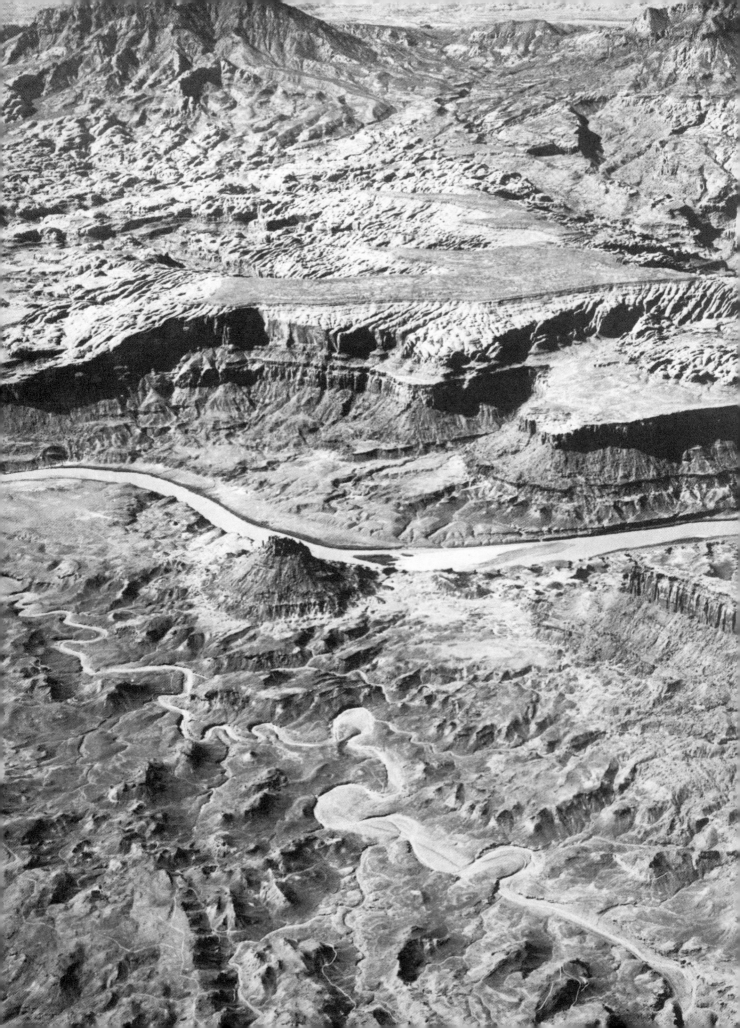

arets, and turrets—colorful rock laid bare by erosion. Not so easily seen from the rim at Bryce are the deep canyons. The short Bryce Creek, that heads in the maze of eroded pinnacles just below the rim, and is called Bryce Canyon, is not characteristic of the canyons found along the main water courses. But the parent stream, the Paria River, is.

The Paria quickly gathers its headwaters which then flow through a canyon cut down through the White Cliffs. Another has been cut through the Vermilion Cliffs. Not satisfied, the river has broken through the jagged Cockscomb, a local name for the East Kaibab Monocline. Within a short distance it enters a deep gorge in the Paria Plateau and finally reaches the Colorado just below Lee's Ferry. Buckskin Gulch, its main branch, runs an even more spectacular course before joining the main stream deep in a canyon.

Arbitrarily we use the Paria to mark the southwestern boundary of the canyon country. Beyond it the Arizona Strip, between the southern rims of Utah's High Plateaus and the Grand Canyon, stretches away to the west. This is more open country, there are fewer canyons, and man has been able to get about with greater ease. North of the Paria, dramatic landscapes and rugged canyon scenery appear on every side. North of Bryce Canyon the 11,000-foot-high Aquarius Plateau dominates the skyline. Aquarius is seldom heard; instead, local names are used for its main segments—Table Cliff Plateau, Escalante Mountain, and Boulder Mountain. From its lava-capped rim half the canyon country is visible. To Captain Dutton of the Powell Survey the view was "a sublime panorama. . . . It is a maze of cliffs and terraces lined off with stratification, of rambling buttes, red and white domes, rock platforms gashed with profound cañons, burning plains barren even of sage—all glowing with bright colors and flooded with sunlight."[2]

Off to the south are the long Straight Cliffs of the Kaiparowits Plateau, called locally Fifty-Mile Mountain because it extends from the base of the Table Cliff Plateau over fifty miles to the Colorado

THE LITTLE ROCKIES. *Mount Ellsworth and Mount Holmes and Glen Canyon. Utah 1962. [A. E. Turner, Bureau of Reclamation]*

River. North of Kaiparowits and paralleling it is the remarkably intricate meandering canyon of the Escalante River. Indeed the entire watershed of the lower basin, almost denuded of soil, is one of the most elaborately sculptured parts of the canyon country. There at the very foot of Boulder Mountain is the high, huge elliptical depression about twenty-five miles long, ringed around with the inward-facing escarpments of Circle Cliffs. Water drains out to the lower country through the canyons, the heads of which appear as wide notches in the circle.

Bounding the Circle Cliffs and Boulder Mountain on the east is Waterpocket Fold, a high monoclinal ridge running continuously for eighty miles from Capitol Reef National Monument, its northern extension, to the Colorado River. Heading on the timbered slopes of Boulder Mountain, Thousand Lake Mountain, and adjoining plateaus, the Fremont River has cut a deep canyon through the sharp western face of Capitol Reef just as lesser streams have done elsewhere. The eastern slope of the Fold, a hogback boldly visible throughout its length, everywhere deeply notched by erosion, is a spectacle of great beauty.

Beyond Capitol Reef the Fremont River, kept in its course by sharp-rimmed mesas, flows through brightly colored country. Near Hanksville it comes out briefly into the open, picks up the Muddy River and then, taking as its name the Dirty Devil, it turns south, drops into a sinuous canyon, which it follows until it reaches the Colorado.

In the area bounded by the Waterpocket Fold, the Fremont-Dirty Devil River, and the Colorado, rise the splendid group of five laccolithic peaks called the Henry Mountains. Three of them—Mt. Ellen, Mt. Pennell, and Mt. Hillers—stand close together, forming a mass twenty miles long and ranging up to over 11,000 feet in height. The Henry Mountains, together with their counterparts on the east side—La Sal Mountains, Abajo Mountains, and Navajo Mountain—are the highest isolated elevations in the canyon country. They look like conventional mountains and, as all of them may be seen from great distances, they long have been landmarks in a country where the general horizon otherwise appears to be flat. The two southern peaks—Mt. Holmes and Mt. Ellsworth—are isolated from the main mass of the Henrys and from each other. Called locally the "Little Rockies" they are lower in elevation than the main group but they still rise about 4,000 feet over the Colorado River, which winds about in Glen Canyon a short distance away.

Beyond Thousand Lake Mountain the High Plateaus continue northward over ninety miles to Price River. Stand on the high eastern rim of the Wasatch Plateau. Half a dozen streams fall from it to water Castle Valley, a farming belt at its base sixty miles long. The green areas of irrigated land stand out sharply in contrast to the gray soil and the yellowish rock of adjacent mesas. But look beyond. There, stretching for seventy miles north and south, is the remarkable San Rafael Swell. As the name suggests, it is an upwarp or swell in the earth's surface, in the form of an elongated, kidney-shaped dome about thirty miles wide. Approach the Swell from any direction and you will soon encounter the hogback ridges, or reefs, which completely encircle it. The outer surface of these ridges conforms to the dip or slope of the Swell; this is steep on the eastern and southern slopes where it is called the San Rafael Reef. The inner face of the reef consists of cliffs ranging from hundreds up to 2,000 feet in height. The encircling reef is an effective barrier; only a few natural breaks occur in it sufficiently wide to accommodate vehicles or even horses.

Within the encircling reefs, and rising gradually above them, is a gently domed open area dotted with low mesas, knobs, and rocks about ten miles wide and forty miles long, known as Sinbad. This recalls the *Arabian Nights* story of the second voyage of the traveler from Baghdad who was flown by the Roc to a "valley exceeding great and wide and deep, and bounded by vast mountains that spired high in the air." At either end Sinbad is cut into mesas and steep canyons where it drains off to the San Rafael and Muddy rivers. After gathering together the creeks in Castle Valley, these two streams flow through spectacular canyons directly across the Swell. The San Rafael River breaks across the steepest part of the San Rafael Reef and then flows through relatively open country to the Green River.

PLUNGING SLOPES OF SAN RAFAEL REEF. *San Rafael Swell. San Rafael River in foreground. Utah.* [*Courtesy American Museum of Natural History*]

The Muddy emerges and, after passing through a barren but colorful landscape somewhat typified by the grotesque Goblin Valley, it joins the Fremont to form the Dirty Devil near Hanksville. Between the southern slopes of the Swell and Thousand Lake Mountain a few intermittent streams, emptying into the Fremont River, drain a wild and rugged land including Cathedral Valley and its stately formations.

Between the San Rafael Swell and the Dirty Devil on one side and the Green and the Colorado rivers on the other side, there lies the Green River, or the San Rafael, Desert. Roughly in the shape of a huge parallelogram tilted toward the north, its surface is one of low relief, low mesas, low rounded knobs of stone, and also occasional areas of dune sand, a rather rare sight, oddly enough, in the sandstone country. Other unusual sights are extensive grass-covered areas and the soil-filled valley of the San Rafael.

The northern half of the parallelogram may have little to command your attention, but the southern half is of striking beauty. Let us use the name Land's End Plateau, a name once employed but seldom heard nowadays. There, beyond Robber's Roost a few miles, the plateau narrows and then suddenly on three sides it literally breaks off and in a series of irregular and magnificent steps drops over three thousand feet into the great gorges of the Colorado and into the canyon of the Dirty Devil. These, the Red Rim, or Orange Cliffs, the Black Rim or Ledge, and the White Rim, support terraces of varying widths, frequently surmounted by spectacular remnants, and elaborately dissected by deep, straight-walled canyons. That portion of the plateau between Happy Canyon, draining into the Dirty Devil, and Millard Canyon, draining into the Green River, is indeed one of the most thoroughly eroded areas in the entire canyon country. The Maze and the Land of Standing Rocks are parts of it. The panorama from Land's End—and from other neighboring points, at the extremity of the plateau—of the rugged terrain immediately below and of its equally rugged counterpart on the opposite side of the Colorado is one of exceptional grandeur.

Bounding the canyon country on the north is

GROVE K. GILBERT. *Geologist for the Powell Survey.* [*U. S. Geological Survey*]

ROAD IN SINBAD. *San Rafael Swell. Henry Mountains in background.* [*Parker Hamilton, Flagstaff*]

the high, southern escarpment of the Tavaputs, or Roan Plateau. This, said Powell, is "one of the most wonderful façades of the world."[3] It is actually a sinuous zone of cliffs up to fifteen miles wide called at its lower elevation, the Book Cliffs, and at its higher level the Roan Cliffs. The single name Book Cliffs is commonly applied to the entire structure. It runs on an east-west axis from Castle Gate in Utah to Grand Mesa in Colorado. An airline distance of 150 miles the cliffs wind about like an inverted S for 215 miles. From a crest that ranges up to ten thousand feet above sea level, the descent on the north to the Uinta Basin is gradual. On the south the descent is rapid through a weird, barren labyrinth of short, steep canyons, lined with cliffs, mesas, sharp ridges, and isolated rocks, to the broad open valleys that are to be found at the base two to four thousand feet below.

East Side

FROM THE TOP OF THE BOOK CLIFFS at the southern extension of the Uintah and Ouray Indian Reservation you might draw a line toward the south passing through Arches National Monument, going between the La Sal and Abajo mountains, to the area where Utah, Colorado, New Mexico, and Arizona meet. From there continue the line to Kayenta in northeastern Arizona. This line can be considered the eastern boundary of the canyon country, though it is an arbitrary choice. All of the bounds used here are in fact, arbitrary. The western boundary, marked by the line of High Plateaus is the most definite. The Uinta Basin and much of western Colorado from Grand Junction to Mesa Verde, northwestern New Mexico, and part of northeastern Arizona, have the landscape features so commonly found within our circle, but we intend to embrace only the compact heart of the Colorado Plateau where the canyon and the mesa and the slick rock are the predominant features in the landscape.

But even where these dramatic formations are predominant, there is some open country; soft soil in some depth occurs and streams run in open

REMNANTS OF EROSION. *The view from The Spur, Utah.* [*Parker Hamilton, Flagstaff*]

courses. One such area is the continuous open low-land between Price and Grand Junction at the base of the Book Cliffs. This is the route of both a transcontinental highway and the Denver & Rio Grande Western Railroad between Denver and Salt Lake. This is the zone of access to the northern part of the canyon country, both west of and east of the Green River.

South of the Book Cliffs between the Green River and Arches National Monument there is a huge wedge of country between the Green and the Colorado structurally similar to the Green River Desert-Land's End Plateau, and also tilting toward the north. Travel south over the plateau. The topography works up to a climax: On either side the canyons of the two rivers get deeper as the streams flow toward each other; the land on top narrows as it grows higher and then it pinches out altogether, as the two rivers, far below several miles to the south and out of sight, meet quietly.

Gray's Pasture, Grand View Point, and the detached Junction Butte, the highest point of the wedge at its southern extremity, look out over an eroded landscape of incomparable beauty. Distant views are matched by those close at hand. Walk out on the top of Grand View Point. It drops away over a thousand feet to the broad White Rim. See how canyons have been cut in it by tributaries to the rivers. Look over there at the one that opens into the Colorado. Those weird and fantastic white-capped pillars of sandstone give it its name— Standing Rock Basin, also known as Monument Canyon.

Adjacent to Gray's Pasture, Upheaval Dome is a multi-colored eroded conical dome surrounded by a ring-like syncline about two miles in diameter. Erosion has broken through the northwestern section of the ring and this forms the head of Upheaval Canyon which empties out in the Green River five miles away. Once called Christmas Canyon Dome, it is regarded by geologists as "the most peculiar structural feature that has yet been found in southeastern Utah."[4]

The view from the Utah State Park at Dead Horse Point matches that of the high places overlooking the confluence of the two rivers. This point is on the high rim of the plateau overlooking the Colorado River more than 1,800 feet below. Look off to the southwest past Grand View Point. You can see in profile the eroded valley of the Colorado for many miles. Nowhere can the horizontal-vertical lines of the canyon country be seen with greater ease. Toward the east stand the lofty La Sal Mountains, one of the laccolithic groups.

Arches National Monument is well named. Over eighty stone arches and large windows and openings in huge slabs of vertical rock have been counted in the monument. Some of these are so prominently displayed that from the highway north of Moab they may be seen although nine miles away. But there is far more to the monument than the arches. Cliffs, spires, alcoves, balanced rocks, fins, and other formations common to the canyon country abound, but there is also a difference. Features are spaced widely apart, so you can catch your breath between them. In the country to the west and south the concentration of scenery can be overwhelming.

Southeast from Arches National Monument the Colorado runs through a canyon at the base of the La Sal Mountains. Where it opens out in the Richardson Amphitheater and Castle Valley there are the exquisitely eroded Fisher Towers together with buttes, mesas, and other characteristic canyon-country formations. Downstream in a red-walled valley adjacent to the Colorado River is the little town of Moab.

South from Moab to the foot of the Abajo Mountains and west to the Colorado River is another wedge-shaped dramatic sandstone landscape. Largely drained by streams that head on the slopes of the Abajo Mountains and Elk Ridge, flowing northwest to the Colorado, the crescendo of intricate erosion is reached among the branches of Indian Creek, Salt Creek, and Butler Wash. The best way for you to see this unbelievable landscape is to take a low-altitude flight over it. The upper-middle reaches of these water courses are scarcely distinguishable as such: an incredible maze of canyons, and canyon compounded upon canyons, covers many square miles. Here is found the greatest profusion of arches in the entire canyon country outside Arches National Monument.

UPHEAVAL DOME. *This "most peculiar" formation is out of character with the mesas bordering Green River in the background. Utah.* [M. *Woodbridge Williams, National Park Service*]

Below this labyrinth a few miles, turn westward toward the Colorado, where the country opens up a bit, and you are flying over The Needles. Rows and clusters of rounded spires stand above small grassy parks and parallel graben valleys not far from the head of Cataract Canyon. Across the river, only a few airline miles away, is the Land of Standing Rocks.

The Abajo Mountains, called locally the Blues, or the Blue Mountains, is a compact group of laccolithic origin which dominates the skyline for many miles on every side. Half a dozen peaks range upwards of eleven thousand feet and from four to five thousand feet above the base of the group. One of the "island mountains," like the La Sal group to the north, and Ute Mountain and the Carrizo visible to the southeast in Colorado and Arizona, respectively, the Abajos with their conventional green slopes stand high above and in sharp contrast to the great sandstone canyon country west of them.

Immediately to the west of the Abajos is the deeply dissected Elk Ridge, or Bear's Ears Plateau as it was first called. Twenty miles long on a north-south axis, this upland towers above and broods over the profound Gypsum Canyon and Dark Canyon, which have cut deeply into its steep western face. Indeed, Dark Canyon is the greatest of the tributary canyons of the entire region. From its head to its mouth near the foot of Cataract Canyon, an airline distance of about twenty-five miles, there is a fall of five thousand feet. The heads of Dark Canyon have almost cut Elk Ridge in two. A very narrow place known as "The Notch" separates the "North Elks" from the "South Elks."

Drive up the dirt road to the Bear's Ears for one of the grandest of panoramic views in the canyon country. The Ears are two huge buttes over four hundred feet high standing on the south rim of Elk Ridge, itself over eight thousand feet in elevation. From a distance the buttes faintly resemble the ears of a bear. They are one of the prominent landmarks in the Four Corners country.

Look off to the east and let your eye swing around

CHESLER PARK. *The Needles country, Utah.* [*M. Woodbridge Williams, National Park Service*]

IN THE COURT HOUSE TOWERS SECTION. *Arches National Monument, Utah.* [*Philip W. Tompkins Photograph, California Academy of Sciences*]

the horizon to south-southeast. You have just seen parts of four states. The San Juan Mountains, Mesa Verde, Ute Mountain in Colorado, and the Carrizo Mountains in northeastern Arizona form the sky-line. Spread out in the foreground, and somewhat marginal to our area, is what appears to be a flat lowland—the Sage Plain. Actually it is gashed by numerous northern canyon tributaries of the San Juan. Here are McElmo Creek and Montezuma Canyon, where prehistoric peoples lived and built substantial dwellings, best seen in the structures preserved in Hovenweep National Monument on both sides of the Utah-Colorado line. On the opposite side of the river, and also marginal, a broad country of scattered mesas, sand dunes, and shallow canyons at the base of the Carrizos falls away toward the San Juan or into Chinle Valley, which empties into the San Juan at Comb Ridge.

Now let your eye swing south. Spread out before you is a broad, high land sloping off to the east and to the west—the Monument Upwarp. Standing on its crest in the distance are the slender pinnacles which give Monument Valley its name. Closer at hand and spread out immediately beneath you is the immense Grand Gulch Plateau. Bounding it on the east is the thousand-foot high Comb Ridge, a sharply upturned monocline that runs a hundred miles from Elk Ridge to Kayenta in Arizona. Water draining from the eastern slope of the plateau is deflected by this ridge, flowing along Comb Wash to the San Juan. The highest branch of the Wash has nibbled away at a corner of the southeastern shoulder of Elk Ridge where it has carved out Arch Canyon in bright orange-colored sandstone.

The western slope of the plateau is drained by the white-rimmed Grand Gulch, its upper tributaries eating into the base of Elk Ridge. These quickly drop into straight-walled canyons; they gather together finally into one main canyon, a narrow, meandering trench until it reaches the San Juan River. Though less than a thousand feet deep, Grand Gulch, even at its heads, is almost inaccessible even by foot. Off to the southwest is the long line of Clay Hills and the Red House Cliffs capped nearby by the imposing Moss Backs, or, as H. E. Gregory called them, "The Tables of the Sun."[5]

Now turn west, still looking off from near the Bear's Ears; you are at the head of White Canyon. Almost within sight below are the three stone bridges of Natural Bridges National Monument. Two of them bridge White Canyon and the third, the largest, crosses Armstrong Canyon, a tributary. White Canyon, a Colorado River tributary, is actually a narrow, straight-walled, but shallow canyon in white rock. It is at the base of a larger, open valley bordered by red cliffs and mesas which is a main access route to Glen Canyon. Open also and a riot of color, Red Canyon, a few miles away to the south, parallels White Canyon but is separated from it by cliffs impassable save at one point called, appropriately, Blue Notch.

Bordered by Red Canyon and the Colorado River, and by the Clay Hills and the San Juan River, is another wedge called sometimes the San Juan Triangle, or the Red Rock Plateau. The whole is a knobby, bumpy, moundy, slick-rock country sliced by deep canyons. The northern part is drained by Cedar, the long and beautiful Moqui, and Lake, canyons emptying into the Colorado, and by Castle Creek flowing to the San Juan. Beyond Lake Canyon and the lower reaches of Castle Creek a number of short, straight-walled canyons pitch off the steep slopes of Nakai Dome into the San Juan and both ways off the elevated Grey Mesa.

Some of the roughest terrain in the entire canyon country is found south of the San Juan River in the Navajo Reservation. Much of it is drained by the northern tributaries of the San Juan River. Between Chinle Valley on the east and Navajo Mountain on the west, Gypsum Creek, Oljeto Wash, Copper Canyon, Nakai Canyon, Piute Creek, and lesser streams have cut back into the lofty tablelands astride the Utah-Arizona boundary. The high, parallel mesas: the finger-like Piute, and Nakai, No Man's, Skeleton, Zilnez, and Hoskininni mesas facing north with sheer impassable cliffs, are separated from each other by profound and always highly colored canyons, reaching to the San Juan.

Much better known is the open country between Copper Canyon and Hoskininni Mesa, and the long serrated Comb Ridge that sweeps like a huge arc from the San Juan River above Mexican Hat to

Kayenta. Standing in isolation are numbers of high remnants, among them Monitor Mesa, Oljeto Mesa, Boot Mesa, and Train Rock. The whole is climaxed in Monument Valley where a cluster of isolated and thin pillars of rock reach into the sky a thousand feet. Not to be outdone, Agathla Peak, or El Capitan, a volcanic neck near Kayenta, shoots into the air 1,300 feet above its base.

The gigantic rounded dome of Navajo Mountain on the edge of Glen Canyon just below the mouth of the San Juan River is the grandest natural edifice in the southern end of the canyon country. It is a single laccolite, an island mountain, which rises to over ten thousand feet in elevation. It may be seen from points a hundred miles away and has long been a prominent landmark in the Southwest. From its summit much of the canyon country can be seen. Stand on the western side of the peak and look northwest toward the long extended fingers of the Kaiparowits Plateau. Spread out before you is an indescribable fantasy of bare sandstone. At one place you can see the Colorado River. That place is nine air-miles away and seven thousand feet lower in elevation, the greatest downward departure in the entire canyon country. The whole mountain is heavily eroded on every side but particularly so on the northern and western sides. Steep rugged canyons line the slopes, plunging toward the San Juan and the Colorado. Forbidding Canyon gathers the drainage from the southern slope and from most of the western side and carries it in Aztec Creek to the Colorado. Walk down a short distance on the western slope of the mountain. Look carefully and you will be able to see the canyon of Bridge Creek. Now you can see it, the great vaulting arch of stone that spans it, Rainbow Natural Bridge.

South and west of Navajo Mountain in the huge triangle formed by Aztec Creek, the Colorado River, and the lower part of Navajo Canyon, is the Rainbow Plateau. The dominant feature is flat-topped Cummings Mesa, tilting toward the Colorado and cut up into almost inaccessible parts by the deep slot-like canyons emptying into the river. Between Cummings Mesa and Navajo Canyon the country opens out but it is dotted with isolated remnants like the stately Tower Butte and the massive Leche-e Rock.

South and east of Navajo Mountain about the heads of Navajo Canyon, Begashibito and Shonto washes, and Piute and Laguna creeks, there is a canyon complex tilting three ways: The waters from these streams flow west to the Colorado, north to the San Juan, and south to the Little Colorado. Below the mouth of Kaibito Creek, Navajo Canyon is a long, narrow trench in the rock whose walls are broken in only a few places by side canyons. If the main canyon is the trunk, the upper drainage resembles a huge arching oak tree with many limbs and small branches. The upper tributaries have bitten into the plateau, separating the headwaters of Navajo Creek, Piute Creek, and Begashibito Wash, and in places only a narrow divide remains. Begashibito and Shonto washes slope gradually toward the southwest and are much less entrenched, although Shonto Canyon at Shonto is one of beauty. The Shonto drainage heads on a divide overlooking the deep Keet Seel and other canyons that have been cut into the back of Skeleton Mesa. They unite to form the highly colored Segi Canyon whose stream, Laguna Creek, flows northeast from Marsh Pass, through Kayenta to Chinle Wash. These intricate canyon systems offered homelands to prehistoric people who built many masonry dwellings in a number of places within them. Three have been preserved as units in Navajo National Monument: Inscription House in Navajo Canyon; Keet Seel and Betatakin in the Segi.

The southern extension of the canyon country, as we have defined it, is reached at White Mesa. Standing alone on top of Kaibito Plateau, unknown to the world though its white eastern and northern escarpments are visible for many miles, White Mesa tilts to the northwest and, through a network of beautiful white canyons, it drains largely into Kaibito Creek in Chaol Canyon and to the Colorado through Navajo Canyon. To the east of White Mesa, separated by the Klethla Valley, is the brooding bulk of Black Mesa. West is open country to the Echo Cliffs, a long high monoclinal ridge, an almost unbroken line of cliffs from near Moenkopi Wash to Lee's Ferry, where the Colorado has cut a gorge through them. Returning to Lee's Ferry, where the Paria enters the Colorado, we have come full circle.

HAWKEYE BRIDGE. *Navajo Mountain, Utah.* [*William C. Miller, Pasadena*]

The Rivers and the Canyons

AT MOAB THE COLORADO RIVER makes a dramatic entrance to the canyon country: It flows through The Portal, a gate in the eight-hundred foot high cliffs at the head of a canyon 279 miles long. After receiving from both sides the waters from the tributary canyon wilderness we have just explored, it ends just above Lee's Ferry where the river makes an equally dramatic exit through a great gorge in the Echo Cliffs. This long canyon is not the same everywhere; descriptive names have been given to sections of it. There are other canyons of the Colorado. Above Moab the river and its tributaries—notably the Dolores—pass through canyons, and below Lee's Ferry the river enters Marble Canyon which connects with the Grand.

From The Portal to the mouth of the Green River, a distance of sixty-two river miles, the Colorado flows in a canyon, sometimes called Utah's Grand Canyon,[6] and drops one foot every mile throughout the entire distance. The river meanders leisurely along as if to permit those who ride its surface to enjoy to the fullest the scenic beauties it has created. Much of the way, the cliff walls bordering the river are low, permitting views of flat-topped mesas in the distance. Continuing downstream, you will observe that more streams come from the left. Kane Springs Canyon, Lockhart Canyon, Indian Creek, and Salt Creek head back on the La Sal and Abajo mountains and the high country in between. For twenty miles above Lockhart Canyon, open basins near the river permit you to see the outlying ramparts of Hatch Point Mesa. On the right side, tributary canyons are short, heading on the high plateau between the Colorado and the Green that tilts toward the north away from the river. Thirty-two miles downstream from The Portal, Dead Horse Point towers over eighteen hundred feet above the great bend known as The Gooseneck. Below the mouth of Indian Creek, the river canyon gets deeper, tributaries enter through narrow, slot-like can-

HERBERT E. GREGORY. *Geologist, U. S. Geological Survey.* [*Courtesy Edna Hope Gregory*]

overleaf: THE CANYON AND THE MESAS. *The Colorado River from Dead Horse Point, Utah.* [*Norman Van Pelt, Utah Tourist and Publicity Council*]

yons, and you are no longer afforded views of distant mesas. At the confluence of the Green and Colorado, the walls shoot up about thirteen hundred feet almost from the water's edge.

By the time the Green River reaches its mouth, it has already traveled through great canyons: Lodore, Whirlpool, and Split Mountain are one of a series through the Uinta Mountains; Desolation and Gray canyons consist of a single gorge 120 miles long that divides the Tavaputs Plateau. The Green River comes out of Gray Canyon in the Book Cliffs above the town of Green River and flows through an open valley for a few miles before it enters another series: Labyrinth and Stillwater canyons. The names are suggestive. The river drops only about a foot and a half every mile and, like the Colorado, it meanders about after leaving the town of Green River, taking 117 miles to reach its mouth—about half that many miles away as the crow flies. The general surface of the land itself tilts toward the north, so the canyon becomes deeper toward the south. Labyrinth Canyon begins its winding course below the mouth of the San Rafael River; at the Bowknot the river travels over ten miles to reach a point one mile distant from its starting place. Broad bottom lands on the inside of the bends are common. At the head of Stillwater the canyon broadens out. In the vicinity of Millard Canyon, which comes in on the right, you may see on either side the straight walls of the Red Rim. But these soon disappear from view as you drop into an inner canyon below the White Rim. The cliff walls grow higher and the canyon becomes narrower until the mouth is reached.

The Colorado and the Green rivers may be placid and leisurely above their confluence, but all of that is changed below it, in Cataract Canyon. Through Cataract, which is forty miles long, the Colorado drops 425 feet, over ten feet to the mile; there are more than forty rapids. Cataract is the deepest in the Utah canyon country. Only thirteen hundred feet deep at its head, it is over two thousand feet deep near its mouth. The walls are steep, irregular slopes composed of many ledges and but few high and massive cliffs, giving the canyon a ragged look not seen elsewhere in the canyon country.

Only a few short and steep canyons enter Cataract on the right side, but several come in from the high country on the left. Butler Wash in Red Lake Canyon and Cross Canyon enter Cataract near its head and drain much of The Needles country. Gypsum and Dark Canyons are profound gorges that have eaten their way far back into Elk Ridge. Bowdie and Sheep canyons dissect the high plateau on either side of Dark Canyon.

Cataract Canyon has been partly drowned by Lake Powell. At maximum level the reservoir reaches about five miles above Gypsum Canyon to a point approximately 187 miles above Glen Canyon Dam. For all of that distance, the course of the Colorado River may be traced in a general way by the line of cliffs that intermittently protrude above the waters of the lake. Narrow Canyon, seven miles long, between Cataract and the mouth of the Dirty Devil, holds the lake within its walls which are much lower than the cliffs of Cataract. A long narrow and winding arm of Lake Powell marks the inner channel of the Dirty Devil and the beginning of Glen Canyon.

From the mouth of the Dirty Devil to Lee's Ferry, a distance of 170 miles, the river used to flow quietly with now and then a stretch of fast water, but there was nothing to compare with the pounding rapids of Cataract. Most of the way the river flowed between beautiful massive walls. Many tributaries entered through deep, narrow canyons, often not wide enough to permit human passage. Caves, grottos, glens, alcoves, and amphitheaters broke the monotony of majestic cliffs. The serenity of the water and peacefulness of the landscape suggested to Powell the name Glen Canyon.

Today embayments in Lake Powell tell us where Glen Canyon was the most easily approached. North Wash and Trachyte Creek, and White and Red canyons on the opposite side, were the main routes into the upper part of the canyon. Near the

THE MOUTH OF GYPSUM CANYON IN CATARACT CANYON. *The ragged walls tower 2,000 feet above the creek bed. Utah 1962.* [*W. L. Rusho, Bureau of Reclamation*]

mouth of Trachyte Creek, Hite was the only settlement in Glen Canyon but it boasted a post office. Bullfrog Creek and Hall's Creek offered approaches into the river midway between Hite and the mouth of the San Juan River.

Below Hall's Crossing, the canyon, deepening, crosses the Waterpocket Fold. One of the greatest sights in this sector is the Rincon, a huge abandoned hanging meander of the Colorado that is now on the shore of Lake Powell. The narrow winding course of the lake below indicates the depth of the canyon that was a thousand feet deep at the mouth of the Escalante River and Hole-in-the-Rock Crossing.

If you except the Little Rockies of the Henry Mountains, the dominant feature of the landscape adjacent to Glen Canyon, between Hite and the San Juan River, is the clean-swept bare rock.

It is rather common in the canyon country to find streams that pay very little attention to existing topography; they seemingly flow about at will, not stopped by obstacles in their path. These are antecedent streams. They were there first, and as the present land forms rose in their paths, the streams simply cut a passage through them. The San Juan River is a striking example. It heads in southwestern Colorado, finds an open course through the corner of northwestern New Mexico and the southeastern corner of Utah until it reaches Bluff. Just below there, it has sawed right through Comb Ridge. It comes out in the open briefly to receive Comb and Chinle washes and then it enters the precipitous meandering canyon that has eroded at right angles to the wide Monument Upwarp. A few miles farther on it does come to the surface briefly at Mexican Hat. Here the strangely eroded Valley of the Gods and the starkly beautiful Lime Creek amphitheater open out on the north. Beyond the Hat, the San Juan winds about in the Goosenecks, the best known and most accessible entrenched meander in the canyon country. Fifty-seven miles below Mexican Hat, the San Juan once more comes up to the surface at the ford at Clay Hill Crossing and at the adjacent Piute Farms, both now under water at the head of the San Juan arm of Lake Powell. From Chinle Creek the San Juan, in a canyon most of the way,

used to flow a distance of 133 miles to the Colorado and dropped about 950 feet. The steepest part was below Piute Farms where the river tumbled over occasional rapids caused by boulders washed into the river from the tributaries heading on the high mesas on the Utah-Arizona line and on Navajo Mountain on the south side; Nakai Dome and Grey Mesa on the north side look down on a narrow lake today where once there was a deep river canyon.

During the days of river-running, nearly everyone agreed that the most spectacularly beautiful section of Glen Canyon was below the San Juan where the Colorado ran between the Kaiparowits Plateau and Grand Bench on the right and Navajo Mountain and Cummings Mesa on the left. For thirty-five miles towering walls rose on either side of the river. Set back from the rims, you could see the outliers of the Kaiparowits Plateau, and isolated remnants of the Cummings Mesa and Grand Bench. These were drained by narrow, sinuous, and slot-like canyons emptying into the river.

Below West Canyon and Last Chance Creek the river came out into more open country and the walls lowered in the vicinity of the Crossing of the Fathers. There Lake Powell now reaches its greatest width. But then the river soon found itself again in a narrow canyon nearly 700 feet deep where Glen Canyon Dam stands, fifteen miles above Lee's Ferry.

Now walk out on the highway bridge at the dam and look downstream. There you see part of the remnant of Glen Canyon, little changed. But the river is altogether subject to the control of man. In its freer days and in full vigor, the Colorado, as if tired of those high walls and narrow canyon, used to sweep through the thousand-foot-high Echo Cliffs and pass into the open briefly at Lee's Ferry. But only briefly. It picked up the waters of the Paria River and then dropped down into Marble Canyon immediately below.

This is big land, the country upstream from Lee's Ferry. It took men quite a while to learn all about it, even to discover it all. For that matter, they're still at it. The first to look into it and to leave us a record arrived in 1776.

LANDSCAPE ARCH. *Arches National Monument, Utah.* [*Josef Muench, Santa Barbara*]

Last Chance Canyon. *Utah. 1962. [Philip W. Tompkins Photograph, California Academy of Sciences]*

3 / The Mythical River

The Crossing of the Fathers

SPAIN NEVER SENT MORE THAN A HANDFUL of explorers into the great canyon country of Utah and Arizona, but those few left a definite and lasting imprint. They arrived late, near the end of the Spanish era, long after their predecessors had discovered and named the Colorado River. The first Spaniards saw the river near its mouth within fifty years of the discovery of America; and within twenty years after the fall of the Aztecs, Coronado's men were looking down into the Grand Canyon.

Before the end of the sixteenth century, the land discovered by Coronado was colonized and brought securely under the Spanish banner; it was named New Mexico because it was thought to rival in wealth the homeland of the Mexicans and the Aztecs. With great enterprise, Juan de Oñate, the colonizer and first governor, toured his realm from the Great Plains to the lower Colorado, studying the numerous Pueblo Indian towns, looking for mines, and hoping to uncover some information about a strait connecting the Atlantic and Pacific oceans, believed to exist somewhere not far north of New Mexico.

We have forgotten in these days that the quest for a satisfactory water route through the continent impelled much of the pioneer exploration of North America. Columbus had sought a way to India, but discovered America instead and thereby raised a continental barrier blocking commerce between Europe and Asia. Until the coming of the railroads, men kept on looking: a sea-level passage to the Pacific would be best; failing that, next best would be two interlocking rivers with a short land bridge

between them. Since the rivers could not be found, they had to be invented.

Oñate retired from New Mexico without having found a strait or a river connection with the coasts. After his time the province settled down to a more routine existence; few adventurous quests were made in the unknown lands beyond its borders. New Mexico was abandoned during the bloody revolt of the Pueblo Indians in 1680, but Spanish authority was restored eleven years later by Diego de Vargas.

During the eighteenth century there was a revival of exploration. For one thing, Spain found it necessary to defend her realm in North America against European rivals. In New Mexico at mid-century the Spaniards established friendly relations with the Ute Indians, and for the next few decades traders and prospectors worked north from Santa Fe across the upper San Juan basin and reached the Colorado River by way of the Dolores and Gunnison rivers. There is little evidence to suggest that they ventured into the intricate canyon country of the lower San Juan and of the Colorado below the La Sal Mountains.[1]

More imaginative explorers during these same years sought ways to connect with roads the widely separated frontier provinces of Spain in California, New Mexico, Texas, and Louisiana. Among them two Franciscos have earned enduring fame. Francisco Atanasio Domínguez and Francisco Silvestre Vélez de Escalante, of the Order of Friars Minor, sought and obtained permission to explore for a road between Santa Fe and Monterey in California.

Not only would they connect the two provincial capitals, but they would find sites for new settlements and posts and for missions among the tribes. They left Santa Fe at the end of August 1776 and returned to New Mexico five months later on January 2, 1777. They hadn't made it through to California, but their exploration was a magnificent achievement anyway.

The Franciscans and their party made a great circle tour, a pioneer trip that kept them out of the canyon country until they neared the end of their journey. They traveled known trails north from Santa Fe to the Colorado River in western Colorado. Then on ground new to Spain, they swung west through the Uinta Basin and reached the Great Basin at Utah Lake. There they moved south a distance to strike the latitude of Monterey which they expected to follow west. But by then winter was approaching, so they decided to return to Santa Fe. They kept on south and when the mountains on their left lowered, they turned east and headed across the Arizona Strip. With only vague information and without an Indian to guide them, they stayed in the open country, avoiding the few canyons that dropped off in the Colorado on their right, and keeping in sight of the Vermilion Cliffs on their left. At length they reached the Colorado River at the point where, nearly a hundred years later, John D. Lee established Lee's Ferry.

Domínguez and Escalante were probably the first white men to see the spot where they camped during the last week in October. It was at the mouth of the Paria River, called by them the Rio Santa Teresa. They gave the name of San Benito to their camp site, adding the ironic word, *Salsipuedes*— Get out if you can! They must have felt they were boxed in.

The Colorado River ran swift, deep, and cold across their path. Downsteam the yawning mouth of Marble Canyon blocked their way. They looked into the deep mouth of Glen Canyon with the towering Echo Cliffs on either side. Their attempts to ford the river and to paddle across it on crude rafts failed. Desperate now, they went upstream to look for another place to cross.

The first days of November 1776 were among the worst of their entire trip. The Spanish party managed to clamber up over the Echo Cliffs. After that they had to wade through salmon-pink sand. Then rain, snow, and hail drove into their faces. Food was scarce and they feasted on cactus pads with crushed berry sauce. They reached the edge of Glen Canyon to see the river nearly five hundred feet directly below them. No crossing was possible, so they went on. "Doubtless God disposed that we should not obtain a guide, perhaps as a benign punishment for our sins," Escalante wrote in his diary. Almost as he wrote, one of the men scouted ahead and found a passage down to the river through a short side canyon. The river at the canyon mouth was wide and not too deep, he reported. Good news indeed. To keep the animals from slipping off, steps were chopped into the steep sandstone slope of the canyon, and the entire party descended to a sand bar at the water's edge, forty river miles above Camp Salsipuedes.

The bottom was tested and the river was found shallow enough to wade; the friars rode across on horseback. By five o'clock in the afternoon of November 7, the entire party of thirteen men had forded the Colorado. They celebrated, says Escalante, "by praising God our Lord and firing off a few muskets as a sign of the great joy which we all felt at having overcome so great a difficulty." They named the ford La Purísima Concepción de la Virgen Santísima.

From the Colorado the trail to Santa Fe was comparatively easy. They struck off southeast across open but rocky country. The blue, rounded dome of Navajo Mountain bore northeast. They crossed Navajo Canyon where Kaibito Creek came in and, holding southeast, they headed the southern tributaries of Navajo Creek, passing White Mesa on their right. On November 12 they reached open trail and were out of the canyon country altogether. It was smooth traveling now and, by way of the Hopi and Zuñi villages, they reached Santa Fe.

Where the way was difficult for the Spaniards, thousands now live and work and play. A major highway crosses their trail from Echo Cliffs. Both the ford and Padre Creek, where these first white men chopped steps and made a way to the river's

The San Buenaventura

edge, are now deep under the waters of Lake Powell backed up behind Glen Canyon Dam, twenty-four river miles away. The reclamation-built city of Page is near the dam. At Wahweap, not far from the old crossing on the edge of the lake, vacationers enjoy swimming, fishing, water-skiing, and boating. Most of the names the pioneer Spaniards left along their trail have been forgotten, including La Purísima Concepción de la Virgen Santísima, which was replaced sometime later by the Crossing of the Fathers, or, in its Spanish form, El Vado de los Padres. No matter. They were the first Europeans to tackle the canyon country and, since they were not too sinful, God had let them through.[2]

DOMÍNGUEZ AND ESCALANTE DISCOVERED the canyon country. Alexander von Humboldt put it on the map. The Spanish explorers made remarkable contributions to knowledge: Theirs was the first traverse of the Colorado Plateau, and of the Great Basin. The diary that Escalante wrote and the maps that were drawn by Bernardo de Miera y Pacheco are fundamental sources of information. Plant life, animals, minerals, land, weather, the location and names of Indian tribes are given in detail. But this work did not become public knowledge for some time. Escalante's manuscript-diary was transmitted through channels to the Viceroy in Mexico and to the King of Spain. Miera, the expedition cartographer, drew several maps to illustrate their new discoveries, but apparently none was ever printed and it remained for a German scientist to make known to the world the achievements of the Domínguez-Escalante expedition.

Alexander von Humboldt came to Spanish America in 1799 where he stayed five years; the last one was spent in New Spain where he gathered a mass of material from which he wrote his *Political Essay on the Kingdom of New Spain*. The original edition was in French; an English edition in four volumes appeared in 1811. The *Essay*, accompanied by a large folio atlas, contains a detailed description of the northern frontier of New Spain based upon actual exploration. Humboldt himself never visited the northern regions but he talked to those who had and he used the best manuscript and printed sources he could find. Apparently he did not find Escalante's diary but from secondary sources he did bring Miera's geography into his own "Carte Générale."

Miera's multi-colored maps were beautifully done; the relief is shown in actual land forms. His mesas are flat-topped and they look like mesas. The route of the Domínguez-Escalante exploration is clearly shown: every camp site is named and located. The boundaries of named Indian tribes are drawn and he gives us an abundance of ethnological and historical information. Place names abound. The Rio Colorado is prominent, but in its course through the canyon country it is named the Rio de las Zaguaganas after a Ute Indian tribe. Higher up it becomes the Rio de San Rafael. The Rio de Nuestra Señora de los Dolores is identical with the Dolores River, but the San Juan of today was then named the Rio de Nabajoó. The Sierra de la Sal and the Sierra de Abajo are about in their proper places. Navajo Mountain is called El Cerro Azul.

Miera's maps are very accurate indeed, considering the complexity of the terrain and the information available to him, but he did make a few huge and important mistakes. One: From two lakes, Utah Lake and Salt Lake, he made one, calling it Lake Timpanogos, and giving it a navigable outlet to the Pacific on the west. The second mistake is his treatment of the Green River. Miera lifted this stream out of the Colorado basin and emptied it into the Great Basin where it fell into Sevier Lake, which he named Lake Miera. He called his creation the Rio San Buenaventura.

These mistakes are easy to explain. When the Spaniards reached the Uinta Basin they could not imagine that the Green River, which they discovered, breaks directly through the Tavaputs Plateau. Rather they guessed it took a different course and identified it with the Sevier, a bad guess indeed. The explorers heard of Salt Lake, though they did not visit it. They could not conceive of a lake without an outlet to the sea and so Miera gave it one. The Spaniards, in their exploration from Utah Lake south beyond Sevier Lake, were actually on the edge of the Great Basin which has no outlet to the sea. But they did not know this. Instead, they thought of themselves as being on the western slope of the Rockies (known to the Spaniards as Sierra de las Grullas), and therefore they thought that all the streams they saw must eventually reach the Pacific, including the Rio Timpanogos and the Rio San Buenaventura, as well as the Colorado. Humboldt adopted this geography, and its implications, with little change.

These first explorers into the wilderness of the Colorado basin were dreaming the dream of Columbus: they were looking for a road to India. And their dream was published by Humboldt. He went further. In his atlas he published eight small maps indicating possible commercial routes across the North American continent. One showed a projected communication between the headwaters of the Rio Grande and those of the Colorado. He said that this route would not "be interesting for commerce, till great changes introduce colonization into their fertile and temperate regions." Observing the rapid advance westward of the Anglo-Americans, he concluded that "these changes are perhaps not very distant."[3] They weren't.

After 1776 Spain became involved indirectly in the American Revolution, international complications in Europe followed, and she sent no more official explorers to the canyon country. Soon she was plagued by revolution in her own possessions in America; Miguel Hidalgo y Costilla rang the

Near the Head of Cataract Canyon. *Utah.* [*Parker Hamilton, Flagstaff*]

4 6

liberty bell in New Spain in 1810, and eleven years later Mexico emerged free and independent. Mexico inherited from Spain all of the country west of the Continental Divide and south of the forty-second parallel of north latitude. But during the twenty-five years of Mexican control there was little expansion on the frontiers beyond the limits set by Spain. During that time though, the Green River was put back in its place and the San Buenaventura disappeared.

Caravans and Furs

EVEN BEFORE THE END OF THE Spanish era a few New Mexican traders wandered into the country discovered by Domínguez and Escalante. More came after 1821. Although not very much is known about them, they trafficked with the numerous Ute Indians living in the mountain valleys on the eastern edge of the Great Basin between Salt Lake and the Sevier River. A number were slavers who, for guns, horses, and wool blankets, bought or stole Paiute Indian women and children and returned with them to New Mexico, where they were sold as household servants. The Paiutes themselves sold their own children to the Utes, who in turn traded them to the New Mexicans. This trade seems to have grown in scope with the years and was still in operation as late as 1853, and it probably continued for some time after that.

There was little to attract the New Mexicans to the canyon country of the Colorado River since few Indians lived there. But it was a barrier they had to cross and we may thank them for finding a better route to Utah than that of Domínguez and Escalante. It was surely they who worked out a good trail that cut across the southwestern tip of Colorado and, after crossing the Colorado at Moab, reached the Green River at Green River, Utah. A trail from the east, from Colorado, followed the open country at the base of the Book Cliffs and came into the Green River crossing. From this point the traders could follow the Book Cliffs to the base of the Wasatch Plateau. If this were crossed by way of the Price River and Spanish Fork Can-

yon, the traveler would arrive at Utah Lake. If he wished to reach the Sevier Valley from the Green River Crossing, a way was open to him across the extreme northern end of the San Rafael Swell to Castle Valley. Thence he could cross the Wasatch Plateau at Wasatch Pass and reach the Sevier by way of Salina Canyon. This route between New Mexico and the Great Basin, which was extended from the valley of the Sevier southwest to San Gabriel in California, has become known as the Spanish Trail, though it was not developed until the Mexican epoch.

There were minor variations in these routes but it is doubtful if all the trails in the canyon country assigned to Spanish or Mexican origins can be attributed to them. When you find something in the Southwest that cannot otherwise be explained, it is common practice to call it Spanish in origin. The better lost mines, for example, were lost by Spanish discoverers. You hit upon the remains of an old trail. Who made it? The ubiquitous Spanish. Thus a trail that threads The Needles country, crosses the Colorado at the head of Cataract Canyon, and finds its way on to the Land's End Plateau is called a variation of the Spanish Trail. It may have been used by outlaws at a later time, but it would be a most unlikely route for travelers during the Mexican period when, even if you had something to hide, on the established trail you were utterly remote from law and authority. Another variation is found in a route that crosses the very dry middle of the San Rafael Swell from Temple Mountain to Castle Valley; this is actually thought to be a continuation of the route across Cataract Canyon. And there are variations of this trail. Mexican Bend and Mexican Seep are names found within the Swell. If these several cut-offs and variants in the Spanish Trail existed at all during the years when the canyon country belonged to Mexico, their use must have been slight.

The Crossing of the Fathers route was also used to some extent during the Mexican era though, as elsewhere, there is precious little evidence to document the extent of this use. Traveling west to California, Antonio Armijo from New Mexico brought a trading party of thirty-one men across the ford in December 1829. While improving the trail at

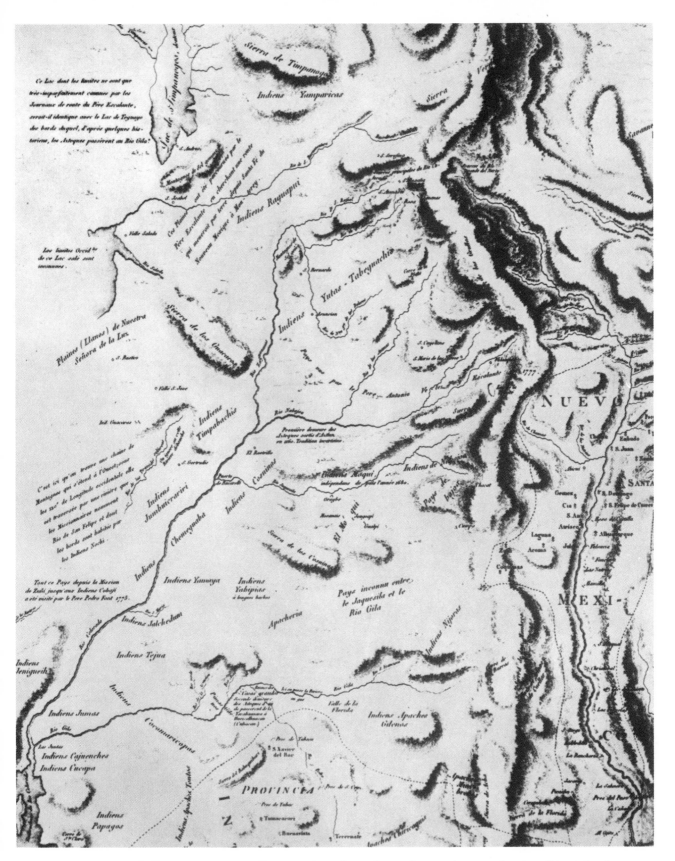

HUMBOLDT'S "CARTE GÉNÉRALE," 1811. *This influential map showing the upper drainage of the Colorado River was based upon Spanish exploration. The "Rio Nabajoa" is now the San Juan. The "Rio de S. Rafael" is the upper part of the Colorado now in Colorado. The "Rio de S. Buenaventura" is the Green River; that it does not connect with the Colorado River was a source of much confusion and gave rise to a mythical river believed to flow to the Pacific. [Courtesy Bancroft Library]*

the ford, they noticed some inscriptions on the cliff wall which they thought had been made by Domínguez and Escalante, whose discovery trip was known to them. (More recently, some inscriptions with a Spanish cast or style about them have been found and were photographed before they were drowned by Lake Powell.) The Spanish friars in 1776 took no time to stop and doodle on the rocks but the inscriptions may be a record of parties that came along before 1829.

Armijo's trip marks the opening of the annual caravan trade between New Mexico and southern California, a traffic that lasted twenty years. Woolens from New Mexico were packed by mules over a thousand miles to the coast and there exchanged for horses and mules, which were driven back over the trail to Santa Fe. Sometimes over a hundred traders would form a caravan. On the return trip as many as a thousand animals would be driven along. Once the trail was open, it became a general thoroughfare between New Mexico and California, and was not limited to traders.

The Crossing of the Fathers cut-off was not suitable for such heavy traffic and was probably not used very much. The longer Spanish Trail via Moab, Green River, and Castle Valley, which avoided the rougher country, was preferred. You could also add Indian slaves to your list of trade goods when passing through the populous Indian country bordering the Sevier River. Slaves were in demand, both in California and New Mexico.

If the Mexican traders traveled quickly through the canyon country, the American fur men stayed to look it over. When Mexico became independent in 1821, Spanish colonial restrictions were lifted, and trade was opened between the Missouri frontier of the United States and Santa Fe. Numbers of Americans traveled with the caravans to California and even entered the trade, but they were more active in the trapping of furs.

The American mountain men literally mapped the central Rockies on a beaver skin. From Santa Fe and Taos after 1821, trappers ranged north and west into the upper basin of the Colorado River, and by 1824 they had reached the Green River in the Uinta Basin, which became an important base

FACTORY BUTTE. *Near the Fremont River, Utah.* [*Josef Muench, Santa Barbara*]

CATHEDRAL ARCH. *White Mesa, Arizona.* [*William C. Miller, Pasadena*]

overleaf: NAVAJOS NEAR GOULDING'S TRADING POST. *Monument Valley, Utah.* [*Frank Jensen, Cedar City, Utah*]

of operations. The canyon country was also trapped. Beaver, the chief animal caught, is plentiful in the canyons even today, and must have been abundant during the great days of the trade between 1820 and 1840.

One of the fur-trade entrepreneurs in Utah was Antoine Roubidoux, who established a trading post at White Rocks in the Uinta Basin in 1831 or 1832; his men traveled from there as far south as the Gila River in Arizona in search of pelts. One of his associates may have been Denis Julien, who inscribed his name and the date, "1831," near Roubidoux's post. Sometime later Julien went south into the canyon country, where he left his autograph on the rocks in a number of places. His name has been found in three different locations. Two are in Labyrinth and Stillwater canyons, and there is one in Cataract Canyon. All are dated 1836. How did Julien get into the canyons? By boat? Or, did he walk in from the rim? The inscription in Cataract Canyon would argue that he was using a boat. The date "1837" has been found in Glen Canyon and this may have some connection with Julien or others.

Little is known about Julien. He was quite probably a typical mountain man, one who would go anywhere after beaver. Like his contemporaries elsewhere, he literally discovered the region he roamed. The Julien inscriptions are the earliest records we have of actual penetration into the deeper canyons. Beyond this we have small evidence of exploration of the canyons by the mountain men. The fur trappers in the canyons wrote little, and the intimate geographical knowledge which they must have acquired was mostly lost; at least little of it became public knowledge.

Certainly we may say that the Mexican traders, opening a route through the canyon country, and the fur men like Denis Julien, corrected the mistakes in geography made by Domínguez, Escalante, and Miera. They connected the Green with the Colorado, they erased the San Buenaventura and other mythical rivers, they determined the scope of the canyon country, and they were undoubtedly the first to make detailed explorations of the actual canyons. The routes opened during the Spanish and Mexican periods are principal roads in use today in the canyon country.[4]

D. Julien Inscription. *In the mouth of Hell Roaring Canyon, a tributary of the Green River, Utah.* [*K. Sawyer, U. S. Geological Survey. Courtesy Southern California Edison Company*]

THE BOOK CLIFFS. *North of Green River, Utah.* [*Courtesy American Museum of Natural History*]

4 / Topographical Engineers

The Road to Cathay

MAY 23, 1844—JOHN C. FRÉMONT OF THE U. S. Army's Corps of Topographical Engineers, on his way home from the second expedition, stopped at Utah Lake, where Domínguez and Escalante had camped sixty-eight years before. There he came to a reluctant conclusion.

On his way out Frémont had traveled the road to Oregon, but then he had turned south to look for the San Buenaventura River—that mistake of Miera, perpetuated by Humboldt—believed it to flow from the Rockies to the Pacific. Frémont first crossed the Sierra Nevada, explored the Central Valley of California, and then came back over the Spanish Trail to Utah Lake. There he admitted what the fur men had known for some time: that the country between the Wasatch Mountains and the Sierra Nevada was indeed a great basin with no outlet to the sea, and he so named it. Frémont also renamed the principal west-bound stream in the Great Basin, calling it the Humboldt River.

Frémont had demolished an influential myth in American exploration. Since 1776, both of Miera's two creations, the San Buenaventura and the river flowing from Lake Timpanogos, had been elaborated upon by imaginative cartographers who blandly carried them across blank places on their maps and emptied them into the Pacific Ocean. Ready-made for those seeking a water road to India, the fictitious rivers of the West had interested nearly all those who came along: Lewis and Clark, Pike, the voyagers coasting Pacific shores, the Hudson's Bay Company, and the American fur men.

Frémont's great maps of the West, drawn by Charles Preuss and published in 1845 and 1848, outlined the Great Basin and disposed of the mythical rivers. On the first map, the canyon country of the Colorado River is white space, but on the second, the Green and the Grand (Colorado) are located, although the mouth of the Green is much too far south. In contrast to the commercial map publishers, the Topographical Engineers, in mapping the new western lands of the United States, exhibited admirable restraint. Areas not known to them were, as a rule, left blank or marked "unexplored." "Hypothetical geography," said W. H. Emory of the Engineers, "has proceeded far enough in the United States." For some thirty years after the publication of Frémont's map in 1848, the canyon country was generally labeled "unexplored" on the maps produced by the Topographical Engineers and on those of other government explorers who came along after the Civil War.[1]

If Frémont had destroyed the illusion of an easy river passage from the Rockies to the Pacific, this was not so important now, since the developing railroads were already replacing river transportation. Rapidly moving events in the West were of great interest to this new industry. After a war of less than two years, Mexico ceded to the United States the entire Southwest below the forty-second parallel. The Mormons had already arrived on the shores of Great Salt Lake. Then, in 1848, gold was discovered in California. The gold rush was a great ten-year-long migration. Nearly all the rushers took up residence in the new El Dorado, or elsewhere in the West when the mining frontier, after 1858, expanded beyond California. Not very long after Humboldt's prediction, great changes indeed were taking place in the West.

The bright lure of golden California prompted an active search for suitable routes thither—for horses, wagons, rails, and boats. The hope of yet finding a river route was not entirely dead. During the gold rush, the Spanish Trail through the canyon country was little used. Why bother with a long winding trail through rough country when you could take the shorter southern routes opened during the war, or the more central Oregon Trail, taking advantage of the Humboldt River cut-off?

Much more attention was given the canyon country during the search for a route for the first transcontinental railroad. Everyone agreed the line would have to be built, but the question was *where*? Sectional rivalry between the North and South delayed the decision, and there was uncertainty about some of the blank places on the map. So Congress in 1853 authorized the War Department to find the best route. Secretary of War Jefferson Davis charged the Corps of Topographical Engineers with surveying four routes—two in the south, one in the north, and the fourth a central route.

Giving up the idea of a river road to the Pacific, both Frémont and his influential father-in-law, Senator Thomas Hart Benton of Missouri, got behind the railroads. They backed the central route in the expectation that its terminus would be St. Louis. Benton tried to get Frémont appointed as head of the official survey of the central route, but when the command fell to Lt. John W. Gunnison, private interests were enlisted to put Frémont on the trail for an independent survey. Meanwhile, to popularize the central route, Benton persuaded E. F. Beale to travel over it en route to his new post as Superintendent of Indian Affairs in California.

Beale got under way first, followed by Gunnison and the official railroad surveyors. Frémont brought up the rear. All of these parties came into the canyon country from Colorado across the open lands at the foot of the Book Cliffs. They all crossed the Green River at the crossing long used by traders on the Spanish Trail. They all continued along the estab-

lished well-worn trail through Castle Valley. Then following the main-traveled route, Beale and Gunnison left the canyon country through Wasatch Pass and Salina Canyon while Frémont took a variant and went south to the head of the Fremont River and reached the Sevier after crossing the Awapa Plateau.

The northern edge of the canyon country came prominently into the public view as a result of these explorations in 1853. In 1854, Gwinn Harris Heap, who had traveled with Beale, published his *A Central Route to the Pacific*, with an accompanying map. The most informative and detailed description of the country traversed was that written by Lt. E. G. Beckwith for the Gunnison survey. Frémont wrote a letter published in a Washington newspaper in 1854. "Europe still lies between Asia and America," he wrote. "Build this railroad and things will have revolved about: America will lie between Asia and Europe—the golden vein which runs through the history of the world will follow the iron track to San Francisco. . . ." Frémont was clearly one with Columbus, Miera, and Lewis and Clark.[2]

Finally, at Promontory, Utah, in 1869, the last spike connected the rails and the dream of a western road to Cathay was realized, even if it didn't follow Frémont's and Benton's central route. But one line was scarcely enough to serve the needs of the rapidly expanding West, and within fourteen years of the completion of the first transcontinental line, the Denver & Rio Grande Western Railroad put a bridge across the Green River right at the crossing of the Spanish Trail.

Meanwhile, along the southern periphery, the Topographical Engineers were edging toward the canyon country. In 1849 Lt. James H. Simpson had joined Lt. Col. John M. Washington's command for a raid into the Navajo country. Leaving Santa Fe, they visited the prehistoric ruins in Chaco Canyon and those in Canyon de Chelly, and returned by way of Zuñi and Inscription Rock. In his report Simpson urged further examination of the country west of Zuñi to locate a route for a wagon road to Los Angeles, since Santa Fe traders with pack trains had made it through years before. And he gleaned

From Grand View Point toward the Abajo Mountains. *Utah.* [*Parker Hamilton, Flagstaff*]

enough information in New Mexico to hint broadly in his report that the valley of the Colorado River might be passable.

Shades of Alexander von Humboldt! Communication between the oceans by way of the Rio Grande and the Rio Colorado! Frémont had pinched off the mythical rivers; but what of the existing ones? Everyone knew the Colorado reached the Pacific. But did it really flow through a canyon? The traders at Santa Fe told Simpson it did, but he was not convinced. Captain Lorenzo Sitgreaves of the Engineers was sent in 1851 to settle the matter. His instructions read to explore the Zuñi River to its mouth and then follow the Colorado to the Gulf of California. Sitgreaves found that the Zuñi discharged into the Little Colorado, which he then followed until it began to drop into a canyon. Unable to proceed farther, he headed west and his first sight of the Colorado was when he reached the Mojave Indian villages in California. Two years later, Lt. A. M. Whipple surveyed a route closely paralleling Sitgreaves' trail, one of the four Pacific railroad routes under investigation by the Topographical Engineers. And the rails followed. So, at the same time that the Denver & Rio Grande Western Railroad was bridging the Green River, the Atlantic and Pacific Railroad (later the Santa Fe) was laying tracks along the Sitgreaves-Whipple route in Arizona.[3]

Gunnison's survey had cut across the northern edge, and Whipple's had skirted it on the south, but the land in-between—the very heart of the canyon country—was still a blank. In 1857 Lt. G. K. Warren, Topographical Engineer, published the great "Map of the Territory of the United States from the Mississippi to the Pacific Ocean." This incorporated the work of the Pacific railroad surveys and many other sources. In it the canyon country was a prominent area of blank paper marked "unexplored."[4]

A Land of Wonder

IF IT HAD NOT BEEN FOR OPEN HOSTILITIES between the United States and the Mormons in Utah, 1857–1858, the Topographical Engineers might have ended their explorations in and near the canyon country with the railroad surveys. The "Utah War," as it is called, grew out of tensions that developed between the Mormons and some of the federally appointed territorial officials. When the situation worsened, President Buchanan sent a force of 2,500 troups under the command of Albert S. Johnston to enforce the authority of the new governor appointed to replace Brigham Young. Fearful that the "invasion" would open the gates to the mob violence that the Mormons had come to Utah to escape, Young took up the gauntlet. As Johnston's "army" approached Utah, its progress was slowed by the guerrilla tactics of the Mormons. In the spring of 1858, after spending a cold winter near Fort Bridger, then in Utah Territory, the army finally entered Salt Lake City, once cooler heads had ne- gotiated a truce. The army remained in Utah and established Camp Floyd forty miles from the city.

The success of Mormon guerrilla warfare in the opening days of the "war," and the logistical isolation of the military forces caused the War Department to seek new supply routes into Utah. The Corps of Topographical Engineers was directed to carry out a number of expeditions which notably supplemented the work of the railroad surveys and increased geographical knowledge of the various approaches to Utah. Captain J. H. Simpson, who as a lieutenant had gone into Navajo Country in 1849, ten years later found a new wagon road across the Great Basin and completed the description of the Basin begun by Frémont. His report of these 1859 explorations also carried a map of the Domínguez-Escalante route plotted from their diary by Philip Harry. The year before, Lt. Joseph C. Ives steamed up the lower Colorado in the U. S. S. *Explorer* and found it navigable as far as Black

KISHPAUGH BUTTE. *San Rafael Swell, Utah.* [*Parker Hamilton, Flagstaff*]

Canyon, where Hoover Dam now stands.[5]

Another important exploration was based in New Mexico. Captain John N. Macomb, in April 1859, was ordered to take an expedition directly into the canyon country. He was to determine the course of the San Juan River, to fix the position of the confluence of the Green and Grand (Colorado) rivers, and to find the best and most direct route between the Rio Grande and the southern settlements of Utah. The canyon country was still something of a mystery, a blank on the map. Indeed the "Map of Utah Territory Showing the Routes Connecting it with California and the East," published by the Topographical Engineers in 1858, carried the bold legend: "Region Unexplored Scientifically." There were few changes to record during the ten years since Frémont had published his map of the West, but the Gunnison railroad survey route was shown, and from Gunnison's map the Spanish Trail was located. From the same source a second Spanish Trail, labelled as the "South Trail in Winter Season," runs south of the first, crossing the Green and the Grand not far above their confluence.[6]

Macomb was in the field from mid-July to the end of September 1859. His party, which included John Strong Newberry, who had been geologist with Ives the year before, followed the well-defined Spanish Trail past Mesa Verde, across the Sage Plain to the "Ojo Verde," a spring on the route between the La Sal and Abajo mountains. Here they established a base camp and Macomb, Newberry, and some of the others headed west to find the confluence of the Green and the Grand. They traveled about thirty miles, probably down Indian Creek, judging by Newberry's description. Following this stream, they soon found themselves in a canyon and did not succeed in reaching the river, so they climbed out to the rim and found a high point where they could see the Colorado, and the explorers were able to satisfy themselves that they were only a short distance from the confluence.

Newberry was highly impressed by what he saw. Turning full circle, there was a beautiful landscape in every quarter. He wrote: "Toward the west the view reached some thirty miles, there bounded by long lines and bold angles of mesa walls similar to those behind us, while in the intervening space the surface was diversified by columns, spires, castles, and battlemented towers of colossal but often beautiful proportions, closely resembling elaborate structures of art, but in effect far surpassing the most imposing monuments of human skill. In the southwest was a longer line of spires of white stones standing on red bases, thousands in number, but so slender as to recall the most delicate carving in ivory of the fairy architecture of some Gothic cathedral; yet many, perhaps most, were over five hundred feet in height, and thickly set in a narrow belt or series some miles in length. The appearance was so strange and beautiful as to call out exclamations of delight from all our party." This is a first description of The Needles country, probably the first to be published.

Bearing in mind the objective of the exploration, Captain Macomb wrote: "I cannot conceive of a more worthless and impracticable region than the one we now find ourselves in. I doubt not that there are repetitions and *varieties* [sic] of it for hundreds of miles down the cañon of the Great Colorado, for I have heard of but one crossing of that river above the vicinity of the Mojave Village, and I have reason to doubt if that one (El Vado de los Padres) is practicable, except with utmost care, even for a pack-mule."

Unable to reach the San Juan by following the Colorado, from Ojo Verde the full expedition turned south toward the San Juan River. From one elevated point, a short distance south of the present town of Blanding, Newberry tells us the explorers obtained a beautiful view of the country bordering the San Juan. This included Mesa Verde, Shiprock, the Carrizo Mountains, Monument Valley, and the Bear's Ears. Looking off to the west, Newberry wrote that they could see a great gap: "through which the San Juan flows to its junction with the Colorado. The features presented by this remarkable gate-way are among the most striking and impressive of any included in the scenery of the Colorado country. The distance between the mesa walls on the north and south is perhaps ten miles, and scattered over the interval are many castle-like buttes and slender towers, none of which can be

GLEN CANYON TRIBUTARY. *Utah 1962.* [*F. B. Slote, Bureau of Reclamation*]

POTTERY PUEBLO. *Piute Mesa, Utah.* [*Philip M. Hobler, Museum of Northern Arizona*]

NARROW CANYON AND THE HENRY MOUNTAINS. *Utah 1962.* [*A. E. Turner, Bureau of Reclamation*]

VALLEY OF THE GODS. *Lime Creek Basin, Utah.* [*Philip W. Tompkins Photograph, California Academy of Sciences*]

less than 1,000 feet in height, their sides absolutely perpendicular, their forms wonderful imitations of the structures of human art. Illuminated by the setting sun, the outlines of these singular objects came out sharp and distinct, with such exact similitude of art, and contrast with nature as usually displayed, that we could hardly resist the conviction that we beheld the walls and towers of some Cyclopean city hitherto undiscovered in this far-off region. Within the great area enclosed by the grander features I have enumerated, the country is set with numberless buttes and isolated mesas, which give to the scene in a high degree the peculiar character I have so often referred to as exhibited by the eroded districts of the great central plateau. Here and there we caught glimpses of the vivid green of the wooded bottomlands of the river, generally concealed by the intermediate and overhanging cliffs." This is one of the earliest descriptions of Monument Valley as seen from a distance. Having seen from their elevated position the rough canyon country to the west, they realized that they could not travel to the mouth of the river. Therefore, Macomb went directly south down to the San Juan, probably reaching it in the vicinity of the later town of Bluff. The expedition turned upstream and it returned to Santa Fe by way of the tributary, Cañon Largo, and the Pueblo village of Jemez.

The Macomb exploration was an important approach to the canyon country. Macomb had demonstrated to his own satisfaction, at least, that there was no suitable supply route through to settlements in southern Utah. Communication would have to follow existing trails and of these the Crossing of the Fathers was scarcely one practical for military purposes. But, apart from the immediate objective of the exploration, the descriptions left by Newberry are of high value and his geological report is the first of its kind for the eastern side of the canyon country. The location of the confluence of the Green and the Grand, and the course of the San Juan River above the canyon were accurately determined. So were the La Sal and Abajo mountains, and the Bear's Ears, and other places.[7]

The discoveries of the Macomb expedition were first published in a map of the "Territory and Military Department of Utah Compiled in the Bureau of Topograph[1] Eng[rs]. . . in 1860." For example, the Spanish Trail—and there is now only one as opposed to the two on the Gunnison map—is laid down with accuracy for the first time. The Domínguez-Escalante route, plotted by Philip Harry and later published in Simpson's *Report of Explorations Across the Great Basin . . .* (1876), also appears on this map. In greater detail and on larger scale, the Macomb material was shown on the official map of the expedition made by F. W. Egloffstein, and published in the official report which did not appear until 1876. Both Newberry and Egloffstein had been with Ives, and the reports of Ives and Macomb should be regarded as complementary. Egloffstein invented a new technique that delicately illustrated the sculptured land. His beautiful maps portray the Colorado River Canyon country from the Book Cliffs to a point far below the "Big Cañon" (Grand Canyon). These maps very nicely summarize the accomplishments of the Corps of Topographical Engineers since 1848 when Frémont published his map of the West. The Colorado River is made to follow its true course; the geographical fictions of the past have largely disappeared. The canyon country is still largely a blank. But Egloffstein on his map did not write in the revealing phrase that had appeared on the map published by the Topographical Engineers in 1858: "Region Unexplored Scientifically."[8] J. H. Newberry had begun an effective scientific study of the canyon country. As a result of the exploratory work of the Topographical Engineers, and of Newberry's pioneer geological studies, men thereafter were concerned much less with finding a way through the canyons and much more with the country itself.

5 / The Scientists

The Man with One Arm

ONCE THE CIVIL WAR WAS OVER, THE DE-velopment of the West moved forward at headlong speed. Miners, farmers, stockmen, and lumbermen rushed into as yet unexploited areas. Roads and railroads followed, connecting the new towns and cities. Crowded by the great numbers of newcomers, the Indian saw his way of life threatened, and struck back.

The opening of the West after the War was furthered by four separate surveys undertaken by Clarence King, Ferdinand V. Hayden, John W. Powell, and George M. Wheeler. First in the field, King began in 1867 to survey the route selected for the transcontinental railroad. The others chose different areas, but soon they all found themselves drawn to the Colorado River basin. By the time the report of Macomb's exploration was published in 1876, Powell, Hayden, and Wheeler had nearly filled in the blanks left on the map of the canyon country by the Topographical Engineers.[1]

The two voyages of discovery directed by John Wesley Powell constitute the best known part of the history of the Colorado River. Powell examined the long line of canyons between Green River, Wyoming, and the foot of Grand Canyon, together with some of the adjacent country during 1869, and 1871–2.

At Promontory, May 10, 1869, the last spike was driven and the rails were connected. Two weeks later, where the Union Pacific crossed the Green River in Wyoming, Powell's first voyage began. Powell had fought on the Union side in the Civil War and had lost his right forearm at the battle of Shiloh. He was discharged with the rank of major, a title that stayed with him the rest of his life. Undismayed by his handicap, and consumed by an interest in science and a love of adventure, in 1867 and 1868 Powell explored the Rockies of the Colorado, where he developed a great interest in the Colorado River. The river in its lower reaches was still a mystery; men had crossed it but the rumors of canyons, whirlpools, and waterfalls persisted, and no one had tried to navigate the river for any great distance. Powell determined to be the first to do so.

May 24, 1869. Ten men in four boats left Green River, Wyoming. Elevation, 6,100 feet above sea level. By July 13 they were through the canyons of the Uinta Range and the Tavaputs Plateau and had reached the Green River crossing of the Spanish Trail. Elevation, 4,064 feet above sea level. Keeping on, they glided past the mouth of the San Rafael and into Labyrinth Canyon and soon entered Stillwater Canyon. The current was quiet and the river wound about "as if in no haste to leave this beautiful canyon," as Powell wrote. Gradually the walls grew higher until they reached up to 1,200 feet, and the explorers had reached the junction of the Green and the Grand. Elevation, 3,875 feet above sea level.

They spent a few days at the junction. Powell and Bradley climbed out on the east side. "The scenery from the top is the same old picture of desolation we have seen for the last hundred miles. Curiously shaped spires and domes rise everywhere . . ." Bradley observed in his diary. This was a second description of The Needles country. Just ten years before, Macomb and Newberry, from a point about fifteen miles to the east, looked at the same landscape—and turned back.

Powell and his party went on. July 21, they pulled out into the current and were soon in the fast water of Cataract Canyon, a name Powell put on the map. For twelve days they toiled—portaging and lining, while running the forty-mile-long succession of rapids. "Sometimes the waves below would roll over a boat. . . . Now and then the boat would roll over; but, clinging to its sides until they could right it, the men would swim to shore, towing it with them. We found much difficulty in the whirlpools below; for at times it was almost impossible to get out of them. They would carry us back under the falls, they would dash us against the rocks, or they would send us swirling down the river," Powell wrote. Finally, they came out on smooth water at the mouth of a muddy stream which they then and there named the Dirty Devil. July 28, 1869. Elevation above sea level, 3,460 feet.

Now it was easy going through Glen Canyon and they rested on their oars and enjoyed the scenery. After the rough and ragged walls of Cataract, Powell was much impressed by the "mounds and cones and hills of solid sandstone, rising one above the other as they stretched back in a gentle slope for miles," and he named the upper part of the canyon, Mound Canyon. Below the mouth of the San Juan the landscape changed again, and Powell tried to describe it. "We had now run once more into dark red and chocolate-coloured sandstones, with slate-coloured beds below: these usually form vertical walls, occasionally terraced or broken down, and from the crest of these, the orange mounds sloped back, bearing on top of each mound some variegated monument, now vertical, now terraced, now carved by time into grotesque shapes, such as towers, pinnacles, etc. These monuments stood alone or in groups, and spread over the landscape as far as the eye could reach. . . . We named it Monument Canyon." Mound and Monument were good, appropriate names.

On August 1 and 2, 1869, the explorers camped not far below the mouth of the San Juan River. Here, near the mouth of a short, narrow canyon,

they discovered a spectacular grotto-like chamber arched over by high vaulting walls. The sighing wind and the unusual acoustical properties of the chamber suggested the name, Music Temple. While Powell was making observations nearby, three of the men—O. G. Howland, Seneca Howland, and William Dunn—carved their names on the rock wall of the chamber. Powell himself, after his work was done on August 2, took a long nap in the Music Temple, an act repeated by many river travelers until the time when, in 1963, the grotto was drowned by the waters of the reservoir. It was these cool, shady side canyons, so welcome to the traveler, that Powell was remembering when he later gave the name Glen, replacing Mound and Monument, to the magnificent canyon between the Dirty Devil and the Paria. On August 4, after passing the Crossing of the Fathers, the explorers reached the mouth of the Paria River. Elevation, 3,120 feet above sea level.

Twenty-six days later they had dropped through the fast waters and rapids in Marble Canyon and had made it through Grand Canyon to the open country at the mouth of the Virgin River. Elevation 750 feet above sea level. Of the ten to embark at Green River, six men completed the journey. One had left the expedition at the Uinta River. O. G. and Seneca Howland, and William Dunn, having incised their names on the walls in Music Temple, quit just when victory was in sight. They had had enough of the rapids, they said. While walking out toward the settlements, all three of them were killed by Shivwits Indians.

Powell had made good his determination to be the first to travel through the canyons. If others, perhaps, had preceded him—trappers or prospectors—it didn't much matter. Powell was not so much interested in being first as he was to learn. During the 1869 voyage, he learned. He saw everything. He steered the expedition through a thousand miles of the canyons of the Colorado; he climbed out to the rims to study the country whenever there was time; he collected plants and made geological sections and observed the stars at night; he studied Indian ruins; he put names on the map; he appreciated the beauty and grandeur of the land-

CATARACT CANYON. *Utah 1962.* [*Parker Hamilton, Flagstaff*]

scape all the way; he had solved the mystery of the canyons of the Colorado. "Here ended the 'Great Unknown,'" Powell, the scientist, said as the trip ended. Jack Sumner, who made the entire trip, summed it up as he saw it: "Before we started I was called a damned fool for embarking in such an enterprise, for nobody possibly gets through. Since I have got through, I have been called a damned fool for the same thing, because there has been many men long since that have proved that there was nothing to go for as they have it all." But, unlike these stay-at-homes, Jack had seen the elephant. He had helped solve the mystery. He'd been through. "If anybody disbelieves any of this, or wants to know more of the cañons of the Colorado," he said, "go and see it." Years later he was back in Glen Canyon prospecting the river bars for gold— while Major Powell was in Washington directing the United States Geological Survey.

The second Powell voyage, 1871–2, paid for by funds appropriated by Congress, largely duplicated the first, but it was better organized for the collection of information, and less adventurous. Eleven men in three boats left Green River, Wyoming, May 22; they reached the Green River Crossing in Utah August 26; after ten days in Cataract Canyon, on September 30 they arrived at the Dirty Devil; a week later they were at the Crossing of the Fathers where supplies had been left for them by the Mormon scout, Jacob Hamblin. After a few days there, they floated on down to the mouth of the Paria River. This ended the river exploration for 1871. The remainder of the year, and the first months in 1872, were actively spent in surveying and map-making in southern Utah and the Arizona Strip. The river trip was not resumed until August 1872. It was discontinued at the mouth of Kanab Canyon in Grand Canyon where the boats were abandoned and the explorers walked out.

Actually, the year 1871 marks the beginning of the "Powell Survey," making him one with King, Hayden, and Wheeler, who were at work in the American West. From the time Powell received the first federal appropriations in 1871, he patterned his field operations after the others and planned to undertake a broad geographical and scientific ex-

amination of the region assigned to him; this he felt should include the canyons of the Colorado and the vast plateau draining into them. Powell worked under the jurisdiction of the Smithsonian Institution (he named the Henry Mountains after Joseph Henry, Secretary of the Institution) until 1874 when his survey was transferred to the Department of the Interior and named officially the United States Geographical and Geological Survey of the Rocky Mountain Region. Until his survey was consolidated with the others in 1879 to form the Geological Survey, Powell and a roster of capable students mapped and studied much of the Colorado Plateau and published books of primary importance.

As for the two river voyages, 1869, 1871–2, Powell's account of them has annoyed many people. He wrote a composite report of the explorations, using data accumulated on both trips. He made no mention of the 1871–2 exploration in the book. But, to Powell, the 1869 trip must have been the most important. He had conquered the unknown; he had accomplished what no man had done before. From the first, the second voyage sprang, a duplication of the first, but with more time to observe and to collect. Why not write a composite report of the two trips? Why not, indeed? Anyway, Powell probably had in mind the general public when he wrote, rather than a scientific audience. If he omitted reference to the second expedition in his own report, it was covered by nearly all of the personnel of the second voyage, who kept diaries that have since been published.

SECTION OF MAP MADE BY F. M. BISHOP DURING THE POWELL EXPEDITION OF 1871. *Map reads from "aa" to "B." "End of Rapids" is at the lower end of Cataract Canyon. Narrow Canyon extends from there to the mouth of the Dirty Devil River. Glen Canyon begins at the Dirty Devil. The first island below the Dirty Devil was the later site of Dandy Crossing, named by Cass Hite in 1883. The "Old Ruins" were visited by the Powell Expedition and were later called "Fort Moqui." F. M. Bishop made a map of all of the canyons of the Colorado from Green River, Wyoming, to Lee's Ferry. His remarkably accurate manuscript map is in the possession of the Utah State Historical Society. [Courtesy Utah State Historical Society]*

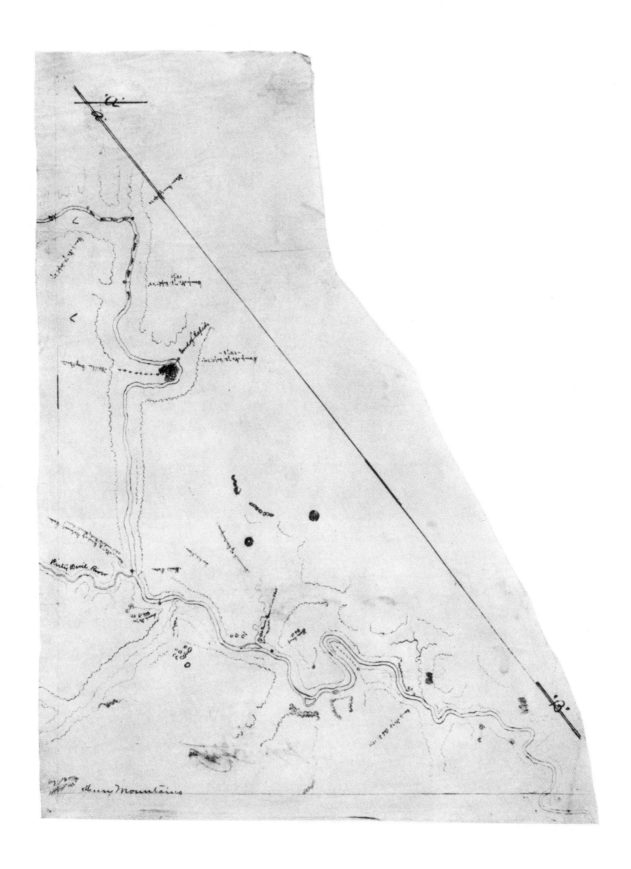

THE LAND OF STANDING ROCKS. *Utah.* [*W. L. Rusho, Bureau of Reclamation*]

IN THE "BIG DROP." *Cataract Canyon, Utah.* [*C. Gregory Crampton*]

Indeed, the second Powell voyage must be one of the most thoroughly documented expeditions in the history of western exploration.

Given the achievements of the Powell Survey, few scientists can be found who will pother and fuss over Powell's reporting of the river trips. The ideas and concepts he developed on the voyages found expression later in works of high value in geology, ethnology, land classification and reclamation. He saw the whole region as few have since. His report on the voyages (1874) contained a broad analysis of the processes and results of land sculpture as revealed in the Colorado Plateau, a basic work in regional geological literature.[2]

In his own studies, Powell found numerous gaps in geological knowledge and he directed his appointees to fill them. Captain C. E. Dutton studied and identified the High Plateaus before going on to the study of the Grand Canyon. Dutton found the canyon country highly appealing and his vivid dramatic prose reflects this. His literary style is of a calibre seldom found in geological literature—and rarely in more recent publications coming from government agencies. Grove K. Gilbert contributed a celebrated report on the Henry Mountains. In it he identified the laccolithic structure so ably that the Henrys have since become one of the classic areas in geology.

The volumes published by the Powell Survey were illustrated by drawings, some by prominent artists like W. H. Holmes and Thomas Moran. E. O. Beaman, James Fennemore, and J. K. Hillers made photographs in the field. The first satisfactory maps of the canyon country were made for the Powell Survey by A. H. Thompson and his associates, who often made important discoveries during the course of their mapping reconnaissance. It was Thompson, for example, who differentiated the drainages of the Paria, Escalante, and Dirty Devil rivers, and who first sketched out the main features of the Aquarius and Kaiparowits plateaus, the Waterpocket Fold, and the Henry Mountains. His geographic contour maps were the base on which Powell, Dutton, Howell, and Gilbert recorded their geological findings.

By 1880 all the reports were published: Powell on the river explorations and the physical structure of the Colorado basin (1876), on the Uinta Mountains (1876), and on the arid lands of the United States with particular reference to the lands of Utah (1879); Gilbert on the Henry Mountains (1877); and Dutton on the High Plateaus (1880).[3]

Wheeler and Hayden

THE WHEELER SURVEY, officially the United States Geographical Surveys West of the One Hundredth Meridian, was an elaborate undertaking of the Army Corps of Engineers, designed to map, examine, and describe the resources of the West. Under the direction of George M. Wheeler, it carried on in the brilliant tradition of the Corps of Topographical Engineers, which had been merged with the Corps of Engineers during the Civil War. During the course of reconnaissances through Nevada and Arizona in 1869 and 1871, Wheeler became enamored of the Colorado River and seems to have tried to vie with Powell in the scientific conquest of the plateau and canyon country.

Wheeler's staff of officers, engineers, and scientists mapped the region northward from the Grand Canyon to the High Plateaus and from Nevada eastward to the Crossing of the Fathers in Glen Canyon. His reconnaissance parties crossed the trail of Powell's men on the Dirty Devil, Escalante, and Paria rivers, at Lee's Ferry and elsewhere. Edwin E. Howell and Grove K. Gilbert first served with Wheeler before joining Powell's Survey.

Although Wheeler's men explored and mapped portions of the canyon country, they were at work elsewhere as well, so that most of their numerous publications did not touch the canyon country. Wheeler's final *Report* (1889) summarizes the entire work of his survey and the impressive volumes on geology, botany, zoology, and archeology are basic reference works. One of the enduring contributions made by the Wheeler Survey was the excellent atlas of hachured and shaded maps, two of which, sheets 59 and 67, cover the region from the High Plateaus to the Grand Canyon.

While Powell and Wheeler were zealously studying the west side of the canyon country, Ferdinand V. Hayden's United States Geological and Geographic Survey of the Territories was busy in Colorado and in an adjoining strip of Utah extending approximately to the longitude of Bluff and Moab and including the Four Corners region in the San Juan Valley. His men, notably W. H. Holmes, A. C. Peale, Henry Gannett, G. B. Chittenden, and W. H. Jackson, in 1874 and 1875 explored, mapped, and studied topography, geology, and archeology, carrying on where Macomb and Newberry had left off. The La Sal, Abajo, and Carrizo mountains, and Ute Mountain, received particular attention. W. H. Holmes anticipated Gilbert in formulating the hypothesis of laccolithic origins of mountains, a fact recognized by Gilbert, who named one of the peaks in the Henry Mountains after Holmes. W. H. Jackson and Holmes described their discoveries of prehistoric ruins in Mesa Verde, Hovenweep, and elsewhere in the Four Corners region. Jackson took the first photographs of these important sites and Holmes made sketches and drawings of them.

The reports of these investigations are found in the annual publications and bulletins emanating from the Hayden Survey. Although these works cannot be compared with the artistic productions of the Powell Survey, they contain information of basic scientific value on the eastern side of the canyon country. Hayden also produced a topographic contour map of Colorado. Extending into Utah and Arizona, it equaled the maps published by Powell and Wheeler. It is unfortunate that Hayden did not extend his survey westward to the Colorado River as this region—the San Juan Triangle and the Navajo country west of Monument Valley and Marsh Pass—was not covered by any of the three great public surveys.[4]

THE DIRTY DEVIL ENTERS THE COLORADO. *The mouth of the Dirty Devil (lower center) is the dividing line between Narrow Canyon (right) and Glen Canyon (left). The Colorado River flows from right to left. Utah 1962.* [*A. E. Turner, Bureau of Reclamation*]

FORT MOQUI IN GLEN CANYON. *This was the name given to this prehistoric structure at the mouth of White Canyon near Dandy Crossing and Hite. It was first seen by Major John W. Powell in 1869. It has long been a primary tourist attraction in the canyon. Utah 1962. [W. L. Rusho, Bureau of Reclamation]*

The work of Powell, Wheeler, and Hayden in the years up to 1879 was a magnificent achievement. For the canyon country, Powell's work bulks the largest because the area was his primary responsibility. Elsewhere the contributions made by Wheeler and Hayden were of comparable importance. As a result of concerted study at about the same time, followed by publication of comprehensive treatises and maps, by 1880 the world could see a region in broad outline as well as in intimate detail where

RECORD OF THE SECOND POWELL EXPEDITION.
During the 1871 trip, Powell left a boat at the mouth of the Dirty Devil River. The next year some of the party went overland to pick it up. They stopped at Fort Moqui at the mouth of White Canyon, and on the rocks nearby left this inscription. The second voyage was sometimes called the "Western Exploring Expedition." Utah 1962. [C. Gregory Crampton]

GLEN CANYON. *The entrance to Hidden Passage. Utah 1962.* [*Tad Nichols, Tucson*]

twenty-one years before, when Macomb and Newberry entered, it was largely a blank.

Powell, Wheeler, and Hayden pointed out that climate, topography, and the behavior of streams impose controls on the vegetation and that these conditions could serve as guides to economic development. In the absence of minerals other than coal, they concluded that the region would be primarily suitable for grazing and that farming on the limited agricultural land was practicable only under irrigation. In the *Arid Lands* (1879), published by the Powell Survey, Powell and Thompson delineated the irrigable lands in the Colorado basin. These lands along the Paria, Escalante, San Rafael and other streams, already being occupied by frontier Mormons, were precisely located on the accompanying map of Utah, the first really accurate map of the territory.

When the Great Surveys were consolidated to form the U. S. Geological Survey in 1879, Clarence King was appointed the first director and John W. Powell was assigned to the Smithsonian Institution to continue the anthropological investigations already begun as a part of his Survey. In 1879 he was named first director of the Smithsonian's Bureau of American Ethnology, a post he held to the end of his life. In 1881, when King resigned from the Geological Survey, Powell was appointed to the directorship of that agency, a post he occupied until 1894. In both agencies Powell surrounded himself with competent men who published an everlengthening series of scientific monographs. Powell had made an epochal exploration of the Colorado River; his brilliant team of scientists went on to explore the canyon country and the Colorado Plateau; from there he went on to his greatest achievement which was to interest the government in the scientific study of the entire nation, particularly in the areas of ethnology, anthropology, irrigation, reclamation, and conservation. Much of this study he directed himself.[5] Major John Wesley Powell's run through the canyons of the Colorado in 1869 was an important trip.

ANGEL ARCH. *The Needles country, Utah.* [*Josef Muench, Santa Barbara*]

NATURAL ARCH. *White Mesa, Arizona.* [*William C. Miller, Pasadena*]

6 / Canyon Country Primeval

The Conditions of Life

A GOOD MANY OF THE PROBLEMS OF LIVING in an arid land had been learned by the Mormons some time before Powell published his book on the subject. Very soon after their arrival in the valley of the Great Salt Lake in 1847, the Latter-day Saints began exploring the mountains, east and west, north and south, to spy out the land in the valleys of the mountains and to appraise the resources of this new desert land. Within ten years a number of outposts had been located hundreds of miles away, and settlements nearer at hand were expressions of a frontier rapidly moving beyond the Salt Lake Valley. Mormon colonization easily and naturally followed the Spanish Trail. In 1855, at the Colorado River crossing, Alfred N. Billings and a company of forty-one men planted a settlement where Moab is now located, the first in the canyon country. In sixteen wagons drawn by oxen, with supplies of flour, wheat, corn, potatoes, peas, oats, and such hardware as whipsaws, axes, scythes, ironbars, trowels, hoes, shovels, and plows, and driving dairy cattle and horses, the expedition left the Great Basin by way of Salina Canyon and traveled the Spanish Trail through Castle Valley to the Green River. There they crossed the dry desert between the Green and the Colorado and, after considerable difficulty with the wagons in the lower part of Moab Canyon, they finally reached the river and ferried across. Arriving in mid-June, they immediately began to build a fort, plant crops, dig ditches, and preach to the Indians.

This was the Elk Mountain Mission, a colony founded primarily to advance missionary work among the Ute Indians. It was named after the La Sal Mountains known at the time as the Elk Mountains (a name later transferred to Elk Ridge west of the Abajos). Fortunately, the Indians seemed friendly, for the colonists' main concern was to get the crops in and a fort up. John McEwan wrote back to his brother describing life in the frontier community. There was no timber, even firewood was scarce, and the land, he said, was sandy. "How this soil will produce, I do not know; there is not much land for farming purposes anyhow. It is thick with sagebrush and greasewood, and nearly all sand. . . ." Not much interest in the landscape beyond the soil. "The Indians call this nothing but a kanyon," he wrote. "It is about three miles wide, mountains high and almost perpendicular where we are, of a reddish cast. . . ." The weather was hot. The sun beat upon them. The rocks around them, even the ground under them, radiated heat. "I have suffered more than I can express at present for want of water to drink; the sun's piercing rays and the sun burning your feet under you, soon dries a man up. I have been sick after being alkalied. I am just getting over it."[1]

The Elk Mountain Mission was gaining the kind of experience that Powell would summarize later. Dry climate for one thing. Look at a rainfall map of the United States and you will find that west of the hundredth meridian there is much less rainfall than there is east of it. Twenty inches of precipitation or less is the rule in most areas, but there are places where it is only half of that. In the canyon country of southeastern Utah and northeastern

THE KITCHEN HOUSE. *Kitchen Canyon, Utah.* [*Philip W. Tompkins Photograph, California Academy of Sciences*]

ABAJO MOUNTAINS. *North of Blanding, Utah.* [*Parker Hamilton, Flagstaff*]

Arizona the rains sometimes add up to ten inches. The West at large is semi-arid and dry; the canyon country is arid and drier. But general statements about canyon country climate can be deceptive. Variations in weather from place to place are so pronounced that it is more accurate to speak of several local climates rather than of one.

Take rainfall: The highest altitudes receive the greatest amounts; the lowlands and the canyons less. Thus you may often enjoy blue skies and sunshine while watching a summer storm break over the Henry Mountains, for example, not over ten miles away. During the summer, thunderstorms of short duration and brief cloudbursts covering a few square miles are frequent, though widely scattered. When a heavy rain falls on slick-rock areas, it quickly runs off: water appears everywhere; it gathers in courses and roars down steep slopes, falls over canyon rims, and fills usually dry washes with roiling water, canyon debris and mud and stones. Within a few hours after the storm, the bare-rock surfaces, except for occasional depressions or natural tanks, may be dry again, and within twenty-four hours the bed of the wash may be only wet sand with here and there a shallow pool.

The lower levels of the canyon country, below about 6,500 feet, are poorly supplied with water. Annual precipitation below this level seldom reaches ten inches and in most places is closer to half that. The few perennial tributaries of the Green, Colorado, and San Juan rivers derive mainly from snows that fall on the High Plateaus, the La Sal Mountains, the Abajos, and Elk Ridge. Some of these, like the Paria, Escalante, Dirty Devil, and San Rafael, are called rivers. During the spring run-off, they may carry a considerable volume of water, but through the remainder of the year, the normal flow is small and this is greatly reduced by irrigation. Small, constant streams, fed by springs, are common in the lower courses of the larger canyons tributary to the Colorado, Green, and San Juan rivers. Life in the canyon country is supported to a far greater extent by waters tributary to these rivers than by the master streams themselves.

As you would expect, the lowest elevations have the warmest weather, although not all places at the

BAKER RANCH. *Hall's Creek. Utah 1962.* [*Parker Hamilton, Flagstaff*]

PREHISTORIC IRRIGATION DITCH. *At the mouth of Cha Creek, San Juan River. Utah 1962.* [*Christy G. Turner II, Museum of Northern Arizona*]

same altitude have the same temperatures. The annual range of temperature in any given locality may be wide: Reaching up to 110 degrees in the summer, the thermometer may drop ten or more points below zero in the winter. Everywhere there is a marked range in the daily temperatures between day and night; during the warm weather months, this may reach 50 degrees. Hot days, even in the deep canyons, are followed by cool, comfortable nights. At the higher elevations, such as Bryce, Boulder Mountain, the La Sal and Abajo mountains, the summer nighttime temperatures can be uncomfortably cold.

Despite these extremes of temperature, the climate of the canyon country, as in many areas of the arid West, is healthful and invigorating. Generally clear skies (prolonged periods of overcast are rare) and gentle winds (severe storms are infrequent) are characteristic. To escape the hot days of spring and summer, all you need to do is to hunt the shade of a rock or a tree. On the open, treeless parts of their reservation, the Navajo Indians put up a simple summer shade consisting of brush thrown over poles, a ramada. They have long known that in the desert country the sharp edge of the shadow is the line between comfortable coolness and enervating heat.

In the arid lands of the canyon country, many forms of plant life are found, but overall vegetation is not abundant. Dark green conifer forests, interspersed with aspen, and here and there a meadowy glade, crown the highest elevations in the canyon country. Lower down, the cool tall pines and aspens give way to the pygmy forests of piñon and juniper interspersed with sagebrush.

Below about the 6,500-foot contour, where rainfall and snow are light, the pygmy evergreens begin to disappear and only the sage remains. At lower elevations, the sage in turn vanishes, leaving scrubby plants of lesser size, such as shadscale and blackbrush; here and there you may see several species of cacti. You may also see grass, at all elevations, but

BIG RUIN, SALT CREEK. *The Needles country, Utah.* [*M. Woodbridge Williams, National Park Service*]

only at the highest levels does it carpet the soil. At springs and along the courses of intermittent streams at the lower elevations, you may occasionally see a leafy cottonwood tree standing alone, offering summer shade to man and animals. Along the perennial streams and on the wet floors of the deeper canyons, cottonwoods are common. They are also plentiful in the major canyons of the Green and Colorado, but the banks of those streams are more often lined with willows.

The general sparseness of vegetation permits uninterrupted vistas over great distances, even on level terrain. At many points on the rims, at the breaks, and on the crests of folds and reefs, your eye may quickly travel through three life zones (Boreal, Transition, Upper Sonoran) as it moves from the timber-capped plateau, to the lighter greens of the pygmy trees and sage, to the open areas where low scrubby plants dot the soil and, through their very insignificance, dramatize the bold and sharp sandstone landscape. High landmarks may be seen from great distances and from many different points. Given some familiarity with the canyon country, you seldom feel lost. Travel very far and you will see the familiar welcome profile of a piece of standing up country: the blue-green dome of Navajo Mountain; the Bear's Ears; the La Sal, Abajo and Henry mountains; the long, straight line of the cliffs of the Kaiparowits Plateau or Piute Mesa; the dark, forest-covered, brooding brow of Boulder Mountain. Indeed, if you are used to the wide and open spaces, and love the magnificent distances of the canyon country, you are likely to feel hemmed in and lost in the green wooded areas of the East, and to long to see an acre or two of bare rocks again and breathe some dry air.

Wild animals live in the canyon country. Mule deer in large numbers graze the highlands in the summer and drift down to the pygmy forest and sage brush to winter. The inquisitive antelope favor life in the more open, lower country, while the mountain sheep, now rarely seen, prefer the rougher rimrock areas overlooking the canyons. In the low areas, where vegetation is scarce, animal life is scarce. Lizards skitter about, an occasional snake is seen, and at night bats fly and rodents prowl. Most animal species living in open-desert conditions,

where cover is light, are protectively marked with natural camouflage. The yellow rattlesnake, for example, when he moves into an environment where pink soil predominates, will change over and become a pink rattlesnake.

Beaver is common along the Colorado and Green rivers as well as in the cold streams formed by melting snows in the tall conifer forests. Larger species of fish are limited to the master streams and to a few of the perennial tributaries, like the Fremont and San Rafael rivers, where trout are caught near the headwaters. Carnivorous animals—coyotes, foxes, skunks, and badgers—range widely in the canyon country. In any location you are seldom out of sight of birds, ranging from the graceful, circling hawk to the horned lark, darting about in the brush by your trail or road.

Although the entire region is a product of erosion, arable land in the canyon country is scarce. Soil is formed as the rock disintegrates, but it soon washes away into water courses. Much of the soil suitable for agriculture has been formed mostly by stream action; it is likely to be loose in character, often shallow, though in some areas quite fertile. The alluvium-floored upper valleys of the perennial streams heading on the High Plateaus on the western side of the canyon country are extensive enough to support a number of towns and settlements. The limited soil in the deep canyons at the lowest levels has been unstable. Where at one time there was enough land to support limited numbers of prehistoric farmers, these marginal lands have later suffered from erosion.

Between the water courses, soil consists of eroded material filling spaces between projecting rocks, or it appears as the soft surface of the disintegrating formations such as the extensive shale soils found in Castle Valley and at the base of the Book Cliffs from Price to Grand Junction. There are only a few areas of extensive open land and these, like the Green River Desert and the Kaibito Plateau, may be loose and sandy, although you will see only a few areas of dune sand in the canyon country. Many areas consist of bare rock which have no soil covering at all.

Arable soil resources have been developed most extensively where they can be put under the ditch.

In a land of little rain, modern man lives where irrigation stretches the annual flow of water. Dry farming also has been practiced successfully, notably on the Sage Plain stretching from Monticello and Blanding, Utah, eastward into Colorado.

For human settlement, the best of the lands in the canyon country were around the edges, at the base of the High Plateaus and the Book Cliffs, at the feet of the La Sal and Abajo mountains, and Navajo Mountain. Water was not far away; even though it didn't rain enough, the streams fed by snows had not yet disappeared into the canyons below or sunk into the loose soil, and could be diverted for irrigation. There the big game animals ranged and there cattle and other stock would thrive. The first settlers were in sight of the life-giving uplands—the High Plateaus and the laccoliths along the eastern periphery. But they were also on the edge of a slick-rock wilderness below, where the soil, if any, thinned out, the vegetation nearly disappeared, and the streams dropped out of sight in canyons.

It was a beautiful country to live in, but when, as in the pioneer period, you were almost entirely dependent on the land, it was hard to see it that way.[2]

The Ancient Ones

CLEARING SAGE, BREAKING GROUND, looking for timber, digging ditches—the Mormons of the Elk Mountain Mission were probably the first white men to put to test the arable resources of the canyon country. They were aware that they were not its first inhabitants. In October 1854, Brigham Young had sent W. D. Huntington to establish contact with the Navajo Indians and to explore the southeastern part of the territory by way of the Spanish Trail. Huntington accomplished his objective, but found the Indians hostile, though willing to trade. En route the party explored a section of the San Juan River about fifty miles long and twenty-five miles wide, where they found many ruins. In his account of the exploration, Huntington wrote: "The walls of many buildings are still standing entire, some of them three or four stories high, with the ends of the red cedar joists set in the wall, some

projecting eight or ten inches, but worn to a point at their extremities . . . the first ruins we discovered were three stone buildings, crumbled to mere heaps. One appeared to have been a pottery, for in and around it were loads of fragments of crockery of fine quality, ornamented with a great variety of figures painted with various colors as bright as if put on but yesterday. . . . From here we traveled ten miles, with occasional ruins by the way, and entered a deep kanyon with projecting shelves of rock and under those shelves were numerous houses or fortifications. The one we examined was divided into twenty-four rooms, each nearly square and enclosing an area of about 144 square feet. The front wall was built up to the overhanging cliff, which formed the roof, and was curved, and full of portholes. The stones were all squared and faced, were of an equal thickness, and laid up with joints broken in a workman-like manner."

Huntington added that for three or four miles up the canyon from where they saw these remains, "buildings were everywhere in view, of various forms and dimensions, and in almost every stage of decay." After traveling twelve miles northeast of the San Juan River they came to the head of a canyon, "whose sides or banks, even to the very head, were perpendicular, and shelving, and near the banks there was no soil on the rocks . . . all around the head of this kanyon, and down on either side, as far as we could see, were houses of every conceivable form and size. . . . In the centre of this kanyon, and near the head, was a building 16 or 20 feet square; four stories high, and built upon a flat rock about 4 feet higher than the level of the bed of the kanyon. . . . One large building which we entered, stood on the edge of the precipice, with its front wall circular and flush with the bank which formed the back part, making the ground plan of the building like a half moon. . . ."

No precise locations are given but these descriptions, and others in Huntington's account, make it sound very much as if the first ruins they came to were in Montezuma Canyon, a northern tributary of the San Juan, draining much of the Sage Plain; the second group must have been one of the imposing groups of ruins now in Hovenweep National Monument. Huntington noticed there was no water at the latter site and he asked their Indian guides "how the former inhabitants could have managed;—they told us they had heard that a very long time ago there was water running here. We asked them who had built these houses. They smilingly shook their heads and said they had never heard. . . ."[3]

From the time of the arrival of the Spaniards in the sixteenth century to about 1880, the white man was very much intrigued by the prehistoric ruins of the Southwest and freely speculated about their origins. Using Spanish sources, the scientist, Alexander von Humboldt, made the startling suggestion that the Aztecs, after leaving their homeland in Aztlán in 1160, may have traveled across Utah and remained a time on the San Juan River before going on to the Gila River in Arizona. Humboldt's hypothesis was taken as fact by some who read his book and thereafter scattered "Aztecs" and "Montezumas" over the map. W. D. Huntington found his explanation in the *Book of Mormon*. W. H. Bell, whose work carried Powell's account of his 1869 voyage, wrote a chapter on "The Aztec Ruins of New Mexico and Arizona."[4]

John W. Powell and his men in 1869 and 1871 made the first observations of the ruins in the canyons of the rivers. Jackson and Holmes for the Hayden Survey mapped and described the imposing ruins of both Mesa Verde and Hovenweep. Powell developed a profound interest in both prehistoric and modern Indians and, as director of the Bureau of American Ethnology, he furthered much archeological research in the Southwest. Quite naturally, archeologists concentrated at first upon the more dramatic and spectacular ruins, and even then much of the work was reconnaissance in character. They were slow to carry their research into the canyon country until after the turn of the twentieth century, but as more systematic studies were undertaken, they began to edge into it. Since 1956 the comprehensive studies of the prehisory of man in Glen Canyon and the San Juan River canyon, undertaken for the National Park Service by the University of Utah and the Museum of Northern Arizona, have tied in with the earlier work and filled in the gap.[5]

Prehistoric man, the archeologists have found, has been in the West for a long time. For thousands of years the pioneer people (the Desert culture) lived the simple life, hunting and foraging and possessing few material goods. From archaic beginnings, they gradually developed a more sophisticated way of life. By the opening of the first century A. D., the Pueblo people, who had a distinctive culture, were living in the Southwest. The northern branch of the Pueblos, who by then had occupied all of the canyon country of southeastern Utah and northeastern Arizona and adjacent regions, has been called the "Anasazi," a Navajo word meaning the "ancient ones." The Anasazi Pueblos, who lived in separate localities, differed somewhat in their way of life and cultural development, and to these variations names have been assigned. The Fremont culture is found west of the Colorado River and north of the Waterpocket Fold; the Mesa Verde culture, east of the Colorado and north of the San Juan River; the Kayenta culture, east of the Colorado and south of the San Juan; and the Virgin River culture, west of the Colorado and south of the Waterpocket Fold. These boundaries, of course, are generalized and each of the four variants of the Anasazi culture extended beyond the limits of the canyon country, as we have defined it.

After passing through several stages, the Anasazi culture reached a climax in its development during the Great Pueblo period, a golden age that came to a rather abrupt end about A. D. 1300. Agriculture was a fundamental characteristic of these sedentary prehistoric people. Although they enjoyed hunting, their menu was largely vegetarian, consisting of corn, beans, and squash. These canyon-country farmers developed irrigation. They flooded some areas and built ditches to carry water from streams and springs to small plots of land. The land could support more farmers than hunters and so urban centers developed. In the Great Pueblo era there had already been a gradual evolution from the small one-room pit dwellings to the large apartment houses built of stone, adobe, and wood. Primary illustrations of architecture in this great era are Betatakin and Keet Seel in the Segi drainage, Inscription House in Navajo Canyon—all in Navajo

Columns at the Head of Capitol Gorge. *Capitol Reef National Monument, Utah.* [*Philip W. Tompkins Photograph, California Academy of Sciences*]

National Monument—and the splendid structures in Hovenweep National Monument, to say nothing of those in Mesa Verde National Park. Many lesser villages, built in the open or in recessed walls of cliffs, are scattered about over the canyon country.

Although they are best known for their architecture, the Anasazis also developed a significant material culture. Basketry of fine quality was one of their earliest skills; the use of wood and pottery followed. The storage of crops gave them leisure time to contemplate the universe, to develop art forms, and to complicate their lives. They painted figures on the rocks and cliffs (pictographs) and pecked out others (petroglyphs); they used turquoise, shells, and feathers to make objects of adornment, and they decorated some of their pottery with geometrical designs. Religious practice centered around the sacred kiva, the circular, subterranean chamber, which was restricted to men. Of the four divisions of the Anasazi culture—Fremont, Mesa Verde, Kayenta, and Virgin River—the Mesa Verde people in the canyon country seemed to have reached the highest development.

The Anasazi occupation of the canyon country was largely peripheral to the remote and nearly inaccessible canyons, particularly those close to the rivers. These Indians lived for centuries in the upland areas where the conditions of life were better, but during the tenth century they began to work down into the deeper canyons. They built their houses in recesses and protected places on cliff walls and farmed the limited lands on the canyon floors. This was a prehistoric frontier movement caused perhaps by a swelling population and by crowding in the more favored areas upcountry. On the canyon frontier, people were scattered, communities were smaller and they were occupied for relatively brief periods. Maybe the canyon Anasazis were restless or perhaps, being frontiersmen, they thought there was something better over in the next canyon. Nearly any place you go in the canyon country you will see some reminder of the Anasazis: rock chippings, a small granary, part of a house, a pictograph. They made use of the entire area.

Then something happened—before A.D. 1300. Probably it was the sustained drought of the pre-ceding twenty-five years; possibly it was the appearance of hostile nomadic peoples. Whatever the cause, by 1300 the Anasazi had pulled out of the canyon country, even out of the peripheral areas, and had moved south, abandoning their dwellings and leaving many tools and utensils behind them. Just what the ancient ones may have thought of the scenic qualities of the canyon country before they abandoned it, would be hard to say. From the location of some of their dwellings on cliffs and other high places, one is tempted to believe that they sometimes sought a room with a view.

The history of man in the canyon country until the coming of the Spaniards is nearly a blank. By the time Domínguez and Escalante arrived in 1776, the modern Indian tribes had taken over some of the areas once occupied by the prehistoric people. The Utes north of New Mexico early acquired the horse and modern weapons from the Spanish, and by the time the Mormons reached the Great Basin in 1847, the numerous Ute bands held the territory from the boundaries of New Mexico through Colorado to central Utah. Athwart the Spanish Trail, they aided and abetted the slave trade and taxed the caravans. But as the white man began to move south from Salt Lake and encroach upon their lands, and stop the slave trade, the Utes became alarmed. The Walker War in 1853, a series of serious incidents and killings in central Utah, was one result. Another incident occurred in the summer of 1855. At the Elk Mountain Indian Mission on the Colorado, things were going well. A stone fort sixty-four feet square had been completed; the corn and vines were doing nicely in the hot weather, irrigated with water from Elk Mountain and Pack-saddle (now Mill and Pack) creeks. Then on Sunday, September 23, a band of Elk Mountain Utes killed three men while they were outside the fort. Isolated and remote from the Mormon frontier, this first canyon country settlement was promptly abandoned.[6] Twenty-two years later the whites returned and founded a settlement at Moab. But by then, from several directions, the whites were moving into the canyon country, into areas where prehistoric people centuries before had tried their hand at farming.

7 / Mormon Frontier

Mission to the Hopis

THE MORMON THRUST, IN 1854, SOUTHEAST along the Spanish Trail to the country of the Navajos, and the founding of the Elk Mountain Indian Mission the next year was matched by a counter thrust southwest along the Spanish Trail. By 1855, with their settlements at Las Vegas and San Bernardino, in California, the Church of Jesus Christ of Latter-day Saints had secured a southern route—a corridor—to the coast. By this time the pioneers had begun to settle in the valley of the Virgin River in the extreme southern part of the Territory. In the narrow Santa Clara Valley in 1854, the Southern, or Santa Clara, Indian Mission was established among the Southern Paiutes.

The homeland of the Paiutes, who were closely related to the Utes, extended from central Utah south across most of the Arizona Strip to the Grand Canyon and southeast along the Virgin River. Some of them were to be found along the San Juan River between Navajo Mountain and Monument Valley. They seem to have been fewer in number than the Utes and their land was less well-endowed with water and game. Poor, politically and socially weak, the Paiute bands were easy prey for the Utes who exploited and enslaved them. They hunted and dug for food (hence the name Digger Indians), and efficiently got the most out of their stingy environment.

With the arrival of the Mormons, the Paiutes found that they must share an already over-taxed land with the newcomers. The farming methods of the Mormon farmer, however, increased the productivity of the soil, so things ran smoothly for

a few years. But the white men kept on coming. The Utah War brought them in increasing numbers and when the Civil War broke out, a Cotton Mission was sent in 1861 to grow cotton and to produce sugar, wine, and other products. Thus was founded Utah's Dixie in the Valley of the Virgin.[1]

One of the pioneers in Dixie was doughty Jacob Hamblin; three years after he had arrived at Santa Clara in 1854, he was named president of the Indian Mission. For twenty-nine years he served his church as missionary, Indian agent, explorer, colonizer, and peacemaker. Among his notable achievements was the opening of a route from the Mormon settlements on the Virgin River across the Arizona Strip, and from the Colorado, first to the Hopi villages and, later, to the upper valley of the Little Colorado. The expansion of the Mormon frontier into northern Arizona followed the way opened by Jacob Hamblin.

The groundwork for this Mormon expansion was laid in 1858 when Brigham Young instructed Hamblin to take a company of men to open relations with the Hopi towns in northeastern Arizona. Living on three imposing mesas drained by northern branches of the Little Colorado, the Hopis had long been of interest to the white man. Coronado's men saw them; Father Escalante in 1775 visited them before taking the long tour through Utah with Father Domínguez; Humboldt located them on his map of 1811. Since the time they had been brought into the United States by virtue of the Mexican cession in 1848, the Hopis had not been visited by any official exploring party until Lt. J. C.

THE VIEW FROM HOSKININNI MESA. *Agathla Peak (upper left), Arizona.* [*Tad Nichols, Tucson*]

Ives, en route home from the lower Colorado, stopped in to see them in the spring of 1858.

Hamblin's party from Santa Clara left late in October and traveled across the open country at the base of the Vermilion Cliffs by way of Pipe Spring to the northern end of the Kaibab Plateau where they encountered a band of Paiutes. Chief Naraguts, and about eighteen of his men, guided Hamblin's party to the Crossing of the Fathers, following practically the same route taken by Domínguez and Escalante eighty-two years before. The Paiutes knew best how to make the crossing. They all clasped hands and waded into the water, forming a line nearly a hundred feet long. On horseback, the whites followed the shallowest route as indicated by the depth of the weaving line of Indians ahead of them. Thanks to this guide service, the crossing was made without mishap. The Mormons rode out of the water and went on. The date was November 2, 1858. They were aware that the ford was known as the Crossing of the Fathers (though it was better known in Hamblin's day as the Ute Ford). They probably knew nothing of Domínguez and Escalante nor about the Catholics who had staged a little celebration there, November 7, 1776, praising the Lord and firing off a few musket shots.[2]

The wilderness of America was rapidly dwindling. Domínguez and Escalante and Miera had traveled two thousand miles without seeing any other Spaniards; they were indeed thankful to cross the last formidable barrier that stood between them and home. They returned to urge colonization by Spain of the land of the Yutas, recommending particularly that Catholic missions be established among the Indians in the valleys around Utah Lake. Within what seems only a few years now, another people, based in the valleys around Utah Lake, were planning Mormon missions to the Hopi Indians.

Hamblin successfully bridged the gap between the Mormon frontier and the Hopi villages, the practical limits of Spanish-Mexican influence west

of New Mexico. Leaving the Crossing of the Fathers, the explorers reached the village of Oraibi, where they were banqueted on "bean soup without a spoon," Hamblin said later. They visited the seven Hopi towns and, leaving four of their number to preach among the Indians, Hamblin and the others returned to Santa Clara by the same route. Before the winter was over the four missionaries had also returned to the Mormon settlements. The mission had not been a great success but, at least, the door was open. This was something of an achievement; the Hopis had not permitted Catholic missionaries since the Pueblo Revolt in 1680. In the fall of 1859, the Mormons sent a second mission to the Hopis led by Hamblin, but it made little progress. Still another mission to the Hopis was organized by Hamblin in the fall of 1860. As in previous trips, the party, consisting of nine men, forded the Colorado at the Crossing of the Fathers. Three days later, on the trail near Tonalea, George Albert Smith, Jr., was killed by hostile Navajos.[3]

War with the Navajos

GEORGE ALBERT SMITH, JR., killed on November 2, 1860, was the first casualty in a conflict between two frontiers that met in the canyon country. The Mormons moving eastward from their base settlements along the Virgin River, bent upon missionary work with the sedentary Hopis, ran into the vanguard of the Navajos who were moving into the canyon country of the Colorado and the San Juan to escape the power of the United States. Since 1846–8, when they found themselves under a new flag, the Navajos had been troublesome. Fort Defiance, a U. S. Army Post in Navajo country, had been founded in 1850, but the Indian raids and robberies led to a warlike state in 1858. Military expeditions in 1858, 1859, and 1860 ranged north and west of Defiance and forced recalcitrant Navajos into retreat and hiding. It was some of these who stopped the Mormon party and killed young Smith. Hamblin said later that the Indians were avenging the death of some relatives "who had been killed by pale faces like us."

Trouble between the United States and the Navajos continued until a state of open war was reached in 1863; this did not cease until January 1864, when Colonel Kit Carson and the New Mexico Volunteers starved the Indians out of their stronghold in Canyon de Chelly in the heart of their tribal territory, and forced them to capitulate. But not all of the Navajos surrendered. Many of them earlier had headed north into the canyon country of the San Juan—where they moved in among the Paiutes —and west toward Glen Canyon, and these escaped the long forced-march and the concentration camp at Bosque Redondo in New Mexico in the years 1864–8.[4]

In central Utah trouble was also developing between the whites and the Utes, and by 1865 an uprising of Indians threatened the entire Mormon frontier. This, the Black Hawk War, caused the abandonment of many of the isolated Mormon communities; it cost about seventy lives and over a million dollars before it was brought under control by the Utah Territorial Militia in 1868.

The Navajos joined in the war and prolonged it for another year. At times they aligned themselves with Paiute bands who were smarting under the advancing of the Mormon frontier. Early in 1865, Navajos stole some horses from the new settlement of Kanab. Paiutes raided Kanab in December of the same year, and in January 1866, Paiutes and Navajos killed J. M. Whitmore and Robert McIntyre near Pipe Spring. A force of the Iron Military District, Utah Territorial Militia, with headquarters at St. George, chased the marauders to the Crossing of the Fathers. They found the river frozen; the Indians had made a trail of sand on the ice from shore to shore, over which they had led the stolen stock and made good their escape.

The situation became worse. In the spring of 1866, Joseph, Robert, and Isabella Berry, living on the East Fork of the Virgin in Long Valley, were killed by Indians. Outlying settlements were abandoned and once more the militia gave chase. Five platoons of cavalry—sixty-two men—were called out. Captain James Andrus was put in command and ordered to examine the country bordering on the Colorado River from the Kaibab Plateau north

STORM OVER THE DESERT. *Utah.* [*Philip W. Tompkins Photograph, California Academy of Sciences*]

to the mouth of the Green River. They were to search out all of the crossings of the Colorado within this distance; they were to punish the enemy and to conciliate the friendly Indians. And they were ordered to learn as much as possible about the resources of the country they saw.

Mustered into service at St. George on August 16, 1866, the command was in the saddle for about thirty days. It carried out an important exploration. Traveling by way of Pipe Spring and Kanab, one detachment then headed northeast across country new to whites and met another detachment in the open valley of the Paria River near the later village of Cannonville. Near there they had their only encounter with the Indians. On August 26, Elijah Averett, leading two animals, was crossing a shallow but precipitous canyon, when, from ambush, he was shot and killed. The Indians escaped in the rough country and the victim was buried in a lonely spot now known as Averett Canyon, or Hollow.

While in the valley of the Paria, the militiamen took note of the deeply eroded cliffs since known as Bryce Canyon, and then with some difficulty they crossed over to the upper valley of the Escalante River. From there they worked their way up to the flat top of the Aquarius Plateau. After riding through groves of pine and aspen, they came out on Bown's Point, or Deer Point, on the eastern rim where they had an unparalleled view of the canyon country spread out below them like a map. Adjutant F. B. Woolley said of the view: "Below . . . to the S. E. is the Colorado Plateau, stretching away as far as the eye can see, a naked barren plain of red and white Sandstone crossed in all directions by innumerable gorges. . . ." He noted occasional high buttes standing above the general level and he could

TRACHYTE RANCH AND MOUNT HILLERS. *Henry Mountains, Utah.* [*Parker Hamilton, Flagstaff*]

see here and there "the country rising up to the ridges marking the 'breakers' or rocky bluffs of the larger streams. The Sun shining down on this vast red plain almost dazzled our eyes by the reflection as it was thrown back from the fiery furnace." They could clearly see the Pot-se-Nip Mountains, the earliest known name of this spectacular group which Powell, thinking them unknown, named the Henry Mountains. From the top of the Aquarius, Andrus thought he could see the mouth of the Green River. (He could not; it was eighty miles away.) Having carried out his instructions as nearly as practicable, the command returned to St. George by way of the Awapa Plateau, Grass Valley, Circleville, and Parowan.[5]

The war dragged on. Armed patrols, often assisted by friendly Paiutes, guarded the trails between the Colorado and the Mormon frontier, a vigilance that was necessary for several years. The Indians often eluded these guards, and even the detachments of militia sent to punish them. In the fall of 1869, Jacob Hamblin, with a party of forty men including some Paiute Indians, ferried the Colorado on rafts at Lee's Ferry and visited the Hopis once again, hoping to learn if other Indians besides the Navajos were raiding the Mormon settlements. He was told the Navajos were planning another raid and he hurried home by the same route. Had he returned by the Crossing of the Fathers, he would have met face to face a Navajo raiding party driving 1,200 to 1,500 head of stolen stock.[6]

Not long before, Major Powell had come down through Glen Canyon on his first voyage. He saw no one at the Crossing of the Fathers nor at the mouth of the Paria. The voyagers went on. In the Grand Canyon C. H. Howland, Seneca Howland, and William Dunn left the expedition to walk out. It was a cruel fate that they should walk into a war. The Paiute Shivwits killed them a few days after they left the river. The next summer Powell, with Jacob Hamblin as guide, went out to the Shivwit country to see if they could find out what had happened to Dunn and the Howlands. The Indians readily admitted the killing. Powell's men had been mistaken for miners who had killed a squaw in a

drunken brawl on the other side of the river. No one had ever come down the river; therefore, the Indians concluded, they must have crossed the canyon. "When white men kill our people, we kill them," the chief explained.

Powell next prevailed on Hamblin to guide him to the Hopi villages where he enjoyed a lengthy stay, and then Hamblin prevailed on Powell to go with him to Fort Defiance to try to make peace with the Navajos. The two men made a good team. On November 9, 1870, peace was signed at Fort Defiance between the Mormons and the Indians. Trade sprang up after the war. On his second trip through the canyons of the Colorado, Powell arrived at the Crossing of the Fathers the first week in October 1871. While he was camped there, the first Navajo party came by en route to the Mormon settlements to trade; this began a business relationship that continued for many years. The peace was almost broken when three Navajos were killed in Grass Valley on the east fork of the Sevier, but Hamblin again met the war-minded chiefs near Moenkopi in January 1874 and made the peace.[7] One of the first Mormons to engage in the Indian trade was John D. Lee who, in 1873, opened a ferry downstream thirty-nine miles from the Crossing of the Fathers, and that historic ford was soon forgotten.

Lee's Ferry

LEE'S FERRY, the dividing point between the upper and lower basins of the Colorado River, and closely associated with developments in both, is a place of historic and scenic importance. Here the Colorado dramatically breaks through the Echo Cliffs and leaves the walls of Glen Canyon behind as it sweeps out into the open with low banks on either side, half a mile long on the left side and two miles on the right. Here the river tumbles over the huge boulder delta at the mouth of the Paria and is then swallowed by Marble Canyon. This was the one place where the Colorado was readily accessible. It was the only open place of this kind throughout the entire canyon system of the Colorado below Moab, and below the town of Green River, on the

Green, until you passed entirely through the Grand Canyon, a distance of over five hundred miles.

The Colorado at Lee's Ferry could not be forded: Domínguez and Escalante found that out in 1776 and so they went on to the Crossing of the Fathers upstream. Later Jacob Hamblin rafted across a couple of times but it was a dangerous undertaking. The first Powell expedition camped one night here in 1869 without giving the place much notice. The next year, Powell and Jacob Hamblin brought in with them some lumber on mule back to build the first ferry, a crude boat, the *Cañon Maid*, on which the party crossed the river. In 1871 the second Powell expedition ended its run for the year here; before Powell returned in the summer of 1872 to continue his voyage into Marble and Grand Canyon, John D. Lee had arrived. In hiding for complicity in the Mountain Meadows massacre, he had learned from Jacob Hamblin of the remote spot at the mouth of the Paria. With one of his wives, Emma, he moved there in December 1871. The place was inadvertently given its name by Emma when she first saw it and exclaimed, "Oh, what a lonely dell!" And Lonely Dell it was for years. Lee then went to work: He put up a house and when spring came he selected some level ground, put in crops, and dammed the river for irrigation water.

Through the year 1872, John D. Lee occasionally ferried people across the river, using first a crude raft and later the *Nellie Powell*, one of Powell's boats which he had discarded as being unseaworthy. Formal service was opened on January 11, 1873, when a ferry boat, the *Colorado*, built on the spot, was christened. Thus it began: a new crossing of the Colorado, replacing the historic ford upstream found by Domínguez and Escalante. Lee's Ferry served as a major crossing of the Colorado until it was replaced in 1929 by Navajo Bridge built across Marble Canyon six miles below.

Ownership passed from Lee to the Church of Jesus Christ of Latter-day Saints, to the Grand Canyon Cattle Company, and finally to Coconino County, Arizona, in which it is located. These

GLEN CANYON AND GRAND BENCH. *Utah 1962.*
[*Tad Nichols, Tucson*]

97

changes were indications of the major interest served: Following the exploratory work undertaken by Jacob Hamblin, who in the winter of 1873-4 opened a road to the Moa Ave-Tuba City-Moenkopi oasis and to the San Francisco Mountains, the Mormons in the 1870's trekked from Utah and crossed by the ferry on their side to settle the valley of the Little Colorado. Broad economic development of the Arizona Strip followed, including the opening of public roads between Utah and Arizona.

The ferry business was not the only activity at Lee's Ferry. Lee opened trade with the Indians—they were among his first customers on the ferry in 1872; during the Glen Canyon gold rush it was a departure point by horseback and boat for the mines upstream; here in 1897-8 the Hoskaninni Company, the biggest gold operation in Glen Canyon, set up one of its headquarters; here Charles H. Spencer set about placering for gold in the colored Chinle shales in 1910; here was the beginning point for the detailed survey of the Colorado River (upstream to the mouth of the Green River, including the San Juan River up to the mouth of Chinle Creek), undertaken in 1921 by the U. S. Geological Survey and the Southern California Edison Company. The 1921 survey was in anticipation of reclamation development in the upper basin. The year 1922 was an important date in the history of the Colorado River for then the Colorado River Compact was signed. This compact divides the available water of the Colorado between the upper and the lower basin states. The point of division between the two basins, as established in the Compact, was fixed at Lee's Ferry, or, more precisely, at a point one mile below the mouth of the Paria River.

Although John D. Lee and Emma Lee called their ranch at the mouth of the Paria, Lonely Dell, Lee's Ferry has since become the accepted name for this rugged and historic crossroads where the Echo Cliffs face the towering Vermilion Cliffs and where the Colorado comes to the surface briefly between two great canyons. The name is an appropriate monument to a man who, with Jacob Hamblin, opened the way between Utah and Arizona.[8]

RIPGUT FENCE. *Boulder, Utah.* [*Parker Hamilton, Flagstaff*]

LEE'S FERRY IN OPERATION, 1910. *Arizona.* [*A. H. Jones*]

CAINEVILLE. *Utah.* [*Parker Hamilton, Flagstaff*]

8 / Hole-in-the Rock

Villagers Under the Rim

THE EXPANSION OF THE MORMON FRONTIER of settlement, moving outward from Salt Lake City after 1847, was the work of a people determined to extend their spiritual and temporal realm —to build the Kingdom of God in the wilderness. It was a co-operative, planned movement, best described as colonization, in contrast to the haphazard, individualistic character of frontier growth elsewhere in the West. Brigham Young exhorted the members of his church, saying to them that the Kingdom would have to be *built*; and under his vigorous direction, the colonization of new lands, the tilling of the soil, the reclaiming of barren places, and redeeming of the earth took on religious significance. The remarkable success of Mormon pioneering in Utah and neighboring areas in the West is a tribute to resourceful men of faith, accepting ecclesiastical direction and submitting to group discipline, in order to promote the building of their Zion.

Mormon colonization followed an accepted pattern. The church issued "calls" to those who were expected to perform "missions." This was commonly done where the church desired the settlement of areas which would not have readily filled up in normal frontier growth. Individuals thus appointed formed a company to found new industries (the Cotton Mission in Dixie), to settle among and to preach to the Indians (the Elk Mountain Indian Mission), or to establish new farming communities. Individual members of the mission were chosen to include men of diverse skills and crafts to insure the self-sufficiency of the new settlement. Upon reaching its destination the company was expected

to lay out a community after the model of Salt Lake City, which in turn had been modeled after the "Plat of the City of Zion," used by the Mormons first in the Middle West. This plan called for a village laid out on a square, with wide streets, a central public area, and lots of equal size. The lots were large enough to support a cow or two, chickens, a vegetable garden, and fruit trees. Thus, within the village, the settler raised enough to support his family. He would go out daily to work on his fields, often located some distance from town. Even when places were colonized without the necessity of forming a mission, villages were still laid out, though some of them in the canyon country never got very big.

Although the plan of the village was developed before the Mormons moved to Utah, it was well suited to the needs of the frontier colonies: It facilitated defense (the first building in many new villages was the fort) and co-operative action; it afforded an intimate social and cultural life centering about the church; it was the pattern adopted nearly everywhere by the Mormons in their settlement of the West. Thus, the formally organized farm-village, by no means common in the United States, became an important frontier institution.[1]

It is interesting that three distinct peoples in the Southwest developed and perpetuated village life: the prehistoric Pueblos were the first; they were followed by the Spaniards, and then came the Mormons. Though Spanish explorers were the first Europeans to visit the canyon country of southeastern Utah and northeastern Arizona, they founded no settlements there. The Anasazis built substantial

HOLE-IN-THE-ROCK. *Utah 1962.* [*Al Morton*]

communities, especially during the Great Pueblo era, but they abandoned them before A.D. 1300.

The beginnings of Mormon settlement in the canyon country were made in 1855, but, as we have seen, the Elk Mountain Mission was abandoned when attacked by the Utes. Forced back in one sector, the Mormons returned again by way of the Virgin River settlements, following the route opened by Domínguez and Escalante, and Jacob Hamblin. By 1865, when the war with the Indians began, the frontier of settlement had been pushed to the middle course of the Paria River where Peter Shurtz (frequently spelled Shirts) was working a small farm right on the trail to the Crossing of the Fathers.

Now Shurtz liked to go it alone; he must have felt crowded where the population exceeded two persons per hundred square miles. About three miles below the Cockscomb where the Paria breaks through it, the river flowed through a canyon about six hundred feet deep but in a valley that is almost half a mile wide. Here, well over a hundred miles from St. George, Shurtz squatted on the land, put up a rock house for his family and prepared to spend the winter. As the war began, he was among the first to face troublesome Indians; during the winter, hungry Indians drove off and ate his ox. Something of a diplomat, Peter Shurtz reasoned with the Indians, explaining that since they had killed the animal, they all would now go hungry, as he could not plow and plant. His argument was so clear that the Indians became convinced of their error, and when spring arrived, they turned to and pulled the plow, in relays of four at a time, and thus the first crops were put in on the Paria. But the war soon got too close and Shurtz was forced to move back to civilization—but not for long. He is next seen on the San Juan River. In 1877 he built a cabin at the mouth of Montezuma Creek so he could get away from the crowd. But his peace was soon disturbed; within three years the Mormon frontier had caught up with him.[2]

The Mormon-Navajo war, 1865–70, cleared the way for settlement of the canyon country at the eastern base of the High Plateaus. Once the Indian troubles were over, the Mormons began pushing eastward into the canyon country to exploit the lands discovered during the campaigns. Across the Arizona Strip they came, from the Virgin River settlements; and from the older settlements in the Sevier Valley in the Great Basin, they crossed over to the Colorado drainage, where they founded isolated settlements and small villages under the rims of the High Plateaus. Thirteen years after Hamblin and Powell made peace with the Navajos at Fort Defiance, in 1870, practically all of the agricultural lands on the western side of the canyon country had been taken up by the Mormons.

There were three places along the Paria River where farming was possible: One of them was Lee's Lonely Dell. Another was near the Peter Shurtz farm which had been abandoned at the outset of the war. Paria was begun in 1870 and Adairville downstream from it was occupied three years later. The most successful settlements were those founded in the Paria amphitheater at the base of the Paunsaugunt and Table Cliff plateaus. From beginnings made in 1874, a cluster of villages developed, including Clifton, Cannonville, and Henrieville.

In 1875, settlers from Sevier Valley crossed over the 9,000-foot-high saddle between the Table Cliff Plateau and the Aquarius Plateau to settle Potato Valley on the upper heads of the Escalante River. Boulder, on one of the forks of the Escalante, was an offshoot of Escalante. From the Great Basin, settlers crossed the Awapa Plateau and began colonizing the Fremont River valley. Traveling downstream through Rabbit Valley, past the Red Gate between Boulder Mountain and Thousand Lake Mountain, through Capitol Reef, and along the northern base of the Henry Mountains, the settlers found sites for a number of settlements and villages. These included Fremont, Loa, Bicknell, Caineville, and Hanksville.

The Spanish Trail passed through Castle Valley at the base of the Wasatch Plateau. The region had been known since the day when it came under Mexican jurisdiction, but it had never been settled. During the Black Hawk War the possibilities of the region as a place for settlement were noted by militiamen as they pursued Indians into the valley. In 1877, colonization began and a number of vil-

DANCE HALL ROCK. *Hole-in-the-Rock trail, Utah.* [*C. Gregory Crampton*]

lages were soon strung along the headstreams of the Muddy and San Rafael rivers and along the Price River. Ferron, Castle Dale, Orangeville, Huntington, and Price were among the earliest settlements. Most of the permanent communities were nestled about the bases of the life-giving High Plateaus where water brought by ditches was spread out over the land. Green oases against the bright-colored backgrounds of eroded sandstone dramatically marked the location of Mormon villages, from the Paria River on the south to the Price River on the north.[3]

Hole-in-the-Rock

THE VIGOROUS FRONTIER COLONIZATION by the Mormons, following the closing of Indian hostilities in 1870, was partly motivated by the growing hostility between Saints and the non-Mormons—the gentiles. The transcontinental railroad, completed in 1869, and the discovery of gold and silver mines had brought many gentiles into the territory. Tension, developing over such matters as polygamy and politics, suggested the desirability, not only of extending the Kingdom, but of insuring Mormon supremacy in all parts of it.

Brigham Young had energetically pushed frontier expansion, but when he died in 1877, Mormon settlement had not yet crossed the Colorado into the eastern side of the canyon country. After the failure of the Elk Mountain Mission, Mormon colonization had been directed southward to the Virgin River and then eastward from there and across the Colorado by way of Lee's Ferry. But by 1877 there were important stirrings in the Four Corners area. The reports of the Hayden Survey publicized the region and the maps showed trails and roads. Prospectors were rushing about in southwestern Colorado and farmers were beginning to settle along the open valley of the San Juan in northwestern New Mexico. And cattlemen from as far away as

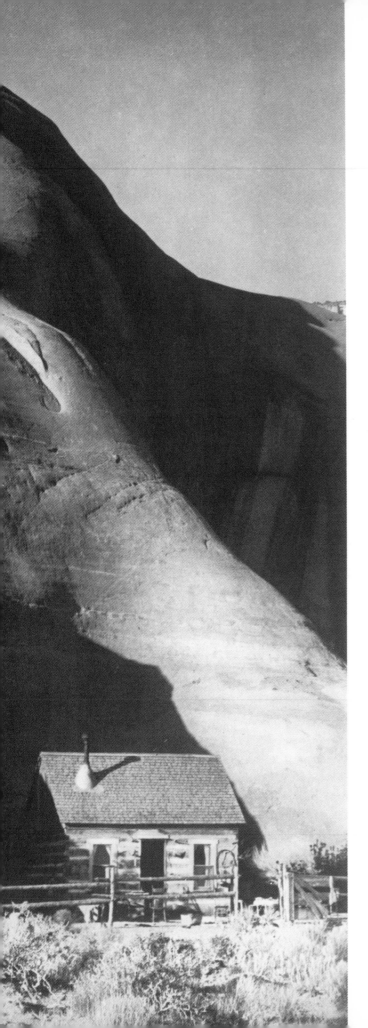

Texas were tapping the range in southeastern Utah. Moreover, the Ute and Navajo Indians were restive.

In order to establish a foothold in the distant southeastern corner of the territory, the Church of Jesus Christ of Latter-day Saints organized a mission, to first select a site, and then to found a settlement. A call was issued by the church in December 1878 at Parowan, and in March 1879 at Cedar City —both older Great Basin towns dating from the 1850's. Under the direction of Silas S. Smith, who favored a location on the San Juan River, a scouting and exploring party including some women and children left Paragonah, near Cedar City, in April 1879 to search for a suitable place to settle.

Smith and his party carried out a notable exploration. They crossed the Colorado at Lee's Ferry and traveled south along the Echo Cliffs to Moenkopi. At that point, where permanent Mormon settlement had just begun they turned abruptly north and opened a wagon road through the Navajo country to the San Juan River. There, at the mouth of Montezuma Creek, they found Peter Shurtz, the pioneer of the Paria, who had arrived in 1877. There were two or three other families living along the San Juan, but Shurtz was the only Mormon, and so Silas Smith decided to locate the colony to follow at Montezuma Creek. Leaving some of their number at the San Juan, the explorers returned by a comparatively easy route that took them north to the Spanish Trail. They crossed the Colorado at Moab, where there were a few settlers, and then followed the Spanish Trail back to their starting point.

The Smith party had traveled nearly a thousand miles in a great circle and it had found roads passable for wagons. The colonizing expedition to follow now faced the prospect of making a long rough journey of five hundred miles to Montezuma Creek. They could go halfway around the circle in either direction, or they could open a shorter, unknown route. They chose to attempt a shortcut. As final preparations were being completed at Parowan, Reuben Collett and Andrew P. Schow of Escalante reported that it was possible to cut across lots by

SODA CABIN. *At the foot of Fifty-Mile Mountain, Utah.*
[*C. Gregory Crampton*]

SLICK-ROCK WILDERNESS OF THE LOWER ESCALANTE RIVER. *Glen Canyon foreground and right. Utah 1962.*
[*A. E. Turner, Bureau of Reclamation*]

way of Escalante. This information was seized upon by the mission and a rendezvous point was chosen —Forty Mile Spring southeast of Escalante. It was no small task to take wagons over the rim to Escalante and thence forty miles over the open desert to the spring, but finally in November 1879 nearly all of the personnel of the expedition, numbering over two hundred and fifty persons—men, women, and children—had assembled and final preparations were made. Eighty-three wagons were to make the trip. A thousand head of stock were to be driven along.

During the wait at Forty Mile, a huge sandstone rock nearby was found to be suitable for dances. With three fiddlers along, some pleasant evenings were held in the place called by the pioneers, Dance Hall Rock. Ominous news began to travel through the camp—the country ahead had not been thoroughly explored. The gorge of Glen Canyon blocked their passage and no one knew what lay on the other side of the river. Could they get through at all? As they were asking themselves these questions, someone brought the news into camp that early snows on the High Plateaus blocked their return. There was little choice now but to go ahead. Under the leadership of Silas S. Smith and Platte D. Lyman, the Mormon colonizers went ahead on what was to be a heroic trek.

Two and a half miles below the mouth of the Escalante River the colonizers found a natural fault on the rim of Glen Canyon. This was just a narrow crack—a slit—at its head but it opened out below into a very short and very steep tributary canyon of the Colorado. By blasting, the Mormons enlarged the crack wide enough to accommodate wagons. They made a "hole" in the rock, the name since given to the site.

The descent over the west rim of Glen Canyon was the most serious obstacle encountered on the entire trek. They not only had to enlarge the fault but, in order to build a road with a grade feasible for wagons, they had to cut back into the solid stone some distance to compensate for the forty-five-foot cliff at the rim. And below the base of the Hole, there was nothing but a narrow declivity at the head of the canyon and steep slopes of bare rock on either side. A road was built along the left side of this declivity some distance above its bed. Narrow places were widened by blasting or by picking away the sandstone rock and heavy talus, and by shoring up the road on the canyon side. At one dramatic place, where there was nothing more than a narrow ledge on a near-perpendicular wall, oak logs were set in holes picked in the cliff, stringers were laid across them, and on these a road wide enough for wagons was built out around the obstacle—a cantilever road on the side of the cliff. Halfway down, the going wasn't so bad—the wagons slid down a steep slope of sand.

The vertical drop through the Hole to the edge of the Colorado River was a thousand feet, this is the distance of three-quarters of a mile. The building of the road from the rim to the river cost the pioneer band six weeks time—about the time they had expected to take for the entire trip. Beginning on January 28, 1880, the entire caravan of eighty-three wagons was driven down through the Hole to the river's edge below. The wagons were braked and the wheels locked, but none was dismantled. The indefatigable historian, Andrew Jenson, visited the Hole in 1928 and forecast the incredulity of those to see the place after him: "How they ever got their wagons down that steep incline will puzzle all future generations."

This was only the beginning. Once in Glen Canyon, it was necessary to get out on the other side. A ferryboat was assembled by Charles Hall and the entire expedition, two wagons at a time, was rowed across. The way out was difficult enough but they did it in stages: A dugway was built from the river up to a 250-foot high bench; then up Cottonwood Creek to near its head—more rock work, the Dugway and Little-Hole-in-the-Rock to get up Cottonwood Hill; from Cheese Camp, it was up the narrow Chute to the base of Grey Mesa, and then a number of short dugways put them out on the flat top of Grey Mesa where they found the snow a foot deep. It was February 1880.

The view from the top of Grey Mesa was breathtaking. The pioneers traveled along the southern rim of the mesa, overlooking the Big Bend of the San Juan River in a canyon a thousand feet deep.

Behind, the Straight Cliffs of the Kaiparowits Plateau reminded them of the weeks they had spent in coming this far. Navajo Mountain boldly stood out on the skyline across the San Juan; ahead of them was an endless confusion of rock and sand, mesas and slick rock. There were few trees. Elizabeth Decker wrote home: ". . . It's nothing in the world but rocks and holes, hills and hollows. The mountains are just one solid rock. . . ." But there wasn't much time for the view, only for necessities of life, and not much for them. On February 21, 1880, during a bad blizzard on Grey Mesa, Olivia Larson, lying on the spring seat of a wagon, gave birth to a boy (named John Rio—he was born within sight of the San Juan River), the third child born since the trek began. Three days later the Larsons had caught up with the train.

When a mountain sheep was started on the mesa, the guides followed it and it led them to a passable, if steep, route down; now across rolling, bumpy rock to a pleasant surprise—Lake Pagahrit on the upper course of Lake Canyon. Sometime in the past a natural dam of sand had formed in the canyon and the flow of water was enough to fill and maintain a clear sheet of water half a mile long. The banks were green and water birds were flying about. After spending time to catch up on their laundry, the caravan drove over the dam and went on.

And so it went. There were a few pleasant, restful stops. But most of the time was spent scouting ahead for the best route—there was not a sign of a wagon track anywhere to guide them; the pulling was slow and there was road work. After leaving the lake, it was rather an easy pull up Castle Wash (named after a prehistoric ruin along the way) to Clay Hill Pass. Here they could look far ahead across the Grand Gulch Plateau but the goal was not in sight. Nothing to do but go ahead. Down Clay Hill, a steep road had to be built all the way. Through the pass, they took a sight on Bear's Ears and headed Grand Gulch.

A new obstacle on Grand Flat—a dense forest of juniper, piñon, and cedar. Trees had to be cut down to let the wagons by. Scouting for a route was exceedingly difficult. As they started down into Comb Wash, the Abajos—already known as the Blues—came into view, a landmark which the settlers had been told was within sight of their destination.

Finally, by way of Snow Flat and the Twist, they reached the bed of Comb Wash only to find the beetling thousand-foot-high cliff of Comb Ridge standing in front of them. Turn down Comb Wash —no other way to go. Mile after mile through the sand of the wash—still no pass through the ridge. They came to the San Juan and found the river had cut a canyon across the Ridge, but the cliffs of this canyon blocked their passage along the river's bank. There was only one way. They had to go up over Comb Ridge. Stop again. Build more dugway. Even the best gradient they could find was almost too steep. Almost, but not quite. Three days were spent on what the pioneers named "San Juan Hill." Seven worn teams to the wagon pulled and clawed at the steep, slick-rock "road," slipping, falling to their knees; but goaded and whipped, finally they topped the grade. Only about twenty-five or thirty miles to go.

After building more dugway to get across Butler Wash, they reached the open sandy banks of the San Juan. Going on, they soon came to Cottonwood Wash, crossed it and camped on the flat bottomlands, April 6, 1880. Only eighteen miles to go and it was open road all the way. But they had had all they could take. They had spent the entire winter on the road. Everyone had come through and three babies were born en route. The decision was made in sheer exhaustion: "We'll stay here." There was water and wood and land. That evening a general site was selected for the village, to be named "Bluff City"; one committee was formed to manage the building of a ditch, another was named to lay out the town site. Platte D. Lyman wrote in his diary: "Wednesday, April 7th, 1880. We began laying off the lots and land and most of the brethren began work on the ditch."[4]

overleaf: GOOSENECKS OF THE SAN JUAN RIVER. *Utah State Park in foreground.* [*Tad Nichols, Tucson*]

9 / The Rock Jungle

Twisting the Mule

FOR ABOUT A YEAR AFTER THE HOLE-IN-THE-Rock colonizing expedition had crossed Glen Canyon, the road they built served as a main link between the new settlement at Bluff and the older communities whence the trekkers had come. Traffic over the road went both ways, though as you look at sections of the road today—many of them are still difficult to reach, San Juan Hill, for example—this seems incredible. But at best, the road between Escalante and Bluff, which crossed some of the most rugged parts of the canyon country, must have been one of the longest roughest wagon roads in the West.

Charles Hall stayed on through 1880 operating the ferry at Hole-in-the-Rock crossing, though there wasn't much business. No one went over the new road unless he had to. Hall began to scout out a new route across the river and he finally found one thirty-five miles upstream at a place since known as Hall's Crossing. This was located just above the mouth of Hall's Creek, which headed on the slopes of the Waterpocket Fold and in the Circle Cliffs. At Hall's Crossing, the walls of Glen Canyon lowered on either side and from here it was indeed much easier to approach the canyon.

It was probably Charles Hall who worked out the wagon road from Escalante to the new crossing. To anyone in Escalante wanting directions, he would have said: Stay on the Hole-in-the-Rock road for ten miles and then turn left into Harris Wash. Follow the Wash—there's no other way to go as it drops down into a canyon. At its mouth you will find yourself at the Escalante River, which you

will have to ford. Before crossing, go upstream nearly half a mile until you come opposite the mouth of a narrow canyon. This is Silver Falls Creek. There's water in it for a ways. There are some steep pitches over slick rock. Then you leave the cliff behind as you come out into the open.

The country around you won't make much sense. It's choppy—piñon and juniper obscure the view—you can easily get lost. Keep on climbing. Soon you will top out. Now stop and take your bearings. You have just come through the rough country enclosed by the Circle Cliffs, which you can see back of you and toward the north and ahead of you. Off to the north is the dark rim of Boulder Mountain; those isolated gray-green peaks to the east are the Henry Mountains.

The roughest part of the road is just ahead. You have stopped on a narrow flat top. Below you is a huge funnel-like opening between two cliffs. Drive down over that steep slope and head for the funnel; it's about two miles to the bottom—you drop a thousand feet. You're in a canyon now. It's deep, narrow, one sharp bend after another, and the cliff walls are undercut at nearly every turn. You might have to do some roadwork in this canyon to get your wagons through. (So typical of the canyon country, this narrow, winding canyon, barely permitting wagons, was later named Muley Twist.)

Keep going. That open sky ahead is the valley of Hall's Creek. When you reach the mouth of the canyon you have passed clear through the Waterpocket Fold. (Powell's men named it.) When you get out into the open, you will be on Hall's Creek.

MULEY TWIST CANYON. *Pioneer road through Waterpocket Fold, Utah.* [C. Gregory Crampton]

CHARLES HALL. *He built and operated a ferry at Hall's Crossing in Glen Canyon, 1881-4.*
[*Courtesy Lillie Hall Denny*]

Turn right and follow the creek about thirty miles to the river. On the other side the road isn't bad—about twenty miles over knobby slick rock and hummocks of sand and you'll reach the Hole-in-the-Rock road. Then it's about seventy-five miles to Bluff by way of Clay Hill Pass, Grand Flat, Comb Wash, and San Juan Hill.

Directions too complicated? They had to be—it was intricate and complicated country. Remember Muley Twist Canyon.

From Escalante Charles Hall brought in materials—logs, planks, and pitch—and made a crude tapered boat thirty feet long. He put it in service in 1881. There was no cable or rope to guide the craft. It was towed upstream and then shoved off with the payload; one steered and two men paddled as the boat-ferry floated downstream, angling, under the two-man power, toward the opposite bank. Ferry charges were about five dollars per wagon and seventy-five cents each for horses. Ferryman Hall lived on the Escalante Road at the base of the Waterpocket Fold, eight miles from the crossing. Here he could divert a small creek of spring water and irrigate a garden plot. When customers came along, he'd walk down to the ferry and put them across; those who came in on the opposite side of the Colorado sometimes had to wait for service.

But there weren't many customers and the ferry went out of business in 1884. By then Bluff and southeastern Utah were no longer so isolated; roads were open to the railhead of the Denver & Rio Grande at Durango in southwestern Colorado. And on March 30, 1883, a few miles west of Green River, Utah, and right on the old Spanish Trail, the last spike was driven connecting the lines that became the Denver & Rio Grande Western Railroad. The same year the Atlantic and Pacific (Santa Fe) Railroad completed its tracks across northern New Mexico and Arizona, passing through Gallup, Holbrook, Winslow, and Flagstaff. The completion of the Denver & Rio Grande Western between Denver and Salt Lake was of particular significance for the settlements south and east of the Colorado River in Utah. The pioneers at Bluff were indeed remote and cut off from the older communities and from events in the territory. In fact, they found it difficult to think of themselves as being in Utah. There was a common saying in pioneer times that when you started for the older settlements west of the Colorado you were going "back to Utah." After 1883, it was no longer necessary to travel the pioneer road across the canyons. It was a comparatively easy trip from Bluff to Thompson on the Denver & Rio Grande Western; from there you could take the cars to Denver or Salt Lake. So, again, the canyons were crossed for the purpose of getting on the other side. There was nothing much in the canyons to attract farmers. The Anasazis had found them marginal—so had the Mormons who

WHITE MESA "MUSHROOM." *Arizona.* [*William C. Miller, Pasadena*]

settled in the more favored lands around the periphery. Roads were built over the easiest routes to connect settlements with each other and the railroads. Who would want to go into the canyons, some of them so winding that a mule could scarcely get through?

But just about the time Charles Hall abandoned his ferry, men were beginning to see something in the canyons besides farming.[1]

The Rock Jungle

THE COMING OF THE RAILROADS helped to sustain the canyon country cattle boom that had begun before the Mormon colonizing expedition reached Bluff. The raising of stock was one of the pillars in the early Mormon economy. Self-sufficiency was to be obtained not only from the farms but from animals that served as food and as a source of power. With an early start in the heart of the intermountain West, the Mormon pastoral industry grew and prospered as markets developed in the mining camps of California, Nevada, Colorado, and elsewhere. The completion of the transcontinental railroad in 1869 opened a wider sale for Utah cattle, beyond the local market. As the Mormon villagers in the 1870's moved from the Great Basin into the western side of the canyon country, cattle and sheep were put on the open ranges. The Mormons took a particular interest in the raising of sheep as they were a source of both food and clothing. The green acres around the village were usually irrigated forage crops to be used as winter feed for range stock as well as dairy herds. Indeed, the prosperity of the nineteenth-century village in Utah Territory was largely dependent on the cattle and sheep market.

When the Mormons arrived at Bluff in 1880, they found that enterprising cattlemen from as far away as Texas were already ranging cattle on the Blues (Abajo Mountains) and the La Sals, where they found excellent grass. These men were in the vanguard of the rapidly spreading cattlemen's frontier that, emerging from Texas after the Civil War, had swept over much of the West and was still spreading. Railroad expansion west stimulated the market, and the unfettered use of the public domain for open range made for high and easy profits. The economics were simple: buy a herd of longhorns in Texas, where prices were rockbottom, and trail them to the nearest unappropriated open range, squat on it, and let the herd multiply. Sell the increase and buy more stock. The range was free, the upkeep small, and the annual profits enormous—they would run up to forty and fifty per cent in the 1870's and 1880's. Foreigners, frequently from England and Scotland, found the western cattle boom an attractive investment field.

Before 1880, Pat O'Donel, Spud Hudson, the Widow Lacey, and the Carlisles (and probably other outfits) had come into southeastern Utah to enjoy the beef bonanza. Harold and Edmund Carlisle managed the Utah operations of the Kansas and New Mexico Land and Cattle Company, an English concern with its home office in London, operating in Kansas, Colorado, New Mexico, and Utah. There was a good market in the mining camps of Colorado for the cattle produced. From the older settlements in Utah and elsewhere, others began to come in search of good range land. The Rays, Maxwells, McCartys, Taylors, and others, traveling the Spanish Trail, arrived at the site of Moab in 1877. The fort of the Elk Mountain Mission was then being occupied by two men who had drifted in to trap and prospect: a mulatto, William Granstaff, called "Nigger Bill," and a French Canadian known as "Frenchie." The new arrivals stayed there a while before moving on to the southern base of the La Sal Mountains, where they founded the settlement of La Sal early in 1878. Still others arrived and settled at Moab which was made a post office in 1880.

The pioneers at Bluff quickly entered the business, working their cattle co-operatively in the "Bluff Pool." Although the colony did not thrive as an agricultural community—the San Juan periodically cut away its own terraces which formed the main farming lands—it prospered as a cow town. But it was some distance from the best ranges and, in the late 1880's people began moving upcountry to Verdure and to Monticello. When irrigation water was brought from the Blues, Blanding was founded in 1905.

The pioneer cattlemen all through the 1880's

SLICK-ROCK JUNGLE. *A wilderness of canyons and mesas. Looking up Aztec Creek in Forbidding Canyon from its mouth in Glen Canyon (lower right). Utah 1962.* [A. E. Turner, Bureau of Reclamation]

grazed the La Sals, the Abajos and Elk Ridge, and the Montezuma Creek drainage east of the Abajos. As the industry expanded, the ranges were extended westward into the broken country sloping off toward the Colorado River: Indian Creek, Beef Basin, Dark Canyon, White Canyon, Red Canyon, and into the wedge-shaped country west of the Clay Hills and north of the San Juan River. Sheep were introduced in the 1890's.

It has often been said of Utah that there were more cattlemen and fewer cattle than in any state in the West. The statement might have applied generally to the western side of the canyon country where there were a number of small, isolated settlements, but not to the eastern side where large companies, like the vast Scorup-Somerville Cattle Company, were formed from the merger of small interests. The La Sals, the Abajos and Elk Ridge, on the east side of the canyon country, and the High Plateaus on the west side were excellent summer ranges. Cattle were wintered at lower elevations and were driven down on both sides of the river into the lower canyons and bottom lands wherever accessible. The country below the pygmy forest belt was tough range for cattle. There was too much rock and not enough grass. It took a lot of it to support the animals. You had to figure on over 200 acres to support just one cow or five sheep. And the animals easily got lost behind the rocks and in the canyons. They could get rimrocked, dying of thirst within sight of water—as a whole herd of horses once did at Dead Horse Point. When Ebenezer Bryce said of Bryce Canyon that he thought it was a hell of a place to lose a cow, he probably voiced the feelings of every cattleman in the canyon country. On the eastern side of the Colorado, Al Scorup, running cattle through the Needles, into Dark Canyon, up on the Woodenshoe, through the Clay Hills, said the range was like a rock jungle.

Apart from the struggle with the environment, the vicissitudes of the cattle industry in southeastern Utah, particularly in the years up to about 1900, were as dramatic and as exciting as any in the West. There was open range warfare, the little man versus the big outfit, Indian troubles, rustling and wild times in general. Here, southeast of the Colorado, a meeting ground of frontiers from east and west located on the border of the Indian country, the times were much wilder than in the canyon country settlements under the rims of the High Plateaus.

The canyon country was a great place for rustlers. You could rope a cow and run a brand—or put your own brand on an unbranded cow—with little chance of being seen. It is told around in the canyon country here and there, with no names being mentioned, that in the early days about all you had to have to get started in the cattle business was a good horse and a long rope. You could get away into the canyons with the stolen stock and even drive them across the Colorado by any one of several crossings and go into business on the other side; or you could sell them. Then you could rustle another bunch on that side to take back with you on the return trip. Rustling became popular after the arrival of the Denver & Rio Grande Western in 1883, for there was a good market for animals along the line; and when times were dull, you could hold up the train. A favorite hideout for assorted train and bank robbers and rustlers was Robber's Roost out near the tip of Land's End Plateau. There was a spring there, and grass; it was remote and practically inaccessible on two of its three sides. Yet it was reasonably close to Hanksville, where you could go for supplies occasionally, and no one was likely to ask any questions. Now a respectable cattle range, Robber's Roost in wilder times was the home of Butch Cassidy and the Wild Bunch. We know the outlaws liked the canyon country because it hid them so well. But beyond that we have little information, for they did not publicize their activities.[2]

The Canyons of The People

FOR SOME TIME BEFORE THE MORMONS began moving into the canyon country, the Navajos had been pushing into it from the east. They called themselves Diné—The People—and were a pastoral

HISTORY AND PREHISTORY. *Trails made by Indians to reach the bank of the Colorado in Glen Canyon. Three separate trails are shown. The small cups at the left were pecked out by prehistoric people to provide a foothold. The larger cups were made in more recent times. The built-up trail on the right was made by Navajos to bring stock down to the river. Utah 1962.* [C. Gregory Crampton]

folk who ranged sheep, goats, and horses, though few cattle; they were also farmers with a fondness for corn, melons, and fruit. For hundreds of years they had lived in the Chuska Mountains on the Arizona-New Mexico boundary. During the time of their troubles with the United States, particularly during 1858–64, a good many Navajos left their homeland around Canyon de Chelly and began moving west into the canyon country south of the San Juan River; many more—estimates run into the thousands—escaped the long walk to Fort Sumner and the subsequent four years of captivity —1864-8. It was during that time that numbers of Navajos crossed the Colorado to prey, with the Paiutes, on the advancing Mormon frontier.

In 1868, the Indians at Fort Sumner were released and a treaty was made with the United States which gave them a large reservation incorporating much of their old tribal territory. The Navajos were glad to be back home, where they could once again roam free. Except for an incident now and then, they have stayed at peace with the world. Thus in 1870, when Jacob Hamblin and John Wesley Powell wanted to talk over bringing to an end the Navajo war with the Mormons, they found the Indians receptive and a treaty was concluded.

A proud people, their enforced residence at Fort Sumner was a severe shock to the Navajos. But it was followed by a period of relative prosperity and population increase. Having given up raiding, they turned more intently to stock raising and agriculture. The coming of the railroad—built near and paralleling the southern boundary of the reservation—in the 1880's, created a demand for the beautiful wool blankets whose distinctive colors and angular designs seemed to mirror the landscape of their homeland. They developed more fully the art of making jewelry and apparel, using silver and turquoise.

Their population increasing and their industry growing, The People were soon moving into areas beyond the bounds of the reservation, which was not as large as their original tribal territory. Though they clashed with the whites on the east and south, the way to the west, toward the canyons of the San Juan and the Colorado, was open to them.

There they found living space, and no whites to challenge them. Nor was it completely unknown to them, for many of The People had gone there during the late 1850's and 1860's.

Though the pattern of Navajo migration westward into the canyon country is not clear, in the ten-year period after 1868 they probably became broadly familiar with the entire region west of Monument Valley, south of the San Juan, including the canyons draining into the Colorado between the mouth of the San Juan and Lee's Ferry. They must have hunted the high mesas west of Agathla and Marsh Pass, and the rugged, wild slopes of Navajo Mountain. They must have looked for farming plots and grazing areas, both of which became scarcer as they moved deeper into the canyons. Before Powell came through on the second voyage, they had brought stock to the banks of the Colorado in Glen Canyon; at the Crossing of the Fathers, Powell met a trading party bound for the Mormon settlements. At his ferry, John D. Lee opened trade with the Navajos in 1872.

As the Navajos moved westward into the canyon country, they managed to obtain, through presidential orders, additional territory for their reservation which incorporated the new settlement. After the additions made in 1878, 1880, and 1884, the reservation extended to the Colorado in the west and included all of the area south of the San Juan River in Utah. Later additions—particularly in the west where the boundaries were extended along the Colorado downstream to the mouth of the Little Colorado—have made the Navajo reservation the largest in the United States.

As the Navajos moved into the land along the San Juan River in Utah, they encountered numbers of Paiutes, and in the Four Corners area, they found themselves on the frontier of the Utes, one of their most formidable Indian enemies. They appear to have gotten along well with the Paiutes, however, and moved in among them, and even crossed through their territory to the north side of the San Juan River. Just above the Clay Hills, the San Juan River comes out into the open for a few miles, with gentle approaches on either side. Here is the Clay Hill Crossing, an easy ford most of the year.

The Navajos may have crossed here before 1860; once across, it was good trail to Clay Hill Pass, Red Canyon, White Canyon, and Elk Ridge. Stories are told that the Navajos used to cross the Colorado River to hunt in the Henry Mountains; the Clay Hill Crossing-White Canyon route would have been the simplest way to make the trip.

Once the Mormons had completed the road across Glen Canyon at Hole-in-the-Rock, Navajos and Paiutes began to use it to travel to the Mormon settlements to trade, and to hunt on the Kaiparowits Plateau. When the Mormons arrived on the San Juan, the Navajos were already running sheep on Elk Ridge. Not long after the founding of Bluff, Kumen Jones went up on the Ridge seeking a summer cattle range. Not far from the Bear's Ears, he found a Navajo Chief, Kigalia, camped at the spring that still bears his name.[3]

The country around the spot where the boundaries of four states now intersect has long been a mingling place. In prehistoric times it was heavily occupied by the Anasazis, a favored land, yet a frontier zone between the culturally advanced peoples living at Mesa Verde and their more primitive cousins who tried to make ends meet on the marginal lands in the canyons. Paiutes, Utes, and Navajos found it a meeting ground. Early in recorded times, Spaniards and Mexicans traversed the region; they were followed by government explorers of the United States. As long as the whites explored and did not linger, the Indians remained peaceful. But then came the settlers, moving into southwestern Colorado, northwestern New Mexico, and southeastern Utah—miners, cattlemen, and farmers. A clash was inevitable. In 1880, just as the Hole-in-the-Rock expedition arrived at Bluff, two prospectors, James Merrick and Ernest Mitchell, were killed by the Indians in Monument Valley.

CABIN DOOR AT ROBBER'S ROOST. *Utah.* [*Charles Kelly Photograph, Utah State Historical Society*]

10/El Dorado

Sierra Azul

IN THE OPENING OF THE WEST, THE GOLD AND silver prospector discovered more places than he is generally given credit for. This was notably so in the arid reaches of the Southwest. The fur men followed only the perennial streams in their explorations; government explorers, railroad surveyors, and overland travelers looked for easy routes in open country; farmers sought land where irrigation was feasible; but the prospector went anywhere he thought he might strike it rich, and thus he was the first to get into a good many areas. Among them was the canyon country of southeastern Utah and northeastern Arizona, where placer gold was discovered in 1883.

Within twenty years the miners had combed the entire country, even though many of them must have found it the most thoroughly difficult prospecting they had ever undertaken. Nevertheless, they worked their way up crooked, straight-walled, narrow canyons, particularly those with gravel bottoms; they scrambled up steep slick-rock slopes and rimrocked themselves on narrow ledges; they built rickety boats and then drowned themselves in river rapids; for supplies they walked up to seventy-five miles across rock, sand, and open desert. In this sandstone wilderness they found, surprisingly enough, lots of "color," even if they could save precious little of it. And they were the first to explore most of the spectacular landscape tributary to the main canyon of the Colorado where only Powell had preceded them.

The sandstone country of the Colorado River canyons had long been a lodestone. Late in the seventeenth century, Diego de Vargas, who had re-established Spanish rule in New Mexico after the Pueblo Revolt, exchanged letters with the Viceroy of Spain about the Sierra Azul, the Blue Mountain. This was reported to be a rich mine of quicksilver somewhere in the province of the Hopis—another story of wealth to be found in an area where Coronado, Espejo, and Oñate had sought fabled lands and dazzling chimera. As the story grew, gold and silver were added to it, but, anyway, quicksilver, essential to the milling of gold and silver, was as valuable as the precious metals themselves. Sierra Azul seemed to elude its seekers, though Father Escalante, before making the trip to Utah, had held some of the quicksilver ore in his hands. While he and Father Domínguez were traveling through the land of the Yutas, they doubtless kept the fabled Blue Mountain in mind. Near the Crossing of the Fathers, the expedition cartographer, Bernardo de Miera y Pacheco, looked off to the northeast where the blue dome of Navajo Mountain stood out on the skyline. The Blue Mountain—he put it down on his map—El Cerro Azul! El Dorado, that myth of easy money![1]

For ten years Americans rushed headlong to California after gold. Just as that El Dorado was beginning to fade, new diggings found elsewhere kept the prospectors on the move. In 1858, the discovery of gold at the eastern base of the Rockies, followed by the great Pike's Peak rush the next year, made it evident to the prospectors that the metal might be found anywhere. From the two opposite poles of California and Colorado gold hunters ranged out through the intermountain country, hoping to strike it rich.

About a year after Pike's Peak rush, Charles Baker was prospecting in the San Juan Mountains of southwestern Colorado. He took time out for the Civil War and then returned to the San Juan country with two companions in 1867. They had prospected some distance down the San Juan River when they were attacked by Indians. The sole survivor was James White who was picked up on a raft below the Grand Canyon in September 1867. Had White preceded Powell through the Grand Canyon, or had he told a whale of a tall tale? No matter.[2] The reports of White's rescue carried the news that Baker's party had been prospecting, and this probably had something to do with the rush to the San Juan Mountains that soon developed. It was only just underway when some welcome news came through: If the diggings played out, you could go looking for diamonds.

During the summer of 1872, the nation was titillated by reports that diamonds, together with rubies and sapphires, had been found somewhere in the West. Henry Janin, a prominent geologist, had visited the field and pronounced it genuine. A company, with Janin as superintendent, acquired the property and prepared to make a million dollars a month. Naturally curious, prospectors up and down the land asked: "Where are the diamond fields?" Most of the early reports, though vague, seemed to locate them in northeastern Arizona, in the vicinity of Fort Defiance, or near the Hopi villages, or along the San Juan River near the mouth of Chinle Creek, or in Monument Valley, or near Navajo Mountain. The few published reports of Powell's 1869 voyage were searched for clues; ex-governor William Gilpin of Colorado delivered an address and announced that the diamond fields were in southwestern Colorado; even South African diamond miners caught the "Arizona Fever." Before the year 1872 ended, Clarence King and his associates on the United States Geological Exploration of the Fortieth Parallel found the diamond fields—in northwestern Colorado—and proved them to be one of the most ingenious salting jobs ever pulled off in the West.[3]

The story was too good to die. So one of the claims had been salted. What about the reports of diamonds and precious stones in other places? They had been popping up all the previous summer! And weren't the diamonds reported in proximity to those ruined cities which some people said had been built by Aztecs? The original treasure trove of Montezuma! Probably many prospectors carried on the search, adding diamonds to their dreams of gold and silver. For years these attractive "Diamond Fields" remained on the maps of northeastern Arizona. Before they had disappeared entirely a lost silver mine had brought a new lot of prospectors into the beautifully rugged country between Monument Valley and Navajo Mountain. The Sierra Azul had been living up to its name.

Pish-la-ki

NEW YEAR'S EVE, 1879. James Merrick and Ernest Mitchell met up with a party of five Mormon scouts who had just come through from the Colorado River. (They had found a route across the forbidding wilderness between the Hole-in-the-Rock and Montezuma Creek and were headed back.) George Hobbs, one of the scouts, striking up a conversation with Merrick, learned that the two were prospectors heading for the Navajo country. Merrick said that he knew where the Indians had a smelter where they were handling ore that assayed ninety per cent silver and that he and Mitchell were going to look for the mine. The prospectors and the scouts crossed Comb Ridge and parted company at the mouth of Comb Wash, where Merrick and Mitchell with their pack string forded the San Juan and headed south toward Monument Valley.

Since 1868, when the Navajos had returned to their homeland, stories of hidden silver mines had drifted off the reservation; these arose from the fact that the Indians had been developing the manufacture of silver buckles, buttons, clasps, and other such items. The question almost any miner would naturally ask was: "Where did they get the silver?" It was easy for the hopeful prospector to conclude that they must have a secret source of silver, per-

haps an old Spanish mine. Merrick thought he knew where it was. When time passed and the two men did not return, an armed searching party went in February to look for them. Scalped and then covered with rocks and brush, the bodies of Merrick and Mitchell were found near the spectacular buttes that now bear their names in Monument (then called Monumental) Valley. Navajos in the vicinity said the Paiutes had killed the white men; Paiutes in the vicinity pleaded innocent. Some specimens of "very rich quartz ores" were found near the bodies. The "facts" were plain: The men had discovered a mine and had been killed on the way out.[4]

The legendary silver mine of the Navajos now became identified with the presumed discovery by Merrick and Mitchell, and one prospecting party after another from southwestern Colorado tried to locate the mine where the two men were supposed to have found the silver ore. Colorado papers played up the story. In April 1882, some prospectors reported that, in one of the canyons leading into the Colorado, they had "found old Indian smelters, but saw nothing of the fabled Myrick [Merrick-Mitchell] mine. They also discovered a large ledge of silver-bearing ore, ten feet in thickness and 100 feet in width in proximity to the smelters. . . . Mortars in which the ore was ground were discovered in the rocks close at hand, also sledge hammers of stone with wooden handles. . . . The fabulous richness of the Navajo mountains is true beyond a peradventure."[5]

In May 1882, a party of seven left Durango, Colorado, to take possession of a "great copper mine which was discovered by Cass Hite on his exploring tour a few weeks ago. This is known to be a lode of mammoth size. . . . A competent assayer finds 49 per cent of metallic copper in the specimens, and about $17. besides in silver and gold. This from the surface. How much richer it will prove from working further in and down, each mining expert will guess for himself."

When it came to a name for the discovery, Hite said the vein "in commemoration of his fallen predecessors . . . should be called the Merrick and Mitchell lode."[6]

THE DIADEM. *Circle Cliffs, Utah.*
[*Josef Muench, Santa Barbara*]

Cass Hite and party, which included George M. Miller, James E. Porter, "both veteran Navajo explorers," Joseph Duckett, and others, may have found some of the copper deposits that do exist in sedimentary sandstone at the northern foot of Hoskininni Mesa at the head of Copper Canyon, a southern tributary of the San Juan. While Hite worked the "Merrick and Mitchell lode," others of the party ranged out through the canyons and over the mesas to Navajo Mountain. At one place at the eastern foot of Navajo Mountain, G. M. Miller carved his name on a rock and the date, 1882. During the summer Hite became acquainted with the Navajo Chief, Hoskininni, head man in the Copper Canyon region. Evidently, Hite's copper mine hadn't panned out well for he queried the chief about the possible location of a silver mine elsewhere which might prove to be the Merrick-Mitchell mine. He was so persistent in this questioning that the Navajos began to call him "Hosteen Pish-la-ki," Mr. Silver Hunter, or Mr. Silver. Hoskininni told Hite that the Navajos had a secret silver mine but that he would not tell him the location of it. If Hite was so anxious to find metal, the Chief asked, why didn't he go to the great canyon of the Colorado? There he would find gold in the sands of the river. Hoskininni would show him the way. The Chief was right. With Cass Hite, he traveled by way of White Canyon to the Colorado and there they found some gold in the banks of the river.

Men kept looking for the Merrick-Mitchell mine long after Cass Hite gave up the search; it came to be known as the Pish-la-ki mine from the name the Navajos had given to Hite. All the elements of a good lost mine story were present: the hazy Spanish background (Sierra Azul); the discovery of the mine and the killing of Merrick and Mitchell; and the wild country where the Indians guarded the secret of their mine. It was a lodestone for prospecting parties for twenty-five years. In fact, the legend still persists. Bring together those who have been in the country for some time, who know the mesas west of Monument Valley and the intricate slopes of Navajo Mountain, and they will always talk of where they think the mine is located. For a

long time the Indians kept a watchful eye on the palefaces. After the boundary between Utah and Arizona had been surveyed, the supervisors made an examination of it in 1911. As they rode past Copper Canyon to Oljeto Canyon, Chief Hoskininni and fifty bucks halted the party to ask them if they had been looking for the "money rock," the silver of "Pash Leki."[7]

Gold in Glen Canyon

PEOPLE HAD BEEN TALKING of the mineral wealth of the canyon country for over a hundred and fifty years, but the reports of discoveries made by Merrick and then by Cass Hite were the first of any significance. These were the opening incidents in the long mining history of the canyon country. The quest quickly shifted from silver to gold when Hite discovered the mineral in Glen Canyon, and during the next twenty years prospectors thoroughly explored the canyons, the plateaus, and the laccolites—and they found some gold.

The *Rocky Mountain News*, May 23, 1882, described Cass Hite as "a mining prospector of sixteen years experience, of superior education, of equal industry and capacity for hardship and toil. . . ." In his thirty-eighth year, Hite went to Glen Canyon and stayed there most of the rest of his life—a time span of thirty-one years. (He died at his ranch at Ticaboo in 1914.) In fact, he probably lived in the canyons longer than any other man. He was there all through the gold rush that began not long after he arrived in Glen Canyon in September 1883.

Hite came into Glen Canyon by way of White Canyon and crossed the Colorado at its mouth; he is said to have named it "Dandy Crossing." Easily reached from the east by White Canyon and from the west by Trachyte Creek and North Wash, Dandy Crossing is the best in Glen Canyon above Lee's Ferry. There are a number of prominent prehistoric sites in the vicinity, including a multi-storied building overlooking the mouth of White Canyon. This building, easily seen from the Colorado River, was visited first by the Powell expedi-

CASS HITE. *"Hosteen Pish-la-ki."* [*Charles Kelly Collection, Utah State Historical Society*]

INSCRIPTION NEAR NAVAJO MOUNTAIN TRADING POST. *George Miller with others prospected the Navajo Mountain region in 1882 looking for the Merrick-Mitchell mine. Utah.* [*C. Gregory Crampton*]

tion; in Hite's day, it became known as "Fort Moqui," and was the most prominent man-made tourist attraction in Glen Canyon, until it was flooded and lost under the waters of Lake Powell. The number of ancient sites in the locality suggest that the crossing was well known to prehistoric peoples, as it was to the Navajos who directed Hite to the locality. Shortly after 1883, the gathering place of the first prospectors to appear was the open bank on the right side of the Colorado, just below the crossing where Hite first camped, and the spot was given the name of "Hite City."

Shortly after his arrival on the Colorado, Hite discovered placer gold in the gravel in the banks on both sides of the river near Dandy Crossing, and more extended explorations soon turned up more gold. Although there probably had been some inconsequential prospecting in the canyons below Moab and Green River and above Lee's Ferry in the ten-year interval between the second Powell voyage and Hite's arrival, Hite's discoveries, however, led to some excitement and resulted in a mild gold rush of prospectors and miners into Glen Canyon.

The first phase of the Glen Canyon gold rush lasted about seven years. During this time several hundred men prospected a region that was probably the most difficult to get about in that they had ever seen. And it was so remote from the arm of the territorial law that the miners promptly set about making their own laws.

Meeting at Hermit Brown's mine on December 3, 1883, nine men signed their names to the laws governing the Henry Mountains Mining District which they had just drawn up. The boundaries of the district followed the Colorado from the mouth of the Dirty Devil to Hall's Crossing, thence along the Waterpocket Fold to the "Big Sandy" (Fremont River), thence to the Dirty Devil, and thence to its mouth. The regulations specified the amount of "discovery work" to hold a claim; qualifications for membership in the district were set out; penalties for "claim jumping," and "other fraudulent or dishonorable conduct" were specified; rules for making amendments were given. The signers included Lewis P. Brown, Chairman, and Cass Hite,

Secretary. In 1887, the White Canyon Mining District, with a similar set of regulations, was organized (Cass Hite, Secretary), which adjoined the Henry Mountains Mining District at the Colorado River and included an area of comparable size east of the river. Far from being a lawless breed, the miners were spontaneous frontier lawmakers, as they had been since the California gold rush; their practices, usages, and common customs have been incorporated bodily into the federal mining laws of 1866, 1872, and subsequent statutes. The Glen Canyon miners observed the federal law and added their own local regulations.

During the 1880's, prospectors in Glen Canyon found gold all along the Colorado from the mouth of the Dirty Devil to Lee's Ferry. But it was extremely fine—gold dust literally—and it was very difficult to recover by ordinary methods of placering—panning and sluicing. The gold was so fine that it would float on the surface of the water and would easily be lost during the washing process. The best locations were found to be on the gravel terraces that are in Glen Canyon above the high-water level. Some of the more productive placers found before 1890 were Dandy Crossing Bar, Ticaboo Bar, Good Hope Bar, and California Bar, but during this time there were dozens of claims filed in the recorder's book of the White Canyon Mining District.[8]

The presence of placer gold in Glen Canyon naturally caused speculation about its source and prospectors from the canyons began working their way into the laccolithic mountains. Even though the land in Utah south of the San Juan River was added to the Navajo Reservation in 1884, occasional prospecting parties climbed about on Navajo Mountain to look for the lost mine of Pish-la-ki. Others hopefully examined the Henry Mountains for gold, despite the fact that Grove K. Gilbert for Powell's Survey had already published his geological study of those mountains in which he pessi-

GLEN CANYON OF THE COLORADO. *At the foot of the Kaiparowits Plateau. Utah 1962.* [Stan Rasmussen, Bureau of Reclamation]

mistically theorized that gold in paying quantities would not be found in them.

Who cared about theory when you could find color in the washes? Not Jack Sumner. Jack had been with Powell on the 1869 voyage, and while Powell studied geology, Sumner kept his eye open for minerals. In fact, Sumner probably panned for gold here and there on the 1869 trip, but like most prospectors, he would not have expected to find good diggings in sandstone country. Nonetheless, he came back to Glen Canyon sometime after 1883. Walking up the slopes of the Henry Mountains about 1889, he and Jack Butler discovered gold in the Bromide Basin on Mt. Ellen. There was a rush to the Henrys, the boom-town of Eagle City sprang up, some gold was found, but the mines soon played out. It would appear that Gilbert had been right.

To the prospector the geology of the entire canyon region was confusing. It was chiefly sandstone, yet Hite had found copper in sedimentary rocks in Copper Canyon, and gold in the sand and gravel of Glen Canyon. What kind of country was this? Powell and his corps of brilliant assistants—Dutton, Gilbert, Howell, and Thompson—had already found out. Their classic monographs on the geologic history of the Colorado Plateau stated many of its fundamental facts, followed by sound interpretations and generalizations, which have been elaborated on by later students.

The canyon country today—indeed the Colorado Plateau—is the result of erosion, mainly by water, of gigantic masses of sedimentary rock. This is not a static condition—erosion is vigorously in progress. This is in geological time, of course; you will not notice much change anywhere from year to year. During the Paleozoic and the Mesozoic eras, which might add up to a mere 490,000,000 years, the plateau of today was a flat area near the sea on which sediments were deposited. As the beds were deposited, they seem to have sunk under water entirely. At the close of the Cretaceous era (the latest period in the Mesozoic), say about 60,000,000 years ago, the plateau area was bodily pushed upward in a huge block. There was not much radical change in the structure of the block; it remained fairly level though there was some warping and folding of the beds. There then followed a long cycle of erosion that wasted away this huge block and reduced it to a near-level plain again at or near sea level.

In the Tertiary period of the Cenozoic era, other beds of sediment of great thickness were deposited over the area. And a drainage system developed across these beds which was the ancestor of the present Colorado River. Again there was an uplifting and the huge block of bedded sandstone was raised to about its present height; during the process there was some faulting. Because of the uplift, the gradients of streams were increased and the rivers began to cut vigorously down through the upraised block. The intricate dissected landscape of the canyon country today is the result of about 20,000,000 years of stream erosion. The wearing away has been so profound that the folds and warping that occurred during the Cretaceous period have come to the surface and are to be seen in the San Rafael Swell, the Waterpocket Fold, Comb Ridge, and in some of the other prominent features of the landscape. During the latest erosion cycle huge masses of molten rock pushed up through the sedimentary strata and bulged them but did not break through the layers. The molten rock cooled and solidified. As erosion proceeded, it left these as laccolithic mountains, standing high above the sandstone plateau all around them.

The gold found by Sumner and Butler in the Bromide Basin came from the hard exposed magma near the top of Mt. Ellen. But if these mines were so unproductive, could this have been the source of Glen Canyon gold? Probably not; geologists seem to think that it was contained in the matter that formed the sedimentary beds during the early periods of the Mesozoic era of geologic time and that it has been washed free as later erosion occurred. Copper and uranium and other minerals were also found in the sandstone country, but until the end of the century, the main quest was for gold.[9]

PIONEER CABIN AT HITE. *Glen Canyon. Utah 1962.* [*C. Gregory Crampton*]

THE TRAIL TO KLONDIKE BAR. *Prospectors in the Glen Canyon gold rush frequently built precarious trails over steep slick-rock slopes to reach gravel bars along the river. A notch was picked in the sandstone, posts were set in, and logs were laid on the posts, making a cantilever trail. Utah 1962.* [*W. L. Rusho, Bureau of Reclamation*]

DARK CANYON RAPIDS. *Cataract Canyon. Utah 1962.* [*W. L. Rusho, Bureau of Reclamation*]

11/Canyon Conquest

Ho! For the San Juan

THE CANYON-COUNTRY MINING BOOM GATHERED speed slowly. It probably took a while for hard-rock prospectors to believe that you could find gold in sandstone; and few seemed to be finding much gold in Glen Canyon. Cass Hite did what he could to stimulate interest by writing letters to the Salt Lake *Tribune* and other papers and by soliciting investment capital. His efforts may have had something to do with the formation of the Denver, Colorado Canyon, and Pacific Railroad Company organized on March 25, 1889, at Denver. As its name suggests, the corporation planned to build a water-level railroad through the canyons of the Colorado from Grand Junction, Colorado, to the seaboard to connect the coal fields of the Rocky Mountains with Southern California! President Frank M. Brown engaged Robert Brewster Stanton, a prominent railroad engineer, to make an engineering survey of the canyons to determine the feasibility of the idea and to assess the resources along the route.

Brown himself took charge of the survey; Stanton was made chief engineer. In May 1889, Brown and Stanton with sixteen men and six boats left Green River, Utah. The expedition reached Hite in June; they had lost some boats in Cataract Canyon but Stanton had doggedly carried the survey through. The expedition ran down fourteen miles downstream from Hite to Ticaboo where Cass Hite was mining in a location that he called the "Bank of Ticaboo." The expedition rested and repaired the badly battered boats, while Brown and Stanton took note of everything of possible interest to a railroad. The party went on and reached Lee's Ferry

early in July, after having surveyed about half of Glen Canyon; they may have concluded the survey at a place now known as Mystery Canyon where some of the men left their names. Shortly after leaving Lee's Ferry, the party met with disaster when Frank M. Brown and two others of the party were drowned in Marble Canyon.

Undaunted by this tragedy, Robert B. Stanton returned before the year was ended to continue the survey. He brought his boats overland into Glen Canyon and launched them above Hite. Stanton saw Cass again and took further note of the gold placers along the way. At one point he met Jack Sumner and had a long talk with him about Powell's trip through the canyons in 1869. Stanton picked up his railroad survey in the lower part of Glen Canyon and carried it right through Marble and Grand canyons to the Gulf of California where it was completed in April 1890.

The whole, breathtaking idea and Stanton's achievement in actually surveying the canyons of the Colorado, including savage Cataract Canyon and Grand Canyon, attracted much national attention. Robert Stanton, the first man through Grand Canyon after Powell, was going to build a railroad! He even argued the practicability of a railroad from an economical and engineering standpoint in a lengthy paper read before the American Society of Civil Engineers, but the company was not able to raise the necessary capital and this scheme was dropped.[1] Nonetheless, Stanton had seen the Glen Canyon gold—it gave him an idea and he was soon back to try it out.

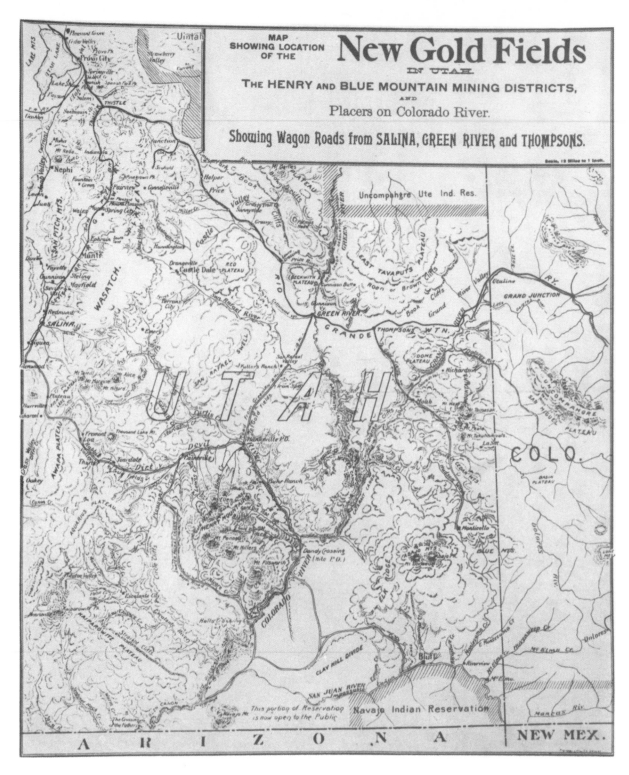

THE CANYON COUNTRY AT THE HEIGHT OF THE GOLD-MINING BOOM. *From the Denver* Mining Age, *1892 (reduced scale).* [*Division of Maps, Library of Congress*]

INSCRIPTION LEFT BY THE SURVEYORS OF THE DENVER, COLORADO CANYON, AND PACIFIC RAILROAD COMPANY, 1889. *Mouth of Mystery Canyon in Glen Canyon. Utah 1962.* [*C. Gregory Crampton*]

The railroad explorations of Robert Brewster Stanton came at a time when considerable development was taking place in Glen Canyon. Capital was being invested and there was a spirit of optimism. Some of Cass Hite's relatives, hoping to strike it rich, followed him into the canyon—brothers John P. and Ben R., and the latter's son, Homer J. Hite. In 1892, gold and other minerals were discovered in the La Sal Mountains, the Abajos, the Carrizos; when the Bromide Basin in the Henry Mountains was booming in the same year, regional interest in the mining potentialities of the canyon country reached its highest peak.

Toward the end of the year 1892, news began to trickle out that rich placers had been found on the San Juan River deep in the canyon somewhere be-

CLAY HILL CROSSING. *San Juan River, Utah 1962.* [*W. L. Rusho, Bureau of Reclamation*]

low Bluff. The San Juan was remote; its canyons had not been tested; so, naturally, people began recalling the lost mine, "Pish-la-ki." There were reports of "secret" discoveries and attempts to stake out the whole canyon before the public learned of the matter. In November, that part of the Navajo Reservation in Utah west of the 110th meridian was restored to the public domain. By Christmas time the papers were full of news from the San Juan, and by January 1893, the rush was at its height.

Along the Santa Fe line in Arizona and New Mexico, the railroad towns were nearly depopulated. Durango in southwestern Colorado went wild. The Denver & Rio Grande Western contemplated extending its line to Bluff, the Mormon town on the San Juan and the last supply point on the road from Colorado, which was now enjoying its first boom. The towns along the Denver & Rio Grande Western vied with each other as the best point of departure for the mines.

Green River had an advantage. Crossing point on the Spanish Trail, it became an important ferry, and even before the railroad was built, it had been founded as the town of Blake. But the river—the heart of the history of the canyon country—was not to be denied its importance to the town, and before long Blake became Green River, Utah, an important stop on the Denver & Rio Grande Western. It had been the jumping-off place for the diggings in Glen Canyon—a road had been opened across the San Rafael Desert to Hanksville and thence down North Wash to the Colorado above Hite—and now it hoped to capitalize on the rush to the San Juan by playing up the route across Glen Canyon by way of Dandy Crossing.

By the end of January 1893, the rush began to slack off. Those who reached the San Juan found that the reports had been exaggerated and that any good claims had already been taken up. The rushers began to straggle back to the settlements. The Salt Lake *Tribune* reported that one disillusioned individual had inscribed his feelings on a sandstone block at Navajo Spring at the base of Comb Ridge: "One hundred dollars reward for the d—d fool who started the gold boom."[2]

Boom Times in the Canyons

THOUGH THE BUBBLE SOON BURST, the mining excitement on the San Juan advertised the entire canyon country and prospectors now began to comb thoroughly through it. They ranged up to the laccoliths, including Navajo Mountain, and drifted back to the canyons—particularly Glen Canyon—to try their luck there. Mining continued on the San Juan, but after 1893 most of the placer mining was centered in Glen Canyon. Outside influences helped to sustain gold mining. The panic of 1893 brought men to placer mining fields where, with little capital, they might make a living through their own individual effort. The election of McKinley in 1896 was a victory for the gold standard and this meant a rise in the price of gold. Finally, the discovery of rich fields in the Klondike, at Nome, and in South Africa were a stimulus to prospectors round the world. So the gold boom in Glen Canyon was sustained beyond the turn of the century.

The gold rush to the canyon country was small by comparison with the rush to the Klondike, but it was unique. Probably there were never over a thousand men in the canyon at any one time. A post office was established at Hite in 1889; it was serving perhaps a hundred men for some distance down the river in 1899. About the same time two hundred men petitioned unsuccessfully for a post office near Hall's Crossing. Where one man remained long enough in one place to receive mail, possibly two would be on the move, never in one place long enough to be counted.

During the years of the excitement, men prospected the full length of Glen Canyon, from the Dirty Devil to Lee's Ferry, and Cataract and Narrow canyons above it, together with their tributaries. The best locations were found in the main-canyon gravel terraces, some of them over two hundred feet above the high-water mark.

It was all placer gold; no coarse gold was found. To recover the fine dust taxed the ingenuity of the Glen Canyon miners. The several placer mining methods were used: the simple pan, sluice boxes, hydraulicking, and dredging. As most of the mines were above the river level, the problem of water supply was serious. Gravity diversion from the river was virtually impossible; there were few tributary streams in the right places and reservoirs in side canyons were likely to be washed out. Pumping from the river met with failure because the sand and silt in the water wore out the pumps. Water wheels were used with some success at Good Hope Bar and Olympia Bar. Over a hundred different types of patented gold-saving machinery were tried out in the canyon, but the best method of all was where one man shoveled gravel into a sluice box and then painfully panned out the residue. How many struck it rich? Who knows? A saying heard during the rush—that the canyon contained enough gold to pay off the National Debt (in 1900!)—showed the buoyancy of the times. A few made thousands, more made hundreds of dollars. The majority, as in most mining rushes, obtained for their pains an exhilarating life in the open air.

It was rugged country to travel. Canyons were a real barrier, the main stem as well as the tributaries which stopped passage—for any great distance—along the main canyon rim. Wagon roads were opened to the river at the crossing points—Lee's Ferry, Dandy Crossing, Hall's Crossing, and Hole-in-the-Rock—and in a few places on either side where crossing was not possible. There were many places accessible by trail; sometimes the miners enlarged or improved those made by the Indians, prehistoric and historic, or they made equally precarious trails of their own. Over the roads and the trails, supplies and equipment were hauled in: foodstuffs from the peripheral Mormon farming communities, lumber and coal from the Henry Mountains, goods and equipment came in by rail to Green River. Then, in order to avoid Cataract Canyon, freight from Green River had to be hauled by wagon over a hundred miles to Glen Canyon.

Once freight reached the river bank, it was frequently necessary to transport it by boat to a mining locality. Many kinds of boats were used: scows, rafts (even double-deckers!), rowboats, skiffs, and power craft driven by screws, side and stern paddle wheels. Sometimes crude sails were used to help push sluggish boats upstream.

Life in the canyon country gold mines was rough, and it was in the open. Men (and a few women) lived in tents, shacks, caves, or under the protective shelter of the overhanging cliff or shelf of rock. Dugouts and small rock houses were built in permanent locations. Lumber was expensive to bring in and there was no local timber, but driftwood could be used ingeniously in building and it also provided fuel. Above Lee's Ferry—where a post office was opened in 1879—the only place that might be called a community was Hite. There the post office was located and one or another of the Hites operated a small store. Mail was brought in from Green River and carried from Hanksville to Hite on horseback. Occasional trappers worked through the canyons during the winter and brought their furs out to Hite in the spring to process them. A few people attempted gardens and some kept chickens. The river produced catfish of excellent quality, but game in the canyons was scarce.

Glen Canyon miners seeking city life had some distance to go. The Mormon villages were the nearest possibilities. There were also the railroad towns—Gallup, Flagstaff, Durango, Grand Junction, Green River—and Salt Lake and Denver, both Rocky Mountain mining centers, were within reach.[3]

ROBERT BREWSTER STANTON. *Trachyte Creek, Glen Canyon. 1897.* [*Courtesy Anne Stanton Burchard*]

HITE IN GLEN CANYON, 1915. *Utah.* [*E. C. La Rue, U. S. Geological Survey*]

GOLD DREDGE OF THE HOSKANINNI COMPANY. *Operating in Glen Canyon in 1901. Utah.*
[*Courtesy Anne Stanton Burchard*]

Robert B. Stanton's Gold Dredge

THE BIGGEST MINING OPERATION in Glen Canyon during the gold rush was undertaken by the Hoskaninni Company, the brain child of Robert Brewster Stanton. Since completing the railroad survey through the canyons of the Colorado in 1890, he had become involved in various railroad and mining projects in California, Utah, and British Columbia. During this time he had not forgotten the prospects he had seen in Glen Canyon, and in 1897 he interested some eastern capitalists in a plan to dredge for gold.

Stanton seems to have looked upon Glen Canyon as a gigantic natural sluice box, its bed lined with gold. He planned to use a big floating dredge, then commonly employed in the western United States; if a pilot machine worked well, he would install several of them at different points in the canyon. He would build dams in the tributary canyons— and even on the Colorado!—to generate electric power to operate the dredges. He would run a series of tests. If these were successful, he would ex-

pect a company to be formed and capital subscribed. Then the dredgers would be installed. Most important: He would stake out and claim the entire canyon from the Dirty Devil to Lee's Ferry! If the claims were contiguous, then the assessment work required by law to be performed on an individual claim could be done on any one, or several, claims. Stanton liked to think big—earlier he had planned a railroad through the canyons; now, for the millions it held in its sands, he would dredge Glen Canyon—a distance of 170 miles. The capitalists liked the idea. Stanton went ahead. Tests measured up to expectations; the prospects seemed to be a good risk and the Hoskaninni Company (named after the Navajo Chief who had directed Cass Hite to the gold of Glen Canyon in 1883) was formed in March 1898. Appointed superintendent of field operations, Stanton ran some more tests to determine the best place to install the first dredge and then he began staking out the canyon. Where others had claims, he would stake out around them to in-

REMAINS OF THE HOSKANINNI COMPANY DREDGE. *Glen Canyon. Utah 1962.* [*C. Gregory Crampton*]

138

OTTO J. ZAHN. *With his brothers he mined for gold in the canyon of the San Juan River at Zahn's Camp for about ten years after 1902. Photograph about 1900.*
[*Courtesy Otto J. Zahn*]

STEAM BOILER AT ZAHN'S CAMP. *Placer-mining locality on the San Juan River. Utah 1962.* [*C. Gregory Crampton*]

sure contiguity of his own claims. In 1899, crews were put to work at separate points, building roads, improving trails in preparation for the installation of several dredges. One crew went to the river at Hole-in-the-Rock, and by cutting steps in the Mormon road, just twenty years old, they made it safer for the use of pack animals. By the end of 1899 the entire canyon had been staked and 145 claims were recorded in the recorders' offices of Garfield, Kane, and San Juan counties in Utah, and Coconino County in Arizona.

Meanwhile a dredge had been ordered from the Bucyrus Company and was delivered to the railhead at Green River in June 1900. The parts were hauled by wagons to the dredging site four miles above Hall's Crossing. From Hanksville, Stanton built a road through the Henry Mountains to accommodate freight wagons; at the rim of Glen Canyon he had to cut a dugway in the rock walls of a tributary canyon to get the equipment down to the river; then it was carried in boats up to a place called Camp Stone where the dredge was assembled.

The huge machine was finally ready to go into operation. Resting on a flat-bottomed hull 105 feet long, it consisted of a chain of 46 three-cubic-foot steel buckets, washing and amalgamating machinery, powered by five gasoline engines. The buckets would scoop up sand and gravel from the river bottom and dump it in a circular screen; coarse gravel would be carried away while the sand was washed over amalgamating tables to hold the gold. The amalgam was then retorted. There were some mechanical failures at first; among other things the boat would stick on the bottom of the river; but finally a general cleanup was made on April 13. The return: $30.15. Cleanup, May 7th: $36.80.

These are the only figures given in the diary that Stanton kept during the life of the Hoskaninni Company. They must have been very discouraging; there may have been additional returns, but not many. The elaborate sluicing and amalgamating machinery was not saving the fine gold dust. The dredge ceased operations probably in the summer of 1901. Stanton was made legal receiver of the company's property. The horses used for transportation were easily sold. To sell the rest of the

property—dredge, claims, and all—was more difficult, but a buyer was finally found who paid $200 for it. Not discouraged for long, Stanton went on to new fields to continue a successful engineering career.

The Hoskaninni Company may have spent $100,000 on the venture. The Glen Canyon gold had defeated the big machine as it had most of the small ones. Years later, in 1938, Julius Stone, who had been the company's first president (Camp Stone had been named after him) came through the canyon on a river trip. The dredge was sitting on the bottom of the river near the right bank. The party stopped, pried off some lumber, and then that evening built a fire with it and made some coffee. Stone appeared to be enjoying the coffee. During the conversation, he told his companions of the Hoskaninni operation and the amount of money he had invested. The coffee tasted fine, he said. It was the only thing he had ever gotten back from his investment. "This cup of coffee," he said, "cost me $5,000.00."

Beyond the one-man-powered shovel, sluice box, and pan, no one ever solved the problem of how to recover the gold from Glen Canyon. For many years the rusting Hoskaninni dredge, visible on the river bed at low water, was a reminder of a valiant attempt. The dredge—and the gold—is now beneath the waters of Lake Powell.[5]

The Zahns and Spencer

THE GOLD RUSH did not last long after the turn of the century. Other fields and other pursuits during the general prosperity of the time looked better, and the canyons were soon empty of miners except in a few of the proven locations. When Emery and Ellsworth Kolb passed through the canyon in 1911 en route from Green River, Wyoming, to the Needles in California, they saw only a few people. John Hite was operating the post office at Hite. Bert Loper, who had been in the rush to the San Juan, was living at the mouth of Red Canyon, the nearest neighbor to Cass Hite across the river at Ticaboo. The Kolbs mentioned seeing no one until they came upon fifteen or twenty men building a large boat at the mouth of Warm Creek twenty-eight miles above Lee's Ferry. The men were employees of a Chicago firm and were working under the direction of Charles H. Spencer, canyon country mining entrepreneur.

Sometime before 1907, Spencer had come into the country via the San Juan River after the big boom of the early 1890's had subsided. Although the rush had subsided quickly, a number of prospects had been found and placer mining continued. The number of mining districts organized—Gabel, Island, Williams, Monumental—is an indication of the continuing activity which probably reached its height in 1895. The best prospects had been found between Clay Hill Crossing and the Big Bend, a distance of twenty miles in the central portion of the canyon of the San Juan River. During the first boom, there had been considerable activity in the upper part of the canyon in the vicinity of the Goosenecks. The gold excitement along the San Juan hastened the opening of roads through the Navajo country to connect the mines with the towns along the Santa Fe Railroad, particularly Gallup in New Mexico and Flagstaff in Arizona. Over these roads heavy machinery was brought in to work the placers along the river.

Perhaps the largest gold mining operation on the San Juan River was undertaken by the Zahn Mining Company, formed by the Zahn family of Los Angeles in 1902. The company acquired a property on the south side of the river that had already been developed. Brothers Hector and Otto Zahn set up extensive sluicing operations at Zahn's Camp and attempted to utilize the heavy equipment that had been brought in previously from the railhead at Flagstaff. To bring in the huge steam boiler and other equipment, a primitive road had been built from Oljeto down Copper Canyon across the mouth of Nakai Canyon to the camp. The Zahns had reasonably good success with their mine. They found enough placer gold to justify patenting the property (one of the very few patents issued in Glen or San Juan canyons), which they worked intermittently until the opening of World War I, or later.

Charles H. Spencer followed the Zahns into the canyon; from the primitive road leading to their camp, he built an even more primitive one four miles farther down the canyon, where he set up an operation to crush sandstone rock. The idea was to recover the gold directly from the source rather than from the sand and gravel of the streambed. Heavy machinery was brought in from Colorado by ox team, and an elaborate plant was set up at the river's edge at Spencer Camp. A first cleanup in June and a second in December 1909 showed that the prospect was not profitable. Indeed, gold values can be found in some of the "red beds," but they are exceedingly minute and Spencer's machinery could not handle enough rock or save enough gold to make the operation pay.

He then became interested in the Chinle shales, which he first tested near Spencer Camp on the San Juan. He found that there were thick beds of this formation at Lee's Ferry and he determined to try to make a fortune from them. Moreover, if Stanton had been right, and the Glen Canyon was a gold-lined sluice box, then Lee's Ferry should be a good place to try another dredging operation. He interested eastern capital and went to work: To operate steam power at Lee's Ferry, where he would hydraulic the Chinle beds and dredge the river, he developed coal prospects on upper Warm Creek over twenty miles from the Colorado; he had coal hauled in wagons to the mouth of the Creek; to move it down to Lee's Ferry, he hauled in by ox team the parts of a huge boat, the *Charles H. Spencer*, and assembled it at the mouth of Warm Creek.

Everything went wrong. The *Charles H. Spencer*—92 feet long and with a 25-foot beam—was the largest boat ever launched in Glen Canyon. It was too big. It got stuck on sand bars. Most of the coal hauled down to Lee's Ferry was consumed to power the boat back up to Warm Creek. The pneumatic dredges did not work well; the Chinle shale was too sticky to sluice. Spencer operated a few months in 1911, possibly briefly into 1912, and then quit. Spencer's gold mining operations at Lee's Ferry were the last of any size in Glen or San Juan canyons. The boom had ended. When Clyde Eddy voyaged through Glen Canyon in 1927, he saw

Oxen-Drawn Freight Wagons. *En route to Spencer Camp, San Juan River canyon, Utah. A gold-mining operation.* [*A. H. Jones*]

only one person, William Carpenter, living at Loper's Cabin at the mouth of Red Canyon.[5] Hite, Ticaboo, Good Hope Bar, Olympia Bar, California Bar, Boston Bar, Gretchen Bar, Schock Bar, Klondike Bar—once busy placer diggings—were now ghost camps on the Colorado.

The canyon-country gold rush, 1883–1911, was probably unique in the history of American mining. This was so, not because the gold was so fine and resisted most attempts to recover it, but because of the locale. With the exception of Lee's Ferry, practically the entire gold mining area in both Glen Canyon and San Juan Canyon has now been inundated by Lake Powell.

The Conquest

THE GOLD RUSH had closed the frontier. Before then men had worked into the canyon country from all sides but had, in general, not stayed in the deeper canyons until gold was discovered. The gap was now closed, the climax reached in the first cycle of exploitation. Gold had had its day but new interests countered its decline. Indeed, the twenty-six years from the time Utah was admitted as a state in 1896 to the signing of the Colorado River Compact in 1922 were most important in the further economic development of the region. It was a time of important beginnings.

Oil, for example. The burgeoning automobile industry that took shape after the turn of the century created an oil fever that was felt in Utah. An early well had been drilled near Green River in 1891, and this gave incentive to oil prospecting that was somewhat fitful, however, until after World War I. E. L. Goodridge brought in a gusher at Mexican Hat in 1908, but sufficient oil to be of commercial value was not found. There was a general quickening of interest all through the canyon country in 1920, produced by the expansion of the automobile industry after the war. Within the next ten years, wells were drilled at Monument Valley, Elk Ridge, Beef Basin, Dark Canyon, the Colorado River below Moab, Robber's Roost, San Rafael Swell, Circle Cliffs, Glen Canyon (at Bennett's Oil Field), and Mexican Hat. These early wells were shallow and no big commercial gushers were located, but a beginning had been made. Today's rich Aneth field along the San Juan in Utah is not far above Mexican Hat.

And copper. Constantly in need of turquoise, the Indians may have been the first canyon-country copper prospectors. Cass Hite probably found copper in Copper Canyon in 1882 while looking for the Merrick-Mitchell mine; this was the same year that Thomas V. Keam discovered some copper outcrops on the Kaibito Plateau where the White Mesa, or Keam, Mining District was formed. Copper was found in association with gold and silver ores of the La Sal, Abajo, and Henry Mountains, but it was most commonly found in the sandstone beds, often in association with radioactive minerals.

When, in 1898, gold prospectors in the La Sal discovered carnotite ore, a new phase of canyon country mining began that passed through three stages—radium, vanadium, and uranium. The first ended in 1924 and the others came later; the uranium boom, following World War II, enveloped the canyon country in its greatest mining rush. The beginning had been made years before: Uranium prospectors often found high uranium values in old abandoned copper mines (White Canyon, for instance) or vanadium prospects (San Rafael Swell).[6]

The most significant industrial development took place in the northwestern corner of the canyon country where the vast coal resources of the Wasatch Plateau and of the Book Cliffs boomed with the coming of the Denver & Rio Grande Western in 1882. Annual production climbed steadily, taking a big jump during World War I, until 1920, when it reached six million tons. The expanding coal industry and the growing population brought the organization of Carbon County—carved from Emery County—in 1894. Thereafter, Price, the county seat, was the center of the most rapidly growing section of the canyon country. Although coal has suffered a decline in more recent times, the expanding demand for industrial power in the 1960's may revive the industry and cause its further expansion into the western side of the canyon country where enormous coal reserves are located.[7]

Elsewhere there was slow growth in population and expansion of economic activity. Except for the intermittent mining developments, the canyon country remained essentially a grazing and farming area; once the limited agricultural land was taken up and the range divided, there was little opportunity for growth. In the 1880's there had been noticeable increases in the population of the Mormon villages along the edge of the canyon country, under the rim of the High Plateaus. As the anti-polygamy campaign worked up to a climax, following the passage of the Edmunds-Tucker Law of 1882, numbers of persons, threatened with prosecution for "unlawful cohabitation," found the canyon country, with its small secluded valleys, a good place to continue living according to their conscience. Zealous United States marshals found it difficult to rout out the "cohabs" from these areas. One result was further federal legislation, and finally polygamy was outlawed by the church and forbidden in the State Constitution of 1896.[8]

On the eastern side of the canyon country, Moab throve on the intermittent mining excitement in the La Sal Mountains, but the Four Corners area continued to be a buffer zone between the Indians and the advancing white farmers, cattlemen and miners. Following the Meeker massacre in Colorado in 1879, most of the Utes were removed from Colorado but the Southern Utes remained on a reservation in southwestern Colorado. Navajos, Paiutes, and Utes—many of them renegades—frequently flared up against the whites; the killing of Merrick and Mitchell in 1880 was only one of many such incidents. In the 1890's, a proposal was made that the Southern Utes be given a reservation in southeastern Utah, but it met with such hot opposition from Utah residents that it was abandoned. The long-running fight reached a climax during the "Ute War"—the "Polk-Posey War"—in 1915, which the Indians lost.[9]

As always, man's conflicts get the best press. In the country south of the San Juan, the Navajos had remained peaceful; they had admitted the white men as traders. Among them was John Wetherill, whose father, a Quaker, had gotten on well with the Utes and had ranged cattle on their reservation in southwestern Colorado. His boys found some of the magnificent ruins at Mesa Verde in 1888; John, while running stock down along the San Juan River in Utah, kept on the lookout for ruins. He joined in the San Juan gold rush and became familiar with the country south of the San Juan River. In 1906 he opened a trading post at Oljeto, near the Utah-Arizona line, and capitalized on the mining business while trading with the Indians.

In the summer of 1900, Henry N. Cowles and Joseph T. Hall opened a trading post at Hole-in-the-Rock, where they enjoyed a trade with Utes, Paiutes, and Navajos from places as far away as Bluff, Navajo Mountain, and Tuba City. Although Cowles and Hall abandoned the post after two years, the Navajos continued for years to cross the Colorado and to trade at Escalante. Navajo life had changed little since 1868, though the Indians had put their farming and grazing resources to maximum use.

After completing his surveys in the Colorado Plateau, John Wesley Powell had gone on to Washington to become the prophet of federal reclamation. Powell had seen the fundamental importance of irrigation in the life of the small Mormon villages, and it was mainly from his observations in Utah that he wrote the *Arid Lands*, which offered the nation a blueprint for the development of the arid West. Co-operative enterprise, he said, was necessary to insure maximum use of limited water; as Director of the Geological Survey, he initiated an irrigation survey of the West and this was accompanied by withdrawals of irrigable lands—here he ran counter to private interests. Yet, in the long run, Powell's suggestions prevailed. The Reclamation Act of 1902, which set aside revenues from the sale of public lands for reclamation purposes, and subsequent legislation that put the federal government squarely into western reclamation, were extensions of his idea that "co-operative capital" was necessary for maximum development of water resources.

In the summer of 1905, the Colorado River broke its banks and began to flow into the inland Salton Sea in southern California; it was only with great difficulty that the breach was stopped in 1906.

This event set in motion a series of actions that resulted eventually in the taming of the river that was by then being called a "natural menace." Government agencies and private concerns studied the river to determine how best to control and to use its waters for irrigation and power. E. C. La Rue, of the U. S. Geological Survey, assembled the data in 1916 in his paper, *Colorado River and Its Utilization*, which shows clearly that progress in water use in the lower basin was far ahead of that of the upper basin; at the same time demands on the water of the Colorado were rapidly increasing in both basins, and these could be expected to increase after the war.

The upper-basin states became apprehensive that extended use by lower-basin states would establish prior rights. There was this question: Did individual states have the right to regulate the flow of the river within their boundaries? Gradually the idea emerged that a compact between the states was essential to the full development of the Colorado. The lower basin needed the support of the upper basin in obtaining federal support for large main-stream developments, and the upper basin wanted to protect its rights for future development. In 1920, the Colorado River basin states set the machinery in motion, and in 1922 the Colorado River Compact was signed by representatives of the seven states involved.

The Colorado River Compact divided the available water of the river between the upper basin and the lower basin, the point of division being fixed at Lee's Ferry. The Compact cleared away many of the perplexities that involved rights to the water of a river in a land where water is scarce. It established a basis for future agreements between the Compact states, and it opened the way for federal legislation that would authorize the construction of major multi-purpose projects; in the lower basin, these began in 1928 with the signing of the Boulder Canyon Project Act, and in the upper basin in 1956, when the Upper Colorado River Storage Act was approved.[10]

By 1922 the beginnings had been made. The machinery was created whereby the river and the canyons were to be conquered.

THE "CHARLES H. SPENCER" AT LEE'S FERRY, 1911. *The largest boat ever to operate in Glen Canyon, it was built by Charles H. Spencer to haul coal from Warm Creek on the Utah-Arizona line 28 miles downstream to his gold-mining operation at Lee's Ferry.* [Kolb Photograph]

THE RUINS AT WARM CREEK. *Headquarters of Charles H. Spencer's coal-mining operations. Utah 1962.* [F. Finch, *Bureau of Reclamation*]

12/Symphony in Sandstone

Blank Verse

"THE AQUARIUS SHOULD BE DESCRIBED IN blank verse and illustrated upon canvas," were the words with which Captain Dutton opened Chapter XIII of his book on the *High Plateaus*. He went further; he wrote that the explorer who looks from the rim of the Aquarius Plateau over the canyons, who climbs about the lava cap of the rim, who enjoys a campfire and a sleep beneath the pine and spruces, "forgets that he is a geologist and feels himself a poet."

Dutton was unusual. But by 1922, among other beginnings, some awareness and some appreciation for the magnificent natural scenery of the canyon country had developed. It would be difficult to say when this began. Some of the early, articulate visitors, like Father Escalante and Jacob Hamblin, were men of strong faith who probably felt more deeply about God than about His works. Occasionally a subjective word crept into the factual reports of the early government explorers, but it could go either way: Captain Macomb, looking toward the junction of the Green and Grand in 1859, thought of it as an inconceivably "worthless and impracticable region"; but to Dr. Newberry, viewing the same scene, it was "strange and beautiful."

Dutton's monographs on the *High Plateaus* and the *Grand Canyon* are happy combinations of geology and belles lettres. He wrote of the canyon country as he saw it from the rim of the plateaus, but the grand scenes from these lofty rims impelled him to depart from the "severe ascetic style which has become conventional in scientific monographs,"

and to paint with words the things he both saw and felt. So to him the view from the rim was at once a laboratory of rocks and "a sublime panorama," or, "an extreme of desolation, the blankest solitude, a superlative desert." And, of a different view: "The grandeur of the spectacle consists in a great number of cliffs rising successively one upon the other, like a stairway for the Titans, leading up to a mighty temple." Dutton felt the scene demanded such writing and, in the *Grand Canyon*, he departed even further from the "severe ascetic style."

The works of the Powell, Wheeler, and Hayden surveys were enriched by photographers and artists, whose work, quite as much as that of the authors, helped to form the popular image of the canyons of the Colorado. Beaman, Fennemore, and Hillers took pictures for Powell; O'Sullivan worked for Wheeler, and Jackson for Hayden. Artist Richard Kern, of the famous brothers, painted the crossing of the Green River of the Spanish Trail for the Gunnison Survey. J. S. Young made colored lithographs of Dr. Newberry's sketches in the canyon country for the Macomb Survey: "Casa Colorado"; "Head of Labyrinth Creek"; "Head of Cañon Colorado"; and "Lower San Juan, Looking West." Egloffstein's maps illustrating Gunnison's, Ives's, and Macomb's reports were works of art. John E. Weyss made an artistic sketch of the Crossing of the Fathers for the Wheeler Survey in 1872. Illustrations by Thomas Moran and Frederick S. Dellenbaugh appear in the monographs of the Powell Survey; the magnificent panoramas of the Grand

NAVAJO MOUNTAIN DWARFS RAINBOW BRIDGE AT ITS FOOT. *Utah 1962.*
[*A. E. Turner, Bureau of Reclamation*]

Canyon by W. H. Holmes, whose earliest works of this kind appeared in Hayden's reports, have not been equaled.[1]

After 1889, when Wheeler's final geographical report was published, the works of art, like those that distinguish the publication of the Great Surveys, disappeared from official reports. It is doubtful if the art work in these reports did much to fix an image of the canyon country on the public mind. Much of it dealt with the region around the periphery and not with the more spectacular canyons. And Dutton's masterpiece on the Grand Canyon, illustrated by Holmes, and the publication by Hayden in 1876 of Moran's beautiful paintings of Yellowstone and Grand Canyon, deflected the public attention. In later official reports, art work was replaced by the strict realism of photographic illustration, brought within easier reach by improved methods in photography, which suited the requirements of the scientific monograph.

"Holes, Hills and Hollows"

FOR THOSE ATTEMPTING to wring a living from the meager land, the canyon country seemingly held little scenic attraction. The prehistoric Anasazis were probably more concerned with defense than view, though from archeological investigation this is difficult to ascertain. The Mormon villagers, faced with the stern economics of making a living from a narrow strip of marginal land, a precarious oasis in a land of bare rocks and little water, probably did not spend much time in contemplating the aesthetics of that environment. To Elizabeth Decker, who took part in the Hole-in-the-Rock trek, it was all "holes, hills and hollows."

With more rocks than grass, the stockmen were noticeably slow to develop an appreciative spirit for the intricate country. During the pioneer period, it is safe to say, the residents in the canyon country most appreciative of their environment were those who found it a good place to hide: outlaws, fugitives, rustlers, "cohabs," and renegade Indians.

Little has been found in the writings of the gold miners, who moved into the canyon country after

RAINBOW BRIDGE.
[*A. E. Turner, Bureau of Reclamation*]

150

1883, to suggest that they had much interest in the natural scene except to dig gold out of it. The outdoor life may have been appealing, but placer mining on the canyon bottoms was hard work with small reward. Moving about was difficult, even hazardous, and supply points and settlements were reached only after crossing long miles of desert. Constant combat with nature may have provoked admiration for nature, but the miners very seldom said so.

The miners were the first to make a thorough-going exploration of the main canyons and of all the tributaries. The placer region extended the full length of Glen Canyon and it encompassed much of the San Juan Canyon below Bluff. It turned out that the gold-producing area in both canyons was largely restricted to the lateral gravel beds along the river banks, but this was not known as prospecting began. We can be sure that during the time of the canyon-country gold rush, 1883–1911, miners prospected every tributary of Cataract, Narrow, Glen, and San Juan canyons from mouth to source, or at least up to the point where prospecting seemed to be probable of success.

If the gold prospectors found few good diggings, they literally discovered the canyons. They found remains of prehistoric peoples, and they viewed at close range the jumbled and intricate landscape, much of which they were the first whites to see. Generally, the miners worked *up* the canyon tributaries from the rivers and went as far as they could, though they were often stopped by the precipitous head of a box canyon. The stockmen, both Indian and white, ranging their animals, generally worked *down* through the canyons toward the river, though they were often stopped on the rim of the box canyons. Of the two, the miner probably developed the better knowledge of the region. Between them, the miners and the stockmen became intimately familiar with the canyon country and most of its natural features.[2]

Cattlemen discovered the three natural stone bridges preserved in Natural Bridges National Monument. Located near the head of the White Canyon, just below and west of the Bear's Ears on Elk Ridge, the bridges are near a major trail coming

CLARENCE E. DUTTON. *Geologist for the Powell Survey.* [*U. S. Geological Survey*]

into the canyon country from the east and from the San Juan River on the south. Cass Hite claimed to have seen the bridges in September 1883. Later others saw them, including J. A. Scorup who had ranged cattle through the area about 1891, and who visited them in 1895.

In the spring of 1903, Scorup met Horace J. Long who was in Glen Canyon at the time, attempting to operate the Hoskaninni Company gold dredge for W. W. Dyar, the new owner who had purchased it following the receivership. Long took a greater interest in scenery than dredging, and when Scorup told him of the bridges, the two men went to visit them. Long kept an account of the trip that was written by W. W. Dyar, and published it in the *Century Magazine*, August 1904, the first description of the bridges to reach the general public. This was followed by a notice, "Colossal Natural Bridges of Utah," published in the *National Geographic Magazine* in September 1904.

Bridges of Stone

THE APPEARANCE OF THESE ARTICLES, among the first of national circulation to extol the grandeur of the canyon country, was of importance to the area. They drew wide attention to a region that the Powell and Hayden Surveys had passed over. The bridges were pictured as being so much larger than Virginia's famous natural bridge, a standard illustration in elementary geography textbooks and thus a sort of standard measurement, that the story seemed unbelievable. In April 1905, a group sponsored by the Salt Lake Commercial Club visited the bridges. Along with the party went an artist, the English-born H. L. A. Culmer, who took measurements and made sketches from which his famous paintings of the bridges were made. Photographs of the paintings of all three bridges were published in the *National Geographic Magazine* for March 1907. E. F. Holmes, ex-president of the Salt Lake Commercial Club, who had suggested the trip in the first place, advocated in this article the formation of a national park encompassing the bridges. Culmer was already well known as a landscape artist; he was an admirer of the English painter, Turner, and the American, Thomas Moran. His paintings reflected his understanding of geology as well as his profound love for the natural scene. In the canyon country of southeastern Utah, he found the eroded desert landscape stimulating and inspiring, and his paintings of the natural bridges in White Canyon and subsequent oils done in Monument Valley, Arches National Monument, and in the San Rafael Swell will probably endure as his best work. Writing sometime after the 1905 visit to the bridges, Culmer commented that erosion in southern Utah has "created scenes of magnificent disorder, in savage grandeur beyond description. The remnants of the land remain of impressive but fantastic wildness, mute witnesses of the powers of frenzied elements, wrecking a world. These were the powers that fashioned those monoliths that rise like lofty monuments from the southern plains; that shaped those enormous stone bridges in the rim rock region of

San Juan . . . and they strewed over a region as large as an empire such bewildering spectacles of mighty shapes that Utah must always be the land sought by explorers of the strange and marvelous." H. L. A. Culmer helped prominently to fashion the public conception of the canyon country.[3]

In their articles, both Dyar and Holmes mentioned the existence of cliff dwellings in the vicinity of the bridges. This caught the attention of archeologists. In the summer of 1907, Dean Byron Cummings of the University of Utah School of Letters and Science, in co-operation with the Archeological Institute of America, organized a party to investigate the White Canyon bridges and the country north of the San Juan River. Cummings's report of the trip, which included data on the stone bridges and the ruins, was sent to the General Land Office and then brought to the attention of President Theodore Roosevelt. On April 16, 1908, he created the Natural Bridges National Monument. This was the first national monument or park established in Utah; in the general area, it was only preceded by Mesa Verde National Park and Petrified Forest National Monument, both dating from 1906.

The creation of one national monument in the region was soon followed by two more. Dean Cummings had a hand in all three. In the summer of 1908, he returned with a party of students to the San Juan region for an archeological dig at Alkali Ridge west of Blanding. Then, with John Wetherill, he investigated the ruins in the Segi and the Segihatsosi canyons, not far from the Wetherill trading post recently established at Oljeto. During this time he learned from Mrs. Wetherill that the Indians had told her of a natural bridge on the slopes of Navajo Mountain.

Heading a "Utah Archeological Expedition," Cummings returned to the Navajo country in the summer of 1909; he hoped to look for the bridge after the archeological work was completed. Again with John Wetherill as guide, he spent most of the summer exploring ruins in the canyons of the Segi and the Segihatsosi. Although the Segi had been explored previously by Richard Wetherill and Charles Mason in the 1890's, and later by John Wetherill, Cummings was the first archeologist to visit the area. The imposing and dramatic ruined town of Betatakin, built during the Great Pueblo era not long before A.D. 1300, was one of the important discoveries. United States Surveyor W. B. Douglass, who had just completed mapping the natural bridges in White Canyon, learned of Cummings's discoveries in the Segi and elsewhere. His report served as a basis for the creation of Navajo National Monument, proclaimed on March 20, 1909, by President William Howard Taft.

After surveying the ruins in Segi Canyon, Cummings set out for Navajo Mountain to look for the stone bridge. He was guided by John Wetherill and a Paiute Indian, Nasja-begay, who knew the location of it. While they were on the trail, it was learned that W. B. Douglass, of the General Land Office, was en route with a party to look for the bridge. Cummings waited for him and the two went on together, passing around the rugged and dissected north side of Navajo Mountain. On August 14, 1909, the combined party discovered the magnificent arch of Rainbow Bridge. A few men of the discovery party walked nearly five miles down Bridge and Aztec canyons to the Colorado River, where they saw evidence that miners had been there before them.

By 1909 the gold rush in Glen Canyon had spent itself and nearly all the miners had gone. Unquestionably, Rainbow Bridge had been visited before 1909 by prospectors who were working their way up from the Colorado, and by those who were exploring the slopes of Navajo Mountain. The reported Merrick-Mitchell mine had brought men to the Navajo Mountain-Monument Valley region in 1882 or earlier. W. F. Williams some time afterward said that he had seen the bridge in 1884 or 1885, in company with his brother, Benjamin, and their father, J. P. Williams, who organized the Williams Mining District on the San Juan River in 1895. There are other reports of discovery of the bridge before 1909 but they count for little. It was the "discovery" in 1909 that led to the formation of a new national monument, which brought the great stone arch to the attention of the world. It is also to be remembered that the Indian, Nasja-begay, had known of the bridge for some time when he guided the white men to it. Both Paiutes and Navajos knew of the bridge before 1909.

At the scene, W. B. Douglass immediately went to work to take the measurements of the bridge; he found that the arch which spanned an inner canyon, stood 309 feet above the creek bed and 235 feet above the rim of the inner canyon upon which the abutments rested. The span was 278 feet; at the highest point the arch was found to be 42 feet thick and 33 feet wide. These measurements to many later visitors have held little meaning, for the bridge in its natural setting—within a canyon and at the foot of rugged Navajo Mountain—seems smaller than it really is. Douglass was also responsible for choosing the name, "Rainbow Natural Bridge," suggested by the Paiute word, *barohoini*, for "rainbow." The bridge has also been known by the Navajo name, *nonnezoshi*, "great arch," or "great stone arch." On the basis of Douglass's report to the General Land Office, Rainbow Bridge National Monument was proclaimed by President Taft, May 30, 1910. An article by Cummings in the *National Geographic Magazine* for February 1910 undoubtedly had much to do with the proclamation.[4]

After leaving the bridge in August 1909, Cummings had gone on to explore the ruins in the upper drainage of Navajo Canyon and there he discovered the Inscription House ruins. The archeological discoveries made by Cummings during the summers of 1909 and 1910 were studied in greater detail by archeologist Jesse Walter Fewkes and, on the basis of his recommendations, together with those of Douglass and Cummings, the boundaries of Navajo National Monument were enlarged in 1912 to include the great ruined towns of Betatakin and Keet Seel, both in the Segi, and Inscription House.[5]

Besides his interest in archeology, Byron Cummings had a deep appreciation for the natural scene of southeastern Utah and northeastern Arizona; this probably had much to do with his return to the Navajo country, where he excavated in the region around Kayenta for years. He was possibly more impressed by the landscape than he was by the prehistoric ruins. His article in the *National Geo-*

INACCESSIBLE RUIN. *White Mesa, Arizona.*
[*William C. Miller, Pasadena*]

Sɪᴘᴀᴘᴜ Nᴀᴛᴜʀᴀʟ Bʀɪᴅɢᴇ. *Natural Bridges National Monument, Utah. [Parker Hamilton, Flagstaff]*

OLJETO TRADING POST. *1909. [A. H. Jones]*

GOBLIN VALLEY. *Utah State Park. [Ward J. Roylance, Utah Tourist and Publicity Council]*

graphic *Magazine* for February 1910 was the first published account of the discovery of Rainbow Bridge and it appeared before the National Monument was established; he wrote of it again in a *Bulletin* of the University of Utah published in November 1910. Both articles carried photographs by Stuart M. Young, a student at the university, showing the bridges in White Canyon as well as Rainbow. In the latter article, he said his work over the past few summers had been undertaken "to make the great natural wonders and beauties of Utah better known and to investigate . . . the life of the ancient people. . . ." In the next sentence, he said, "Our investigations divide themselves into two parts: the natural wonders and the ancient people." The natural wonders came first. Dean Byron Cummings indeed was a notable pioneer in pointing out to the world the natural beauty of the region, as well as its archeological wealth.

JOHN WETHERILL. *Kayenta, Arizona.* [*Rainbow Bridge—Monument Valley Collection, Museum of Northern Arizona*]

Crescendo

THE FORMATION of three national monuments in the same region within two years, together with the publications of Dyar, Holmes, Cummings, and Fewkes, and the paintings of H. L. A. Culmer, as well as the publications of other scientists—Herbert E. Gregory, T. Mitchell Prudden, and others—popularized the eastern side of the canyon country some time before there was a comparable development on the western side. On the western side there was no lack of great natural features—the Kaiparowits Plateau, the canyon of the Escalante River, the Circle Cliffs, the Waterpocket Fold—but there were no dramatically spectacular bridges to compare with Rainbow and the White Canyon bridges, and there were no romantic prehistoric cities of over a hundred rooms built in caves and cliffs, like Betatakin. Although Zion National Park dates from 1909 (Mukuntuweap National Monument, 1909–19), the establishment of Bryce Canyon National Park (1923–28) and Capitol Reef National Monument in 1937 are indications of the slower development west of the Colorado. By 1937, in addition to those mentioned, there was a ring of national parks

H. L. A. CULMER. *Utah artist, painter of the canyon country.* [*Courtesy Kenneth A. Culmer*]

Touring Monument Valley in a Maxwell, 1918. [*Utah State Historical Society*]

Record of the Eddy Expedition in Upper Cataract Canyon. *Utah.*
[*Stan Rasmussen*]

and monuments encircling the canyon country: Grand Canyon National Park (1908–19), Colorado National Monument (1911), Pipe Spring and Hovenweep national monuments (1923), and Canyon de Chelly National Monument (1931).[6]

Tourist travel to the eastern side of the canyon country began very soon after the creation of the national parks and monuments. In 1910 John and Louisa Wade Wetherill moved from Oljeto to Kayenta and for thirty-three years their trading post served as a base for archeological and exploratory expeditions and tourist trips into the wild country of the Navajos adjoining Glen Canyon and San Juan Canyon. Most of these expeditions were guided by John Wetherill. Across the San Juan River in Blanding, Ezekiel ("Zeke") Johnson, first custodian of Natural Bridges National Monument, handled pack trips into the bridges and to the country west of the Clay Hills. Both men became almost as well known as the region.

Rainbow Bridge became the greatest single attraction and the most difficult to reach by land. Both guided by John Wetherill, Zane Grey and Theodore Roosevelt visited the bridge in 1913. Grey returned several times, the last trip in 1922, since he found in the rugged canyon country inspiration for some of the best-selling novels that came from his prolific pen. *Riders of the Purple Sage*, *Rainbow Trail*, *Heritage of the Desert*, *The Vanishing American*, and *Wildfire* were among the most popular novels of their day. Grey's autobiographical *Tales of Lonely Trails*, published in 1922, opens with an account of his trip to Rainbow Bridge. In another place he wrote: "I love wild canyons—dry, fragrant, stone-walled, with their green-choked niches and gold-tipped ramparts."

In 1921 the United States Geological Survey and the Southern California Edison Company undertook the mapping of the Colorado from the head of Cataract Canyon through Narrow and Glen canyons to Lee's Ferry, including the San Juan River below the mouth of Chinle Creek. This project resulted in the first accurate map of those canyons. One group of the surveyors, headed by K. W. Trimble, walked up to Rainbow Bridge from the Colorado River; they were probably the first to

EZEKIEL ("ZEKE") JOHNSON. *First custodian of Natural Bridges National Monument and guide.* [*Utah State Historical Society*]

NORMAN D. NEVILLS, RIVER RUNNER. [*Hal Rumel, courtesy Gaylord Staveley*]

160

KOLB BROTHERS INSCRIPTION CATARACT CANYON, 1911. *Utah. Emery and Ellsworth Kolb ran through the canyons of the Colorado from Wyoming to California.* [*W. L. Rusho, Bureau of Reclamation*]

FERRY ON THE COLORADO RIVER AT DANDY CROSSING. *Hite. Utah 1962.* [*Parker Hamilton, Flagstaff*]

JEEPING IN THE CANYON COUNTRY. *Utah.*
[*Nelson Wadsworth, Salt Lake City*]

CHARLES KELLY. *Canyon country writer.* [*Utah State Historical Society*]

163

do so since the miners had left Glen Canyon over a decade before.[7]

Charles L. Bernheimer, who described himself as "a tenderfoot and a cliff-dweller from Manhattan," conducted a number of explorations into the Navajo country and into the area north of the San Juan River between 1920 and 1930. Bernheimer was attracted to the canyon country through the writings of Zane Grey. His own published accounts of these trips are interesting and valuable. He employed both Wetherill and Johnson as guides, but he persisted in going beyond well-known routes and into new areas. New geographical information was assembled and he made notes on archeological sites. On the expedition in 1921, Bernheimer made an unsuccessful attempt to locate the Crossing of the Fathers, which had all but faded from men's memories, and in 1922, with a pack train, he encircled Navajo Mountain and visited Rainbow Bridge. His canyon country expeditions through the year 1924 are reported in his book, appropriately entitled *Rainbow Bridge*.[8]

During World War I, the automobile came of age, and after the war the United States became a nation on wheels. Travelers in touring cars began to compete with the railroads, particularly in the West where there were fewer lines. But the only roads in the canyon country were those that connected the small settlements around the periphery; and before 1922 these, for the most part, were better suited for wagons than for automobiles. Distant travelers continued to arrive by train and planned to visit the remote parts of the canyon country on horseback. As a reporter for the New York *Sun*, Cy Warman, the "Poet of the Rockies," came into the canyon country in the San Juan gold rush. Some of the poetry and stories he wrote later—"Valley Tan," "Ticaboo," and "Hoskaninni"—grew out of his Utah experiences; and the Denver & Rio Grande Western used some of his poetry in its promotional literature.[9] The Santa Fe Railroad advertised the Grand Canyon, but the Denver & Rio Grande Western, closer at hand, promoted the scenic attractions along its line and the general public early became acquainted with the Book Cliffs

and such places as Castle Gate at the mouth of Price Canyon.

Very few tourist groups or scientific expeditions ventured into Glen Canyon or San Juan Canyon before 1921, when the first detailed surveys were made, except to cross the rivers at well-known places: Hole-in-the-Rock, Dandy Crossing, Clay Hill Crossing, and elsewhere. Archeological studies, for example, had been confined largely to the upland plateaus and tributary canyons, rather than to the main rivers; there had been few archeologists in the canyons since Powell's day.[10]

After the Powell voyages in 1869 and 1871, travel for scientific purposes on the Utah portion of the Colorado River was not repeated until the first decade of the twentieth century when government surveys in the interests of reclamation were initiated. Recreational use of the river began about the same time. The rivers, of course, had been main routes of travel for the miners during the gold rush and for the trappers, who were probably the first voyagers in the canyons. Among the best-known trappers was Nathaniel Galloway, who traveled with William Richmond in 1895 from Green River, Wyoming, to Lee's Ferry; in 1896 they repeated the trip and went through Grand Canyon to Needles in California, arriving there in January 1897. Beginning in the 1890's, there were some short-lived attempts to use power boats, both for pleasure and business, on the quiet waters of the Green below Green River and on the Colorado below Moab.

Although it was primarily a prospecting venture, the trip through the canyons in 1907 made by Charles S. Russell, E. R. Monett, and Bert Loper may be considered as one of the earliest tourist runs. Loper had been in the San Juan Canyon gold rush and he joined Russell and Monett on the voyage to take photographs of the canyons and to prospect. The party left Green River, Utah, in September 1907, and in the passage through Cataract Canyon, Loper's boat was damaged and he was delayed. He planned to rejoin Russell and Monett at Lee's Ferry, but when he finally arrived, they had gone on into Grand Canyon. Loper went back upstream early in 1908, pulling and rowing his boat 150 miles up-stream against the current to Red Canyon where he established himself at the "Hermitage," known later as Loper's Cabin; Cass Hite, across the river at Ticaboo, was his nearest neighbor.

The publication of Dellenbaugh's *Romance of the Colorado River* in 1902, the same year as the passage of the National Reclamation Act, and the appearance of his *Canyon Voyage* in 1908, the first satisfactory account of the details of the second Powell voyage, went far in stimulating interest in river travel. In 1909, Julius Stone, an associate of Robert B. Stanton in the Hoskaninni venture, made the first trip through the Colorado canyons done solely in the spirit of adventure. He hired Nathaniel Galloway as boatman. The Stone group, consisting of ten men and four boats left Green River, Wyoming, in September and reached Needles, California, in November.

In September 1911, Ellsworth and Emery Kolb, photographers at Grand Canyon, left Green River, Wyoming, on a photographic tour using Dellenbaugh's *Canyon Voyage* as a guide. They arrived at Needles, California, in January 1912, after having made the first significant motion pictures of the Colorado canyons.

During World War I, commercial tours in Glen Canyon began. In 1917, David E. Rust, who had first come to Glen Canyon in 1897 during the gold rush, started conducting annual tourist groups from North Wash to Lee's Ferry; he used folding boats covered with canvas, each boat holding two passengers. River recreation in Glen Canyon was well under way by 1922, a decisive year in the history of the Colorado River, although a similar threshold was not to be reached on the San Juan River until Norman Nevills began river-running about ten years later.

By 1922, the natural beauty of the river canyons was beginning to be appreciated, although no books had yet been written about it. Dr. John A. Widtsoe, en route to Santa Fe that year to represent Utah in the signing of the Colorado River Compact, toured Glen Canyon in company with a distinguished group of Geological Survey and Reclamation Service officials, to look over the most suitable dam sites. The party, led by E. C. La Rue, entered the river at Hall's Crossing and saw the Hole-in-the-Rock crossing, Rainbow Bridge, the Crossing of the Fathers, and other places, as well as the possible dam sites. Reflecting upon the voyage in his diary, Widtsoe wrote: ". . . I quite agree with Major Powell, that it is useless to describe with words or even with pictures the wonders, of surprising magnitude and beauty, that fill the country through which we have passed on this trip."

By 1922, people were indeed beginning to see the canyon country as a place of beauty. But it was still a segmented view. The sharpest focus, as it had been through history, was still fixed chiefly on the area around the edges. That is where the parks and monuments, samples of the great country in between, were located. By 1922, no one had said that not only the parts but the whole sweep of country between the Book Cliffs in Utah and White Mesa in Arizona, and between Bryce Canyon and the Four Corners, was one of unparalleled grandeur—that it was one of the earth's great places.[11]

PREHISTORIC PETROGLYPHS. *Mouth of Piute Creek, San Juan River canyon. Utah 1962.*
[*W. L. Rusho, Bureau of Reclamation*]

Notes

1 / Names on the Land

1. Still the best work on Utah's colorful place names, and otherwise very useful, is *Utah, A Guide to the State*, done by the WPA (1941). The same agency also published a mimeographed *Origin of Utah Place Names* (1940b). Neither one gets very far away from the road in southeastern Utah. *Gannett's Gazetteer of Utah* (1900) is a gathering of the nomenclature from the U. S. Geological Survey reconnaissance topographic sheets that had pretty well blanketed the state by then. Leigh's work (1961) treats of 500 Utah place names. Jenson (1919–22) discusses names of Mormon origin.

The difficult world of Navajo names has yet to find a master. Van Valkenburgh's *Diné Bikeyáh* (1941) (Navajo Country), is a little known guide and gazetteer of high value. The "Geographic Terms" in H. E. Gregory's two works, *The Navajo Country* (1916, 1917), cannot be ignored. Some place-name information is found in the ethnological dictionary of the Navajo language by the Franciscan Fathers (1910). Will C. Barnes's *Arizona Place Names* (1960) updates an earlier edition.

2 / Standing Up Country

1. McBride (1907), 700.
2. Dutton (1880), 286.
3. Powell (1895), 75.
4. McKnight (1940), 124.
5. Gregory (1938), 13. The works of H. E. Gregory listed below, and of Charles B. Hunt (1953) are of exceptional value for a study of the geography of the canyon country as well as its geology.

Indeed the best descriptions of the canyon country have been written by men in the government service. The publications of the United States Geological Survey—bulletins, water-supply papers, and professional papers prepared after time spent in the field—blanket the entire region: H. E. Gregory (1951) on the Paunsaugunt region and Gregory and Moore (1931) on the Kaiparowits region; Gregory (1950) on the Zion Park region is a related work; Charles B. Hunt and others (1953) on the Henry Mountains region; Gregory and Anderson (1939) and Smith and others (1963) on the Capitol Reef region; Speiker (1931) on the Wasatch Plateau and Lupton (1916) on Castle Valley; Gilluly (1929) on the San Rafael Swell; Baker (1946) on the Green River Desert-Land's End Plateau region; Fisher (1936) and Fisher and others (1960) on the Book Cliffs; McKnight (1940) on the triangular region between the Green and Colorado rivers; Dane (1935) on the Arches region; Baker (1933) on the Needles country; Hunt (1958) on the La Sal Mountains; Gregory (1938) on the San Juan country—the southeastern corner of Utah; Baker (1936) on the Monument Valley-Navajo Mountain region; Gregory (1916, 1917) and Harshbarger and others (1957) on the Navajo country. Water-supply papers by La Rue (1916, 1925), Follansbee (1929), Woolley (1930), and Miser (1924) treat of the canyons of the Colorado, Green and San Juan rivers.

The earlier publications by Powell (1875a, 1876, 1895), Gilbert (1877), and Dutton (1880, 1882) have not been equaled by modern writers. Newberry in Macomb's report (1876), Holmes (1877) for the Hayden Survey, and Wheeler's (1889) final geographical report are also valuable items in the early scientific literature of the canyon country.

The comprehensive studies of the Colorado River, one by the Bureau of Reclamation (1946–7) and one by the National Park Service (1950), agencies of the U. S. Department of the Interior, are important sources. Hunt's work on the cenozoic geology of the Colorado Plateau (1956) has an exceptionally good bibliography of geological literature, a whole world in itself. See also notes for Chapter V.

The fifteen-minute topographic quadrangles, recently published by the U. S. Geological Survey, which now cover large parts of the canyon country, are the best maps available. By means of contour lines they show surface features accurately, and each is a work of art. Each quad is named after some prominent topographical feature within the area. Here are the names of a few of them: Clay Hills, Fable Valley, Factory Butte, Fiddler Butte, Gunsight Butte, Leche-e Rock, Mancos Mesa, The Needles, Nipple Butte, No Man's Mesa, The Rincon, Orange Cliffs, The Spur, Upheaval Dome, Wagon Box Mesa, The Wickiup, Wild Horse. Index sheets of Utah and Arizona showing the quadrangles available are obtainable from the U. S. Geological Survey in Washington, and in Denver, Colorado.

6. During the Spanish era the name Colorado was applied to

the river in its lower reaches. Humboldt's map, as we have noted in Chapter III, following Miera, applied the name San Rafael to the upper part of the river. In his 1848 map of the West, Frémont moves the San Rafael over to its present location; by that time the name Rio Grande or Grand River, was in current usage for the Colorado above the Green River. The phrase, "the Green and the Grand" will be used frequently in this book. Feeling that it had a proprietary right in the name, the Colorado State Legislature in 1921 changed the name from Grand to Colorado; the Congress of the United States went along with the idea and wrote it into federal law July 25, 1921. Possibly no one worried very much at the time that the Legislature and the Congress took the namesake away from Grand counties in Utah and Colorado and the city of Grand Junction in Colorado. Of course, all these places are *grand* so the theft was not serious. The canyon of the Colorado in Utah, above the Green, was before 1921, the canyon of the Grand, and it is a *grand* canyon.

3 / The Mythical River

1.   There is little documentation on the Spanish and Mexican approaches to the upper basin of the Colorado River. With regard to the canyon country in Utah and northeastern Arizona, the Hafens, in their *Old Spanish Trail* (1954), have assembled much of the essential evidence on routes, traders, and travelers, which is the heart of the matter. Tyler's pioneer work (1951a) takes up Spanish relations with the Yuta Indians before Escalante.
2.   The Domínguez-Escalante expedition through the unexplored wilderness of Colorado, Utah, and Arizona in 1776, has received scholarly attention and is the best documented part of the Spanish story. Documents and background material are found in the beautiful book by Adams and Chavez (1956). Three editions of the Escalante diary have appeared in English (Harris, 1909; Auerbach, 1943; Bolton, 1950) and one in Spanish (Velez de Escalante, 1854). The Auerbach and Bolton editions are particularly valuable for their editorial notes; both include the report made by Bernardo de Miera y Pacheco as well as copies of his maps. A short summary of the expedition was done by Philip Harry in 1860 from a copy of the diary in the collection of Peter Force. This, together with a map plotted from Escalante's distances, was published in Simpson's (1876) report of his explorations in the Great Basin undertaken in 1859. Bolton's work is the most satisfactory field study of the expedition but he did not cover the trail across Glen Canyon. However, Miller (1958) has done so.
3.   Humboldt's great work in the first English edition is titled, *Political Essay on the Kingdom of New Spain* . . . translated from the original French by John Black (London, 1811), 4 vols. The original French edition appeared in the series of quarto volumes written by Humboldt and Aimé Bonpland, and bears the title, *Essai politique sur le Royaume de la Nouvelle Espagne* (Paris, 1811), 2 vols. It was accompanied by the atlas in folio, *Atlas géographique et physique du Royaume de la Nouvelle Espagne* . . . (Paris, 1811); another (Paris, 1812). An octavo edition of the *Essai* in five volumes was also published in Paris in 1811, and a second edition was published there (1825-7) in four volumes. The most recent edition is one in Spanish, edited by Vito Alessio Robles, *Ensayo político sobre el Reino de la Nueva Espana* . . . (Mexico, 1941), 4 vols., and an atlas. All who work with Humboldt soon

discover the need for an exhaustive study of his immense bibliography. A recent biographer is Helmut De Terra, *Humboldt, the Life and Times of Alexander von Humboldt, 1769–1859* (New York, 1955).

The map bears the title, "Carte Générale du Royaume de la Nouvelle Espagne depuis le parallele de 16° jusqu'au parallele de 38 (latitude Nord) dressée sur les observations astronomiques et sur l'ensemble des matériaux qui existoient à Mexico, au commencement de l'année 1804." This is the map that was drawn up in preliminary form by Humboldt in Mexico in 1804 and completed by him and by Friesen, Oltmanns, and Thulier in 1809. Another general map, "Carte du Mexique et des pays limitrophe situés au nord et a l'est . . ." was adapted from the above and from other materials by J. B. Poirson, but it lacks the detail of the first for the Rocky Mountain region. Both maps appeared, the first in two sections, in the editions of the *Atlas géographique*; because of its smaller size the "Carte du Mexique . . ." is frequently found in the several editions of the essay with a title translated to match the language of the edition. The northern half of the "Carte Générale . . ." has been reproduced by Carl I. Wheat, *1540–1861 Mapping the Transmississippi West, Volume One, The Spanish Entrada to the Louisiana Purchase, 1540–1804* (San Francisco, 1957), as his no. 272, opposite page 134. Wheat's monumental work is now complete and runs to five volumes, volume five, in two parts. It is difficult to see how we have been able to get along without this great work in the past. It will remain an indispensable source for the cartographic history of western North America to 1861 (actually to 1879 when the U. S. Geological Survey was founded).

The geographical misconceptions of Domínguez and Escalante, as picked up by Humboldt, are studied in two of my papers, the discovery of the Green River in 1776 (1952), and Humboldt's portrayal of Utah, 1811 (1958), and in one paper with Gloria Griffen (Cline) (1956) on the San Buenaventura. Dr. Cline in her *Exploring the Great Basin* (1963) develops fully these and other geographical mistakes. DeVoto's work (1952) gives continental perspective to the opening of the West, 1492–1806. See Humboldt's *Political Essay*, I, 71-2, 274, and II, 278, for the quotations and closely related matter.
4.   The caravan and trapping era in the canyon country has found a few writers who have probably nigh exhausted the sparse documentation on the subject. The Hafens (1954) have cited most of the significant literature. Hill's work (1921), later reprinted with few changes (1930), is a pioneer study of Spanish-Mexican interest in the Utah country. W. Snow's article on the Indian slave trade (1929) is appended by important documents. The extent of this trade, also studied by Creer (1947, 1949), needs to be investigated more fully. D. Jones (1890) says there was a systematic slave trade between Utah and New Mexico until 1851. However, we know from other sources that it continued well beyond that time. The Ute Chief, Walker, or Walkara, in the Sevier Valley in Utah, was a principal in the slave and horse trade between New Mexico and California. See Bailey (1954).

In the classic work on the western fur trade, Chittenden (1902) has little to say about the Southwest, a lack made up by Cleland's excellent *This Reckless Breed of Men* (1952). Dale L. Morgan's biography of Jed Smith (1953) is the life of one of the greats in the Rocky Mountain fur trade who first perceived the true nature of the Great Basin and opened the trail across the southern part of it that became better known as the Spanish Trail.

There is probably more to be said about the mountain men in the canyon country but the documents are few. James Ohio Pattie is usually cited as one of the first to get into the canyons of the Colorado, but his narrative (Thwaites, ed., 1905) of the trip in 1826 is so vague that his route has to be guessed at. "De Julien, an Unknown Explorer," was an early article in *Outing* (1905). Charles Kelly (1933a) has identified Denis Julien, quite probably the first to visit Cataract Canyon and the lower canyons of the Green. Near the mouth of Westwater Canyon in the Book Cliffs, near the Utah-Colorado line, there is an inscription in French that reads, "Antoine Roubidoux passed here November 13, 1837, to establish a trading house on the River Green or Winte," a record of Roubidoux's activities in the Uinta basin with which Julien may have had some connection. See the Hafens (1954), 102, and photograph of the inscription in Kelly's article (1933b), 115, and in the Salt Lake *Tribune*, January 10, 1960.

That the mountain men knew much of the canyon country is evident from the book of Warren A. Ferris, who roamed the Rockies from 1830–5. In the Auerbach-Alter edition (1940), chapter 70, he writes that: "The Colorado, a short distance below the junction of the Green and Grand rivers, enters the great chanion, which is a canal in many places more than a thousand feet deep, and bounded on either side by perpendicular walls of rock. . . . This chanion confines the river between two and three hundred miles. . . . Its tributaries are confined by walls from their junctions some distance; which compels caravans [on the Spanish Trail] to travel the plains far from the river. . . ."

During the recent historical salvage program in Glen Canyon, the date "1837" was described. This date, opposite the mouth of Lake Canyon, and now under the reservoir waters of Lake Powell, is believed to have been authentic. If so, it would have been a record of the trapping era and the earliest date located in Glen Canyon. See Crampton, *Historical Sites in Glen Canyon* (1962), 44–5, for a report on this date; also Kelly (1939). Brewerton and Kit Carson traveled over the Spanish Trail from California in 1848. See Vinton (1930).

4 / Topographical Engineers

1. Frémont's role in the exploration of the American West is very well known, although his interest and that of Benton's, in a transcontinental river route, which explains his enthusiasm for the San Buenaventura, has not been appreciated; his *Geographic Memoir* (1849) should be read in this connection. His great "Map of Oregon and Upper California . . . 1848," drawn by Charles Preuss and actually covering the area west of the hundred and fourth meridian, accompanied the memoir; it was also published separately. The 1845 map appears in the account of the first and second expeditions published in that year. See Cline (1963), Chapter 10, and Wheat, III (1959) for discussion of Fremont's geographical ideas and cartographical contributions. The Guddes (1958) have translated and edited the brief diaries of German-born Charles Preuss.

The brilliant work of the Topographical Engineers is brought together for the first time in Goetzmann's (1959) highly useful

work. Emory's remark on hypothetical geography appears in his important *Report on the United States and Mexican Boundary Survey* (1857), 44; the accompanying map of the United States between the Mississippi and the Pacific shows blank spots in the canyon country and elsewhere. It was made from many of the same sources as G. K. Warren's map of the same date, published in his *Memoir* (1861).

2. Goetzmann (1959) and Albright (1921) detail the quest for railroad routes. In their new edition of Heap's *Central Route to the Pacific*, the Hafens (1957) have brought together a long letter of Benton's and his speeches in favor of the central railroad route. Heap's map of the route is an interesting portrayal of the canyon country: Following Frémont, he has the confluence of the Green and the Grand too far south; the San Juan River is shown in a pronounced canyon. John W. Gunnison was killed by Indians in 1853 after he had completed the railroad survey through to central Utah. For Beckwith's report of the Gunnison survey, see Volume II (1855) of U. S. War Department, Corps of Topographical Engineers, *Reports of Exploration and Surveys to Ascertain the Most Practicable and Economical Route for a Railroad from the Mississippi River to the Pacific Ocean . . . 1853–56* (frequently cited as the *Pacific Railroad Report*), the massive twelve-volume compilation of topographical and scientific data accumulated during the Pacific Railroad Surveys. The detailed route maps of the Gunnison survey, drawn by F. W. Egloffstein, who later drew maps for Ives and Macomb, appear in the Volume XI of the *Reports* (1861).

Frémont's fifth expedition over the central route in 1853–4 is summarized in a letter published in the Washington, D. C., *National Intelligencer*, June 15, 1854. Solomon N. Carvalho, artist and daguerreotype photographer, was with Frémont on this trip and wrote an interesting but somewhat general book about it, first published in 1857 and recently edited with an introduction by Bertram W. Korn (1954).

3. Simpson's *Journal* (1850) of the reconnaissance in the Navajo country in 1849 is topographically and scientifically important. The party saw the prehistoric ruins in Chaco Canyon and Canyon de Chelly, where peace was made with one band of Navajos. His descriptive and illustrated report of these places, of Zuñi and of Inscription Rock, is of primary importance. Sitgreaves' report (1853) of his expedition is equally interesting, both as a topographical and a scientific document. Lt. Whipple's survey is reported in the U. S. War Department, Corps of Topographical Engineers, *Reports of Exploration and Surveys . . .* III (1855). Foreman (1941) has edited the Whipple report in a new edition.

4. Warren's map is a landmark in the cartographic history of the West, an accurate summary of the state of geographical knowledge at that time. His *Memoir* (1861) is a valuable summary of exploration from 1800 to 1857 in which he explains (Chapter VI) some of the more puzzling geographical problems confronting explorers in the West. An epitome of this memoir, with added material, appears in George M. Wheeler's final *Report* (1889).

5. The Utah War was an important event in the developing economy of Utah, and there is an abundant literature on the subject. See Creer (1929) on the political background and the distinguished volume by Arrington (1958) on the economic results. Ives took great care with his report (1861) of the 1857–8

exploration of the lower Colorado that took him up to the mouth of Grand Canyon, thence overland over the Whipple-Sitgreaves route to New Mexico.

6. A copy of this rare map, prepared for possible use in the Utah War, is in the Cartographic Section, National Archives, Record Group 77. It is reproduced in Wheat, IV (1960).

7. Newberry wrote several descriptions of parts of the canyon country for Macomb's (1876) account of the 1859 exploring expedition in Chapters Five and Six in his geological report. A number of lithographed plates, made from sketches by Newberry, are included. Plate IX is a view of the lower San Juan River looking west from near camp 35; it shows Monument Valley at a distance. The Bear's Ears, mentioned a number of times by Newberry, appear on the Egloffstein map under their original Spanish name: Orejas del Oso.

8. The 1860 map of Utah Territory is of comparable rarity to that of Utah Territory published in 1858; a copy is in the Cartographic Section, National Archives, Record Group 77. It is also reproduced in Wheat, IV (1960). Egloffstein's map of the Macomb expedition bears the publication date 1864 and was probably issued separately in advance of the official report, delayed by the Civil War.

5 / The Scientists

1. Bartlett's (1962) book on the King, Hayden, Powell, and Wheeler surveys does something that has long been needed: He places them in proper perspective. Powell has attracted most of the writers who have neglected the important achievements of the others. A catalogue of the publications, including maps, of the four great surveys has been made by Schmeckebier (1904).

2. It has seemed to me that the 1869 voyage, in terms of the stimulus to Powell's mind, outranks the second in 1871. His account of it, written before the end of the year, as published in the second edition of Bell's (1870) work, 559–64, is an indication of this; that account is the source for the quotation in this chapter. In volumes 15, 16, and 17 of its *Quarterly*, the Utah State Historical Society has performed an important service by bringing together the journals and letters and other writings, most of them published for the first time, emanating from the two river voyages. Records of the 1869 trip include Powell's account reprinted from Bell and his brief geological journal, Bradley's important and complete diary, and J. C. Sumner's Journal, the source of the quotation used here, together with other matter, edited by Darrah (1947). Nearly everyone on the 1871–2 expedition kept a diary: F. M. Bishop edited by Kelly (1947a); S. V. Jones edited by Gregory (1948–9); Walter Clement Powell, the Major's cousin and a sprightly diarist, by Charles Kelly (1948–9); Darrah (1948–9) has also brought together material on Beaman, Fennemore, Hillers, Dellenbaugh, Johnson, Hattan, and Hall. Dale L. Morgan (1947–9) has provided illuminating introductions for both these volumes. In an earlier issue of the *Utah Historical Quarterly* Gregory (1939) edited the diary of A. H. Thompson.

Frederick S. Dellenbaugh, the youngest member of the second expedition, was stimulated to write a great deal about the Colorado River. Until the publication of the diaries above, his account (1908, second edition 1926) of the second voyage was the standard narrative. I have used the 1926 edition here. His

Romance of the Colorado (1902) a general history from 1540, gives special attention to the Powell voyages. Beaman (1874), photographer on the second expedition, published a popular piece.

Powell's preliminary report of the river trips (1874) anticipates the longer composite 1869–1872 account published in 1875 (1875a). Powell's composite reporting and his handling of the affair at Separation Rapids, where the Howlands and Dunn left the 1869 expedition, have caused the spilling of much ink. R. B. Stanton in his book, edited and published posthumously by Chalfant (1932), looks into the latter; the work contains accounts of the 1869 trip by J. C. Sumner and William Hawkins.

William C. Darrah (1951), who has done so much to unearth the scattered primary documents of the Powell voyages, has written the first comprehensive biography. Wallace Stegner, in an important book (1954), and Darrah have finally shown that Powell's contribution, far beyond the Colorado River explorations and beyond the greater work of the Powell Survey, was his successful struggle to interest the government in the scientific study of the nation, particularly in the areas of geology, anthropology, irrigation, reclamation, and conservation. Powell's bibliography in these fields, and in others, is a lengthy one. See Darrah's (1951) listings, 406–7, 409–11.

3. The topographic work of the Powell Survey is expressed mainly in the maps produced. A. H. Thompson (1875), in charge of the work, wrote a chapter in Powell's composite report on an exploratory trip from the Paria River to the Dirty Devil River in 1872. His diary, edited by Gregory (1939), covers the years 1871–5. Dellenbaugh, Thompson's assistant, wrote of the topographical work in his *Canyon Voyage* (1926). His bibliography has not been compiled but it would be a long one. Extensive collections of Dellenbaugh papers, including, in both cases, material on the Colorado River voyages and related work, are located in the New York Public Library and in the Arizona Pioneers Historical Society at Tucson. The preliminary maps made by the Powell Survey are reproduced by Dellenbaugh (1926); the finished product was incorporated in the map of Utah Territory published with Powell's *Arid Lands* in 1878 (second edition, 1879). That map, compiled and drawn by Charles Mahon, J. H. Renshawe, W. H. Graves, and H. Lindenhall, was constructed from data drawn from the four great surveys: Powell, King, Wheeler, and Hayden. The only blank area is the southeastern part of Utah Territory, roughly the area of San Juan County today. The atlases accompanying the volumes by Powell (1876) on the Uinta Mountains, by Dutton (1880, 1882), on the High Plateaus and the Grand Canyon were products of the topographic survey. The early topographic reconnaissance quadrangle maps issued by the U. S. Geological Survey were largely drawn from the data accumulated in the field by Powell's men. The following sheets, still in use in the 1940's, blanketed the entire canyon country (from north to south): Manti, Price River, East Tavaputs, Fish Lake, San Rafael, La Sal, Kanab, Escalante, Henry Mountains, Abajo, Echo Cliffs, Marsh Pass, and Canyon de Chelly. They have been replaced by the accurate, large-scale topographic quadrangles now being issued by the U. S. Geological Survey.

The publications of the Powell Survey, including drawings, photographs, charts, and maps, were notable productions of the Government Printing Office, in addition to being works of scientific value. Dutton's work on the Grand Canyon is surely one of the finest things ever done by the GPO. The place of the artists and photographers in the western surveys is abundantly detailed in the two books by Robert Taft (1938, 1953).

4. The best index to the publications of the Wheeler and Hayden surveys is the Schmeckebier (1904) catalogue. Gregory's (1945b) "Scientific Explorations in Southern Utah," is constantly useful.

The field survey parties under Wheeler's command often made reports of the most agonizing brevity. Lt. W. L. Marshall made a reconnaissance of the Crossing of the Fathers area in 1872 and Lt. R. L. Hoxie made one of the Hall's Creek area in 1873; these are mentioned in George M. Wheeler's (1889) final *Report*. The field books of the Wheeler Survey, once widely scattered, have been largely reassembled and are in the National Archives, Record Group 77. Geological studies in the canyon country made by G. K. Gilbert and E. E. Howell are published in Wheeler's (1875) report on *Geology*. The atlas sheets made by the Wheeler Survey are, in themselves, valuable historical documents. The historian working in the field wishes that the entire atlas might have been completed before the Survey was dissolved. The overlapping of the Wheeler and Powell surveys has been clarified by Stegner (1954).

The pertinent publications of the Hayden Survey are buried away in his annual reports. Hayden's men, refreshingly, wrote fuller accounts than Wheeler's force, and their works are useful and important. In his reports on the San Juan region and the Sierra Abajo, W. H. Holmes (1877, 1878b) developed his technique for making panoramic drawings that reached perfection in Dutton's book on the Grand Canyon (1882). A. C. Peale (1877) studied and mapped the La Sal Mountains. G. B. Chittenden (1877) made an interesting topographical report on the Grand River district and on San Juan County. He details the wagon road, 347–50, from Salina, Utah, to Ouray, Colorado —much of the way on the Spanish Trail—and published sketches of the fords of the Grand (Colorado), Gunnison, and Green rivers. Of Sage Plain, he wrote, 361, "This whole portion of the country is now and must ever remain utterly worthless." W. H. Jackson took photographs of and wrote important descriptive articles (1876, 1878) about Mesa Verde and Hovenweep, visited in 1874 and 1875, and he (1924) also recounted the 1874 visit much later. See also Holmes (1878a) on the prehistoric ruins of the Four Corners region. The Hafens (1959) have edited several diaries of W. H. Jackson, including the 1874 visit to the ruins in that area. W. H. Jackson wrote an autobiogrpahy (1940) and there is a biography by Clarence S. Jackson (1947). The Hayden (1877) atlas containing geological and topographical maps, and panoramic views, was of a standard to match the best of the mapping by Powell and Wheeler.

5. For Powell's life in Washington after 1879, and his contributions to science, see Stegner (1954) and Darrah (1951), and Wilkins's (1958) life of Clarence King.

6 / Canyon Country Primeval

1. Primary details about the founding of the Elk Mountain Mission are reported in the *Deseret News*, August 1, 22, October 10, 31, and November 7, 1855. Jenson's (1941) encyclopedia is full of detailed information on the founding of Mormon settlements in Utah and elsewhere.

2. In this section I have relied heavily upon the geographical material found in the more comprehensive volumes of the U. S. Geological Survey cited in Chapter II, particularly the works of Herbert E. Gregory. My own long acquaintance with the country has been helpful. Woodbury (1960) succinctly states the physical and biological setting; Woodbury and others (1959) report a detailed ecological survey of Glen Canyon.

3. W. D. Huntington's valuable description of the ruins found near the San Juan River is reported in the Salt Lake *Deseret News*, December 28, 1854. This may be the earliest record of those in Hovenweep National Monument and of others in the vicinity.

4. Josiah Gregg, in the *Commerce of the Prairies*, first published in 1844 (Moorehead, 1954) (Chapter XV), posed an Aztec origin for the prehistoric towns of the Southwest. Humboldt himself, in his *Views of Nature* (1850), 207, repeated his earlier suggestion of Aztec migrations. J. H. Simpson (1850), 83, was aware of Humboldt's hypothesis, made on his "Carte Générale" in the *Political Essay* (1811). Bell (1870) and Beadle (1881), have chapters on the Aztecs in Arizona and New Mexico. W. D. Huntington said this about the ruins: "We very readily came to a conclusion drawn from the Book of Mormon in the second chapter of Nephi that the ancient possessors of these strongholds were robbers of the Gadianton Band. . . ." *Deseret News*, December 28, 1854.

5. There is an enormous literature on the prehistory of the Southwest. I have relied here on works by Wormington (1955, 1956); the summary of southwestern archeology by Rouse (1962) in a new edition of Kidder's well-known "Introduction," first published in 1924; Steward (1938); Roberts (1936); Jennings (1957, 1960).

With the passage of the Upper Colorado Storage Act in 1956, providing for the construction of storage dams and other reclamation developments in the basin of the Colorado River, the National Park Service contracted with the University of Utah and the Museum of Northern Arizona at Flagstaff to undertake a program of archeological, historical, and other salvage studies in the area to be inundated by the reservoir behind Glen Canyon Dam, i.e. Lake Powell. The construction of the dam fifteen miles upstream from Lee's Ferry threatened archeological and historical values in an area extending 187 river miles upstream on the Colorado River and for considerable distances up tributary canyons; the reservoir at full pool will extend up the canyon of the San Juan River seventy-one miles to the mouth of Grand Gulch.

The canyons of the Colorado have been bypassed generally by archeologists since Powell's day; this is evident from the W. Y. Adams' (1960) survey of the history of Glen Canyon archeology since 1869.

The contracting institutions completed virtually all of the field work by the end of 1963, and many of the reports containing the field data have been published. Though it will take years to digest these findings and to generalize upon them, nonetheless the gaps in archeological knowledge of the river canyons and much of the peripheral area, have been filled up in a hurry. As this is written, late in 1963, over twenty papers emanating from the Glen Canyon projects of the University of Utah and the Museum of Northern Arizona have been published (1958–63). Notes taken from this mass of material and a brief summary paper by Lister (1963) suggest the river canyon-land areas as a frontier of the more favored uplands in prehistoric times.

6. *Deseret News*, October 10, 31, November 7, 1855. Hunter's (1940) book on Mormon colonization under the direction of Brigham Young is a basic work.

Spanish relations with the Utes in Colorado before 1776 have been studied: Tyler's (1951b) work is important; see also his (1951a) paper on the Yuta Indians before 1680, and a later piece (1954) that surveys the matter from mid-sixteenth century through the trapper period.

7 / Mormon Frontier

1. Mormon colonization in the Virgin River Valley is covered by Hunter (1940), A. K. Larson (1961), and other standard works. G. C. Larson's (1958) outline history is a very useful guide. Palmer (1933) locates by name thirty-five Paiute bands. Isabel T. Kelly (1934) has published an ethnogeography of Paiute bands. Powell and Ingalls (1874) made a report to the Commissioner of Indian Affairs on the condition of the Utes of Utah and the Paiutes of Utah, northern Arizona, and southern Nevada, that is still useful.

2. Jacob Hamblin has found two biographers, Bailey (1948) and Corbett (1952), who have supplemented from many sources the somewhat meager autobiographical account taken down by Little (1881). Thales Haskell's diary edited by Brooks (1944b) details the 1859 trip to the Hopis by way of the Crossing of the Fathers.

3. Hamblin's own account (Little, 1881) of his trips to the Hopi villages is detailed and interesting. See also his biographers in note 2, and Creer (1958b). Waters (1963), 291, points out that the Hopis liked the Mormons but would not allow them to open a church in Oraibi because of the polygamy issue. Hamblin himself was a polygamist.

4. There is an immense body of literature on the Navajo Indians, most of it written by other than historians. I have found very little material on the expansion of the Navajo frontier toward the canyon country as a result of pressures brought on by war after 1846. Dale's (1949) book covers federal relations with the Indians of the Southwest after 1848. Kluckhohn and Leighton (1958) and Underhill (1956) are useful on Navajo relations with the whites. Brandes (1960) gives details on the founding of Ft. Defiance and campaigns to 1861. Colton (1959) treats of campaigns against the Navajos during the Civil War. There is very little material on the Navajo-Mormon war beyond the work of Brooks (1944a) and especially that of Woodbury (1950). See also the Hamblin biographies. General histories of Utah all have something to say about the Black Hawk war: Creer's (1940) edition of Neff, for example. Gottfredson's (1919) book is useful but it doesn't have much on the Mormon war with the Navajos.

5. I have edited F. B. Woolley's important account of the 1866 reconnaissance for the Utah State Historical Society; it is scheduled to be published in the *Quarterly* in 1964. The Military Records Section of the Society possesses many unpublished records of the Utah Territorial Militia, more commonly known as the Nauvoo Legion.

6. See Little's (1881) Hamblin, Chapter XV. Crampton and

Miller (1961) have edited the journals of two 1869 campaigns by the militia against the Navajos.

7. Powell's (1875a) own account of his visit to the Shivwits (Chapter IX) is the best; this appeared first in *Scribner's Monthly*, October 1875. His visit to the Hopi villages is in the same magazine for December. See also Little (1881), Chapters XVI–XVII. See Dellenbaugh (1926), 147, for the appearance of a Navajo trading party at the Crossing of the Fathers, and other diarists of the 1871 Powell expedition.

8. Powell's crew enjoyed Emma Lee's cooking and helped repair Lee's dam on the Paria before embarking for the Marble Canyon-Grand Canyon run on August 17, 1872. See particularly Clem Powell's diary July 15-August 16, edited by Charles Kelly (1948-9).

Most of the writing about John D. Lee focuses on his involvement in the Mountain Meadows massacre of 1857, another unfortunate event in the strained relations between the Mormons and the nation in the same year that Johnston's army marched on Utah. Much less has been written on the opening of Lee's Ferry or of Lee's experiences elsewhere in Arizona. Juanita Brooks (1950) has written a book of admirable balance on the Mountain Meadows affair. The remarkable diaries of John D. Lee (edited by Cleland and Brooks—1955), covering the time when the ferry was established, are of exceptional value for the insight they give into the mind of a zealous Mormon and a stalwart frontiersman. Juanita Brooks's *John Doyle Lee, Zealot —Pioneer Builder—Scapegoat* (1962) places his life in the perspective of its time.

Brooks (1957), Creer (1958a), Crampton (1960) have details on the founding and subsequent history of Lee's Ferry. McClintock's (1921) book is of first importance for the history of Mormon colonization in Arizona. Many works about the Colorado River refer to Lee's Ferry incidentally. Kolb (1914) reports the Kolb brothers' voyage in 1911 and their stop at Lee's Ferry where Charles H. Spencer was then mining. L. R. Freeman (1923, 1924), who was associated with the U. S. Geological Survey—Southern California Edison Company Survey of Glen Canyon in 1921, has material on Lee's Ferry in two books. The 1923 volume, a general history of the Colorado, is an all-round useful book that may be used to complement Dellenbaugh's (1902) volume published twenty years earlier.

8 / Hole-in-the-Rock

1. In his important work on the Mormon Village, Lowry Nelson (1952) chose Escalante, on the upper Escalante River, as one of the villages for study. See also Arrington's (1958) economic history of the Mormons and G. O. Larson's (1947) book on the conquest of the desert by the Mormons; see also his *Outline History* (1958), Chapter VII.

2. The story of Peter Shurtz and the Indians on the Paria I have taken from Brooks (1962), 290; Mormon explorers in 1879 found Shurtz living on the San Juan, Miller (1959), 25.

3. Mormon colonization of the western side of the canyon country between the Paria and Price rivers has not been brought together between two covers. The general histories of Utah have little to say about the southeastern half of the state. The biographical compilations by Whitney (1892–1904), Warrum (1919–20), Alter (1932), and Sutton (1949), have occasional

chapters of value. Roberts (1930) and Jenson (1941) are very useful for pertinent Latter-day Saint history. The details of frontier advance are in the county histories: Carroll (1960) for Kane County; Anne Snow (1953) for Wayne County; Chidester and Bruhn (1949) for Garfield County; McElprang (1949) and Lever (1898) for Emery County; Reynolds (1948) for Carbon County. Gregory's (1945a) work on the population of southern Utah is detailed but lacks a bibliography.

The broad outlines of Mormon colonziation as formulated by Brigham Young are set out by Hunter (1940); the work contains a list of 358 Mormon colonies, with dates of founding, all but a handful founded under the direction of Young between 1847 and 1877, when he died. Taylor (1962) discusses Mormon loyalty to Brigham Young.

4.   There is a fairly large body of published material on the opening of the Hole-in-the-Rock route by the Mormons in 1879–80. Miller's scholarly book (1959), based upon documentary and oral sources and upon field work, is the best work on this remarkable adventure; it contains photographs of some of the most spectacular parts of the route. Earlier writers of importance are: Anderson (1915), Freeman (1923), Miser (1924), Gregory and Moore (1931), Gregory (1938). Birney's book (1931), with three chapters on the trek, interested Richardson (1940a, b), who visited the Hole. Beck (1940–1) published some original documents; Charles Kelly (1947b) mapped the trail from Escalante to the Hole in 1946. Redd (1950) has written an excellent short piece. Albert R. Lyman (1948–50) has placed the San Juan Mission in broad historical perspective with valuable material on the history of Bluff and southeast Utah after 1880; Lyman has also written (1939) a biography of his father, Platte D. Lyman, whose unpublished journal (1876-1901) is a major contemporary source. Kumen Jones (1929, and two undated manuscripts) was a member of the pioneer band. Albert L. Lyman (1909) spent some time at Lake Pagahrit and has a good description of that oasis. During a heavy rain in 1915, the lake overflowed, quickly cut a channel in the sandy dam, and the impounded water rushed down Lake Canyon to the Colorado. Remnants of the old lake bed, now some distance above the stream bed, may still be seen. See Miller (1959), 133, 135; Crampton (1962), 40–3, 47. In his autobiography, Latter-day Saint historian Andrew Jenson (1938) tells how he got out into the field and saw where things happened; the quote is from this work, 601. I have found his *Church Chronology* (1914) a useful work of absorbing interest.

9 / The Rock Jungle

1.   Very little has been published about traffic over the route through Muley Twist Canyon and Hall's Ferry. The references cited in note 3, Chapter VIII, include most of the sources. Hunt and others (1953), 15, give details on the construction and operation of the ferryboat. See Crampton (1962), 49–61, for additional details about the operation of the ferry and the locale.

Robert Athearn's *Rebel of the Rockies* (1962) is a splendid scholarly study of the building of the Denver & Rio Grande Western Railroad. Greever (1954) writes of the building of the Santa Fe with particular reference to public land subsidy.

2.   The history of the beef bonanza in southeastern Utah has not been written. Excellent studies such as Frink, Jackson, and Spring (1956), Barnes (1913), and Peake (1937) give Colorado background. Walker's (1962) article, "The Longhorns Come to Utah," is a synthesis of events from 1847 to 1890. Developments up to 1880 are reported in considerable detail by Clarence Gordon (1883) in the Tenth Census. Perkins, Nielson, and Jones (1957) have some material on cowboys and cattlemen in San Juan County, Utah, as do Tanner (1937), and Silvey (n.d.), and Albert R. Lyman (1909, 1948-50). J. M. Cunningham's association with the Pittsburg Cattle Company is found in Cunningham (1943). Stena Scorup (1944) has written the biography of J. A. Scorup, whose range at the time of his death in 1959 covered the canyon country from the headquarters of the Scorup-Somerville Cattle Company on Indian Creek (Dugout Ranch) to the San Juan River. "Rock jungle," Al Scorup's name for the roughest part of the canyon country, is mentioned in the Stena Scorup biography. David Lavender (1956) has two chapters on Scorup: he has also written an article on Scorup (1940). Wentworth's immensely valuable work has material on the area's sheep industry.

The founding of new towns and life and wild times in southeastern Utah are found in Tanner (1937), Silvey (n.d.), Perkins, Nielson, and Jones (1957), Freeman (1958), and Albert R. Lyman (1955? 1962). See also Stegner (1942) and King (1940) for a life of Matt Warner. Kelly (1959) sums up the doings of the outlaws at Robber's Roost. Pearl Baker (1963) tells of the hard, good life on the cattle ranch at the Roost after the Wild Bunch had departed.

3.   The Navajo westward movement into the canyons of the San Juan and the Colorado is little known. A study like that of Hester's (1962) for Navajo migrations up to 1805, is needed for the time since. In a study of the Navajos at Shonto, an area occupied by them, 1860-4, Adams (1958b) discusses the shock of the military campaigns against the Navajo. See also Kluckhohn and Leighton (1958) Chapter I. Dale (1949) is a good source for details of government relations, including reservation boundary changes; see also Underhill (1956) and Taylor (1931), and Royce (1899). See Chapter VII of this work for relations between the Navajos and the Mormons. Members of the Powell party in 1871 reported that a trail for stock had been built down over the slick rock to the left bank of the river, five and a half miles above the Crossing of the Fathers. Here toe-hold steps had also been cut. In all likelihood, the trail had been made by Navajos and the toe-hold steps cut by prehistoric peoples. During the course of my field studies in Glen Canyon, a number of places were found where Navajos had followed precarious prehistoric trails (not built for European stock, of course), down to the river's edge. See Crampton (1960), 26-8, for a study of trail seen by Powell's men. Other Navajo and prehistoric trails are examined in the same volume. Navajo use of the region north of the San Juan River is found in historical documents. The Egloffstein map accompanying Macomb's report (1876) of the 1859 exploration through the Four Corners region shows a "Navajo Ford" in the approximate location of Clay Hill Crossing. This would suggest the idea that the ford came into use during the United States military campaigns against the Navajos, 1858-61, but of course it may have been used long before. Once the Mormons arrived at Bluff, the Navajos were constant visitors. Perkins, Nielson, and Jones (1957) wrote that Chief Kigalia was the first to put stock on Elk Ridge.

10 / El Dorado

1. The story of El Dorado—the Gilded Man—born in South America early in the sixteenth century, has come to symbolize man's adventurous quest for easy wealth. The first tall tales in the West, a rich potpourri including a number of fabulous and wealthy places, were first told by the Spaniards. This store of legends relating to the Southwest and with particular attention to canyon country and Sierra Azul has been investigated by Tyler (1952) and Hammond (1956). Espinosa (1934) traces the legend of Sierra Azul.

2. James White's alleged raft trip through the canyons of the Colorado has been seized upon as a "first"; he would have preceded Powell by two years. Much has been written about the matter. Even if the trip could be proved to the satisfaction of all comers, a fact with few consequences would have been established. Farquhar (1950) edited the 1867 Kipp report of White's arrival at Callville on a raft; Lingenfelter (1958) and Bulger (1961) have presented the facts and have essayed interpretations of route. See also Farquhar's bibliography (1953) for additional matter. Freeman (1923), Chapter VIII, discusses White's raft voyage, and in Chapter IX he takes up Samuel Adams, another 1867 voyager. In his history of Colorado, II (1890), 195-6, Frank Hall details the prospecting background of the three men in Colorado.

3. The western press from mid-summer 1872 was full of the diamond excitement. Since the event, a number of writers have touched on the hoax but the last word has not been said: Harpending (Wilkinson, ed., 1913) was one involved in the hoax; H. H. Bancroft (1889), 591-2, wrote not long after the event; Frank Hall, II (1890), Chapter VI, has an excellent detailed summary; T. A. Rickard (1932), Chapter XVII, was close to the event and wrote from the mining engineer's viewpoint; Bartlett (1962), Chapter IX, highlights Clarence King's exposure of the fraud. See also Wilkins (1958).

4. The history of Navajo silversmithing is found in Adair (1944) and Woodward (1946). The meeting between the Mormon scouting party and James Merrick (also spelled Merritt and other ways) and Ernest Mitchell is in Hobbs's account in Miller (1959), Chapter VII. The killing of Mitchell and "Myrach" (Merrick) is reported in the Denver *Rocky Mountain News*, March 16, 1880. This account under a Silverton, Colorado, dateline refers also to the killing of Joe Lacomb and Joe Charest by Paiutes.

5. Denver, *Rocky Mountain News*, April 14, 1882.

6. Denver, *Rocky Mountain News*, May 23, 1882, under Durango, Colorado, dateline.

7. The story of the killing of Merrick and Mitchell and the subsequent search for the mine they were presumed to have found appears in several versions. The newspaper references, cited in notes 5 and 6, give contemporary details of the location of the copper mine, but nothing else. Charles Kelly (1953) has the story direct from the mouth of Hoskininni-begay, son of the Navajo Chief, Hoskininni, the reported original discoverer of the mine located by Merrick and Mitchell, and the one who befriended Hite. Kelly (1940) writes of Hite's search for the mine. Williams, with the Chief as guide, looked for the mine in 1883-4 (Yost, 1958). Buck Lee, grandson of John D. Lee, told a version to the Fifes (1956). In the Copper Canyon region,

J. A. Duckett (the same who had been with Hite in 1882?) and others on April 4, 1898, located the "Pasch-lachee" lode claim Nos. 1, 2, and 3. (San Juan County, Mining Claims, C., 337.) Dyer (1911) reports the meeting with Hoskininni at "Moonlake" (Oljeto) Canyon.

8. The mining history of the canyon country has been treated generally in the several publications of the U. S. Geological Survey, particularly by the monographs by Gregory and Moore (1931), Hunt and others (1953), and Butler and others (1920). My own technical reports (1959, 1960, 1962) represent the first attempt at a detailed reconstruction; they are based on field study and a mass of fragmentary sources. The rules and regulations of the Henry Mountains Mining District and the adjoining White Canyon Mining District are recorded in Garfield County, Utah, Deeds, Book A (1883-4), 71-3, and in San Juan County, Miscellaneous Record B (1884-1906), 81-2, respectively. The very interesting record books of the White Canyon Mining District, with records of location, 1885-97, in two volumes, are on file in the Recorder's Office, Garfield County, Panguitch, Utah. There were a number of mining districts organized in the canyon country before 1900; located in the La Sal and Abajo (Blue) mountains, and along the San Juan River, they all had laws and regulations governing the district. Copies were recorded in the Recorder's Office for San Juan County at Monticello. I have noted regulations among the following districts: St. Louis (1888); Blue Mountain (1892); Big Indian (1892); Gabel (1892); Ida (1893); Bluff City (1893); there were others, notably along the San Juan River when the gold rush thither got under way.

9. The references cited in Chapter II, note 5, are largely technical geological reports. As in other places in this book, I have relied heavily on H. E. Gregory, in his study with Moore (1931), and on his volume on the San Juan country (1938); see also Hunt and others (1953) on the Henry Mountains, and Hunt's study on the *Cenozoic Geology of the Colorado Plateau* (1956). The publications of the Intermountain Association of Petroleum Geologists (1954) and of the Four Corners Geological Society (1955) have been useful.

11 / Canyon Conquest

1. Stanton's railroad survey appears prominently in the history of river running, Kolb (1914) and Freeman (1923), for example, as he was the second to go through the canyons from Green River, Utah, to the Gulf. In his own book edited by Chalfant (1932), there is little on his voyages. The purposes and problems of the railroad survey were discussed by Stanton (1890, 1893) in two magazine articles. His report to the American Society of Civil Engineers appeared in 1892. A recent article by Dwight L. Smith (1960) is the first scholarly reconstruction of the railroad venture.

2. The rush to the San Juan River, in the latter part of 1892 and early 1893, is well covered in the pages of the Salt Lake *Tribune*, from which most of this material has come, specifically the issues from July 1, 1892, to January 11, 1893, when the boom began to fade. The inscription at Navajo Springs at Comb Ridge is found in an article, January 11. During this period there was also much mining actively reported in the La Sal, Abajo, and Henry Mountains, as well as in Glen Canyon.

3. The history of the Glen Canyon gold rush is to be found mainly in my own papers (1959, 1960, 1962) wherein pertinent bibliography is cited. The annual Mineral Resources of the United States issued by the U. S. Geological Survey, 1882 to date, is helpful on some statistical matters, but no satisfactory production figures for Glen Canyon have been found. Lewis and Varley (1919) and Butler and others (1920) offer assistance; see also a railroad promotional piece by Maguire (1899).

4. The diaries kept by Robert Brewster Stanton, the principal figure in the Hoskaninni venture, have been edited by Crampton and Smith (1961); the work contains several pictures of the dredge under construction and a facsimile of the original plan of the huge machine. This work contains most of the published data on the operation. Kelly (1939) records Julius Stone's trip through the canyons in 1938; Stone had visited Glen Canyon during the mining operation, and in 1909 he took his first lengthy river trip through the canyons, the account of which was published in 1932.

5. The sources for Zahn's and Spencer's operations are meager. I have used most of them in my own reports (1959), 22–38, (1960), 94–6. Since these studies were published, I have obtained additional information by interview from both venerable entrepreneurs in Los Angeles—Charles H. Spencer and Otto J. Zahn. Albert H. Jones (1960) has written an account of his association with Spencer, with whom he served as engineer, 1908–11.

One of the important sources of information about boats and navigation (including much data on the *Charles H. Spencer*) is in the testimony taken in the "River Bed Case," a suit brought to the Supreme Court (United States vs. Utah, Number 14, October Term, 1929) to determine ownership of the bed of the Colorado River in Utah from the mouth of the Green River to the state line and including the San Juan River below the mouth of Chinle Creek. Many persons prominent in the history of the canyon country testified in the case. The testimony (United States vs. Utah) takes up 5,536 pages. A printed abstract (1931) in narrative form was prepared, and the Report of the Special Master (1930) in the case was also printed; a number of briefs, not cited here, were also printed.

6. The work by Hansen and Bell, comps. (1949), is an excellent summary of Utah oil drilling, 1891–1948. Gregory (1911) and Woodruff (1912) report the interesting developments at Mexican Hat. Baker (1936) is a later study for the San Juan region with a complete bibliography. Gregory (1917, 1938), and Gregory and Moore (1931) and the other technical reports listed in Chapter II, note 5, discuss drilling history elsewhere in the canyon country. These same sources discuss copper and radium-vanadium-uranium mining. Boutwell (1905) has data on discovery of radioactive minerals; Coffin (1921) and Fischer (1942) discuss vanadium around the La Sals. The earlier reports do not come up to the spectacular uranium boom of the 1950's. Al Look's *U-Boom* is an account of that spectacular rush. Stokes, ed. (1954), is a convenient summary of the geology of radio-active minerals in southeastern Utah. See Crampton (1959) for a fuller historical summary. See Briggs (1935) for copper developments on White Mesa.

7. The technical reports listed in Chapter II, note 5, cover the coal resources of Carbon County. Satisfactory reviews of the history of the region are in the U. S. WPA *Inventory of County Archives, Carbon County* (1940a), and in Reynolds (1948).

8. The anti-polygamy campaign had a notable effect on Mormon colonization in Utah and elsewhere. The details of this, together with an almost daily review of prosecutions under the Edmunds-Tucker Law, can be studied in Jenson's chronology (1914). To my knowledge, the advance of, and in some cases the retraction of, the Mormon frontier of colonization in the canyon country and elsewhere, after the pioneer period, has not been studied in any comprehensive way.

9. A. R. Lyman (1948–50, 1962) of Blanding, Utah, has written on the running war with the Indians in San Juan County. See also the recent book by Forbes Parkhill (1961). The splendid book by McNitt (1962) on the Indian Traders has much of value on those who entered the Navajo country. A standard biography of John Wetherill is Gillmor and Wetherill (1953); see also McNitt (1957) on brother, Richard Wetherill.

Sprague's (1957) work on the Meeker massacre may be supplemented by Rockwell's (1956) book, which has significant coverage of the Southern Utes. See also Emmitt (1954).

10. The literature of reclamation is immense. The general story is found in Golzé (1952); Powell's work is detailed by Stegner (1954). Dana (1959) has a short summary. The Colorado River Compact is the subject of Olson's (1926) book; Allen (1958) studies the role of Utah's Governor George H. Dern. James (1917a) is one of the few authors to recognize the place of Powell in Western reclamation. Kleinsorge (1941) and Force (1936) are works that pertain primarily to the lower basin but contain important historical information.

A significant aspect of the post-World War I interest in the upper basin was the work of making a detailed survey of the Colorado River from Lee's Ferry to the mouth of the Green River, including the San Juan River from its mouth to Chinle Creek, undertaken in 1921 by the Geological Survey in co-operation with the Southern California Edison Company of Los Angeles. The resultant map was printed in 1922 in 22 sheets (16 river plans: scale one inch=one mile, contour interval in the river five feet, contour interval on land 20 feet extending to the level of 3,900 feet above the sea, and six profiles), the first accurate map of the Colorado for the area covered. Similar map series of the Colorado between the mouth of the Green and Grand Junction and of the Green from the mouth to Gunnison Butte (above Green River, Utah) had appeared in 1917. See Herron (1917).

Freeman and Bolster's paper (1910) is the earliest comprehensive description of the water supply of the Colorado River basin based upon actual measurements made by the U. S. Geological Survey E. C. La Rue's paper (1916) contains valuable historical data. The annual reports of the Reclamation Service (1902 to date) (later Bureau of Reclamation), which began investigating the Colorado River in 1904, are a chronological record.

There are several studies of irrigation and reclamation for the canyon country and Utah generally: Brough (1898); Mead (1903); Thomas (1920, 1948). George D. Clyde (1959) has summarized Utah's irrigation history; Bingham (1960) writes of reclamation and the Colorado; Paul Jones (1959) writes of reclamation and the Indian. A chapter in my own work (1959) summarizes reclamation history with particular reference to the canyon country.

12 / Symphony in Sandstone

1. The reports of the Powell, Wheeler, and Hayden surveys are to be consulted for the style of the authors and the artists' illustrations. Weyss on the Crossing of the Fathers was not published until 1889, when it appeared in Wheeler's final report. Thomas Moran probably did not visit the canyon country of southeastern Utah or northeastern Utah but drew his illustrations from photographs or sketches made by others in the field. Moran did visit other places in Utah and Arizona, notably the Grand Canyon. Some of his best-known work first appeared in the beautiful folio manufactured by Prang for Hayden (1876). Fryxell's (1958) biography of Moran is helpful, but a longer, full-dress study is needed. Hine's book (1958) on Edward Kern has much on Richard Kern. The role of artists and photographers in the western surveys is developed by Stegner (1954); Taft's (1938, 1953) books contain abundant detailed information about them.

2. There is a notable absence of subjective comment about the canyon country in the writings of those who lived in it and sought to make a living from it. This statement, of course, does not intend to implicate the entire resident population at any given time. When describing their environment, even today, long-time residents of Utah, stemming from farming and ranching backgrounds, are prone to use pharases like "godforsaken," "wasteland," "good for nothing," especially when the places mentioned cannot be made to "blossom as the rose." Beauty is seen in a green field, the ripening fruit, and the works of man. Robert B. Stanton was deeply interested in the canyon country, particularly in the prehistoric remains. His notebooks of the Hoskaninni Company venture contain many notations about these relics when he encountered them in the canyons; when in the East he lectured on the ancient people. Miller's book (1959) on Hole-in-the-Rock contains Elizabeth Decker's comment made under the strain of the trek.

3. The Dyar piece in the *Century Magazine*, August 1904, contained one color drawing and two black-and-white drawings by Harry Fenn. Cummings (1910b) ascribes the discovery of the bridges in 1883 to Cass Hite, who named them the President, the Senator, and the Congressman. The 1905 expedition received considerable publicity in the local press and people began to visit the bridges. Lakes's (1907) article appeared shortly after that by Holmes (1907). Culmer, regarded by James (1922), Chapter XX, as Utah's greatest painter, kept an informative diary of the 1905 trip to the bridges, not published until 1937. His articles on mountain art and scenery (1892, 1894) indicate his attitude toward nature; the one (1909) in the Salt Lake City *Western Monthly*, from which the quotations were taken, shows the impact of the desert landscape on his thinking.

4. The background events and discovery of Rainbow Bridge are found in a number of places. Cummings's own accounts (1910a, b) are modestly brief and none of the hostility that developed between the zealous surveyor Douglass and the Dean is obvious. In writing about the event years later, Cummings (1952) indicates something of his feelings in the matter. Neil M. Judd, one of Cummings' students in the discovery party, and later Curator of American Archeology, United States National Museum, has written the most detailed account (1927), which is otherwise valuable for the photographs made at the time of the discovery by Stuart M. Young. A somewhat broader article was prepared by Judd in essays written *For the Dean*, edited by Reed and King (1950). This book contains an annotated bibliography of Cummings' writings compiled by Gertrude Hill; the important article by Cummings on the natural bridges (1910b) was somehow omitted from it. Chapter 10 in Gillmor and Wetherill (1953) is a fine piece of writing about the Wetherills and the Navajo country, with John Wetherill's part in the discovery of Rainbow Bridge accented. Dean Cummings' eleven-year-old boy, Malcolm B. Cummings, accompanied his father on the 1909 discovery trip, and he is the only one to admit (1940) that he finished last in the "race" to the bridge. His brief recollections of the discovery were published in 1959; see also Stuart M. Young (1959). Joseph E. Pogue, assisting Herbert E. Gregory in his study of the Navajo country (1916, 1917), visited the Bridge with Gregory in July 1910 and published an account (1911) of the discovery, together with the measurements of the White Canyon bridges and Rainbow, taken from data in Douglass' surveys. Still another account is in Miser, Trimble, and Paige (1923). Kerr (1955) summarizes Cummings' life and contributions. W. F. Williams' statement of his visit to Rainbow Bridge in 1884 or 1885 is in Yost (1958); see Heald's article (1955). See my own works (1960), 98–104, for a somewhat more detailed account of the history of the discovery of Rainbow Bridge.

5. Cummings' archeological explorations in the Kayenta district are reported in the second part of the *University of Utah Bulletin* (1910c), in which his work on the great natural bridges appeared. His work on Alkali Ridge is given by Kidder (1910). Brew on the archeology of Alkali Ridge (1946) contains an excellent summary of the progress of prehistoric research in the Mesa Verde–San Juan area. It might be used in conjunction with an equally excellent summary prepared by the Rainbow Bridge–Monument Valley Expedition by Hargrave (1935), also see Beals, Brainerd, and Smith (1954). Judd (1930) sketches the history of Navajo National Monument. Anyone who has ever had his field plans go astray will appreciate Judd's lament, which introduces this article. Fewkes's little book (1911) is the first detailed published account of the ruins in Navajo National Monument and contains a sketch map of the region, including the Rainbow Bridge area, prepared by W. B. Douglass.

6. Herbert E. Gregory's monograph (1916), the first of his several important works about the canyon country, is the first detailed description of the entire Navajo country; it contains much detailed and valuable information and a map that is, historically, still useful. One of the early archeologists in the San Juan region, T. Mitchell Prudden, traveled about widely over the canyon country, and his work (1906) might be called the first general "travel book" of the canyon country. See also his (1903) article on prehistoric ruins of the San Juan area. Compare this with Alter's book (1927) for changes over twenty years. There are a number of accounts of travel into the region, and most of them touch on the upper Colorado basin; those by George Wharton James are examples (1900, 1910, 1917a).

Butcher's descriptive work on the national parks and monuments (1954) is one of the few that lists dates of establishment. The great work of Stephen T. Mather in building the National Park Service is exceptionally well told by Robert Shankland (1951).

7. Gillmor and Wetherill (1953) list twenty-four scientific reports and seventeen popular books and articles that carry acknowledgments to the Wetherills or tell of their activities. Zeke Johnson, who served for thirty-four years as custodian of Natural Bridges National Monument did not receive quite so much publicity. Kelly and Martin (1947) have a friendly article about him. Theodore Roosevelt's own account of his trip to Rainbow Bridge appeared in *Outlook* (1913). Zane Grey's *Tales of Lonely Trails* (1922) almost entirely treats his experiences in the canyon country; the quote is from his 1928 article. Miser, Trimble, and Paige (1923) wrote an account of the geography, geology, and discovery of Rainbow Bridge.

8. Some of Bernheimer's expeditions were carried out under the auspices of the American Museum of Natural History of New York City. Earl H. Morris (1922), who accompanied some of the expeditions as representative of the Museum, reported on the hitherto unexplored areas visited. Bernheimer's *Rainbow Bridge* (1924) would be twice the size if the unpublished diaries had been included. Typescript copies of the diaries of most of the expeditions are found at the Utah State Historical Society, together with a number of photograph albums. Bernheimer (1920, 1923), wrote separate articles on his trip around Navajo Mountain and Rainbow Bridge.

9. The U. S. Geological Survey issued "guide books" helpful to tourists traveling on the several transcontinental railroad lines. Maps, geological information, and other data made it possible for the passenger to inform himself about the countryside as he traveled along. One guide book by Darton (1916) was issued for the Santa Fe route and one by Campbell (1922) for the Denver & Rio Grande Western route. In earlier years the Denver & Rio Grande employed W. H. Jackson to take photographs of scenic features adjacent to the line. The railroad was more concerned with the several mining excitements in the canyon country than with tourist potentialities. The Salt Lake *Tribune*, in January 1893, makes occasional reference to Cy Warman of the New York *Sun*. He became well acquainted with Cass Hite and even wrote a poem about him, "The Ghost of Hoskaninni," which, as far as I know, was never published. Warman's *Frontier Stories* (1898) and *Songs* (1911), contain some Utah material. See also Becker (1935) for a biographical sketch of Warman.

10. See Adams (1960) for the paucity of archeological investigation since Powell. The Monument Valley-Rainbow Bridge survey recognized this lack and in a measure filled some of the gaps. See Hall (1934), Hargrave (1935), and Beals, Brainerd, and Smith (1945). Neil Judd (1924) reports on a National Geographic Society expedition west of the Clay Hills in 1923.

11. Powell, of course, had seen the country as a whole, and had drawn significant conclusions of great benefit to science. His *Canyons of the Colorado* (1895) was a description of the main canyons of the Green and the Colorado. Speaking of the entire Colorado Plateau, Prudden (1906), 89, said that it is "the world's masterpiece." James Bryce in 1922 discussed American scenery in continental terms. A few later writers on the canyon country landscape: Waters (1946) wrote of the entire river as did the Lees (1962); the writers in Peattie, ed. (1948), *The Inverted Mountains*, restricted themselves to the canyons, including Grand. Kelly (1941) wrote of the proposed Escalante national monument that would have included much of Glen Canyon. Charles Kelly's bibliography on the canyon country is one of the longest. Clyde Kluckhohn's two books, *To the Foot of the Rainbow* (1927) and *Beyond the Rainbow* (1933), contain much appreciation for the canyon country. Everett Ruess was a sensitive young man who lost his life while wandering in the canyon-country wilderness; see his assembled writings (1950). Klinck (1953) has written on Monument Valley. The *National Geographic Magazine* has continued to publicize the region, notably so since World War II: See articles by Breed (1945, 1947, 1949, 1952), Bailey (1947), Gray (1957), Moore (1955, 1962). Many articles on southeastern Utah and northeastern Arizona have appeared through the years in *Desert Magazine* and *Arizona Highways*. Two special issues of the *Utah Historical Quarterly* (July 1958, July 1960) were devoted to Utah's parks and scenic wonders and to the Colorado River of the West. Eliot Porter's *The Place No One Knew* (1963) was intended as a requiem for that part of Glen Canyon lost under the reservoir of Lake Powell which began to form in January, 1963.

Bibliography

Adair, John (1944): *The Navajo and Pueblo Silversmiths*. Norman: University of Oklahoma Press.

Adams, Eleanor B., and Angelico Chavez, trans. and eds. (1956): *The Missions of New Mexico, 1776: A Description by Fray Francisco Atanasio Domínguez with other Contemporary Documents*. Albuquerque: University of New Mexico Press.

Adams, William Y. (1958a): "New Data on Navajo Social Organization." *Plateau*, XXX (January), 64–70.

——— (1958b): Shonto: A Study in the Role of the Trades in a Modern Navajo Community. Unpublished Ph.D. dissertation, University of Arizona Library.

——— (1960): *Ninety Years of Glen Canyon Archeology, 1869–1959: A Brief Historical Sketch and Bibliography of Archeological Investigations from J. W. Powell to the Glen Canyon Project*. Museum of Northern Arizona Bulletin 33, Glen Canyon Series No. 2 (Flagstaff).

Albright, George Leslie (1921): *Official Explorations for Pacific Railroads, 1853–1855*. Berkeley: University of California Press.

Allen, Richard Cardell (1958): Governor George H. Dern and Utah's Participation in the Colorado River Compact, 1922–1933. MS, M.S. thesis, University of Utah.

Alter, J. Cecil (1927): *Through the Heart of the Scenic West*. Salt Lake City: Shepard Book Company.

——— (1932): *Utah the Storied Domain* . . . 3 vols. Chicago and New York: American Historical Society.

Anderson, Joseph F. (1915): "Pioneers and Pioneering in Southeastern Utah." *Improvement Era*, XVIII (June–August), 710–16, 870–5.

Arizona Highways, XL (January 1964). Special issue on Lake Powell, Glen Canyon Dam, and the Glen Canyon National Recreation Area.

Arrington, Leonard J. (1958): *Great Basin Kingdom: An Economic History of the Latter-day Saints, 1830–1890*. Cambridge: Harvard University Press.

Athearn, Robert G. (1962): *Rebel of the Rockies: A History of the Denver and Rio Grande Western Railroad*. New Haven and London: Yale University Press.

Auerbach, Herbert S. (1943): "Father Escalante's Journal with Related Documents and Maps." *Utah Historical Quarterly*, XI.

Auerbach, Herbert S., and J. Cecil Alter, eds. (1940): *Life in the Rocky Mountains, 1830–1835*, by Warren Angus Ferris. Salt Lake City: Rocky Mountain Book Shop.

Bailey, Alfred M. (1947): "Desert River Through Navajo Land." *National Geographic Magazine*, XCII (August), 149–64.

Bailey, Paul (1948): *Jacob Hamblin: Buckskin Apostle*. Los Angeles: Westernlore Press.

——— (1954): *Walkara: Hawk of the Mountains*. Los Angeles: Westernlore Press.

Baker, Arthur A. (1933): *Geology and Oil Possibilities of the Moab District, Grand and San Juan Counties, Utah*. U.S. Geological Survey Bulletin 841. Washington, D.C.: Government Printing Office.

——— (1936): *Geology of the Monument Valley-Navajo Mountain Region, San Juan County, Utah*. U.S. Geological Survey Bulletin 865. Washington, D.C.: Government Printing Office.

——— (1946): *Geology of the Green River Desert-Cataract Canyon Region, Emery, Wayne, and Garfield Counties, Utah*. U.S. Geological Survey Bulletin 951. Washington, D.C.: Government Printing Office.

Baker, Pearl (1963): "The Hard, Good Life at Robber's Roost." *Desert Magazine*, XXVI (May), 27–31.

Bancroft, Hubert Howe (1889): *History of Arizona and New Mexico, 1530–1888*. San Francisco: The History Company.

Barnes, William C. (1913): *Western Grazing Grounds and Forest Ranges: A History of the Live-stock Industry as Conducted on the Open Ranges of the Arid West, with Particular Reference to the Use Now Being Made of the Ranges in the National Forests*. Chicago: Breeder's Gazette.

——— (1960): *Arizona Place Names*. Revised and enlarged by Byrd H. Granger. Tucson: University of Arizona Press.

Bartlett, Richard A. (1962): *Great Surveys of the American West*. Norman: University of Oklahoma Press.

Beadle, J. H. (1881): *Western Wilds, and the Men Who Redeem Them: An Authentic Narrative, Embracing an Account of Seven Years Travel and Adventure in the Far West; Wild Life in Arizona; Perils of the Plains; Life in Cañon and Death on the Desert; Adventures Among the Red and White Savages of the West; the Mountain Meadow Massacre; the Custer Defeat; Life and Death of Brigham Young*. Cincinnati, Chicago: Jones Brothers.

Beals, Ralph L., George W. Brainerd, and Watson Smith (1945): *Archeological Studies in Northeast Arizona: A Report on the Archeological Work of the Rainbow Bridge-Monument Valley Expedition* . . . Berkeley and Los Angeles: University of California Press.

Beaman, E. O. (1874): "The Cañon of the Colorado, and the

Moquis Pueblos: A Wild Ride through the Cañons and Rapids; A Visit to the Seven Cities of the Desert; Glimpses of Mormon Life." *Appleton's Journal*, XV (April 18–May 30, 1874).

Beck, D. Elden (1941): "Mormon Trails to Bluff." *Utah*, IV–V (Salt Lake City, October 1940–June 1941).

Becker, May L. (1935): *Golden Tales of the Far West, Selected With an Introduction*. New York: Dodd, Mead.

Beckwith, E. G. (1855): "Report of Explorations for a Route for the Pacific Railroad, by Capt. J. W. Gunnison, Topographical Engineers, near the 38th and 39th Parallels of North Latitude, from the Mouth of the Kansas River, Mo. to the Sevier Lake, in the Great Basin." In *Reports of Explorations and Surveys to Ascertain the Most Practical and Economical Route for a Railroad from the Mississippi to the Pacific Ocean . . . Vol. II*. Washington, D.C.: Beverley Tucker, Printer. Pp. 9–114.

Bell, William A. (1870): *New Tracks in North America: A Journal of Travel and Adventure Whilst Engaged in a Survey for a Southern Railroad to the Pacific Ocean, 1867–8*. Second edition. London: Chapman and Hall.

Bernheimer, Charles L. (1920): "From Kayenta to Rainbow Bridge." *Natural History*, XX (November–December), 552–9.

———(1923): "Encircling Navajo Mountain with a Pack Team: A New Route to Rainbow Natural Bridge." *National Geographic Magazine*, XLIII (February), 197–224.

——— (1924): *Rainbow Bridge, Circling Navajo Mountain and Explorations in the "Bad Lands" of Southern Utah and Northern Arizona*. Garden City, New York: Doubleday, Page.

Bingham, J. R. (1960): "Reclamation and the Colorado." *Utah Historical Quarterly*, XXVIII (July), 232–49.

Birdseye, Claude H. (1938): "Exploration in the Grand Canyon." *Reclamation Era*, XXVIII (August), 170–1.

Birney, Hoffman (1931): *Zealots of Zion*. Philadelphia: Penn Publishing Company.

Bolton, Herbert E. (1950): *Pageant in the Wilderness: The Story of the Escalante Expedition to the Interior Basin, 1776, Including the Diary and Itinerary of Father Escalante Translated and Annotated*. Salt Lake City: Utah State Historical Society.

Boutwell, J. M. (1905): ". . . Vanadium and Uranium in Southeastern Utah." U.S. Geological Survey, *Contributions to Economic Geology 1904*. Washington, D.C.: Government Printing Office. Pp. 200–10.

Brandes, Ray (1960): *Frontier Military Posts of Arizona*. Globe, Arizona: Dale S. King.

Breed, Jack (1945): "Flaming Cliffs of Monument Valley." *National Geographic Magazine*, LXXXVIII (October), 452–61.

——— (1947): "Utah's Arches of Stone." *National Geographic Magazine*, XCII (August), 173–6.

——— (1949): "First Motor Sortie into Escalante Land." *National Geographic Magazine*, VCXI (September), 369–404.

——— (1952): "Roaming the West's Fantastic Four Corners." *National Geographic Magazine*, CI (June), 705–42.

Brew, John Otis (1946): *Archeology of Alkali Ridge, Southeastern Utah, With a Review of the Prehistory of the Mesa Verde Division of the San Juan and Some Observations on Archeological Systematics. . . .* Papers of the Peabody Museum of American Archaeology and Ethnology, XXI. Cambridge: The Museum.

Briggs, Walter De Blois (1935): *James Phillips, Jr., By His Grandson*. San Francisco: Grabhorn Press.

Brooks, Juanita (1944a): "Indian Relations on the Mormon Frontier." *Utah Historical Quarterly*, XII (January–April), 1–68.

———, ed. (1944b): "Journal of Thales H. Haskell." *Utah Historical Quarterly*, XII (January–April), 69–98.

——— (1950): *The Mountain Meadows Massacre*. Stanford: Stanford University Press; 1950. Second edition, Norman: University of Oklahoma Press; 1963.

——— (1957): "Lee's Ferry at Lonely Dell." *Utah Historical Quarterly*, XXV (October), 283–95.

——— (1962): *John Doyle Lee, Zealot-Pioneer Builder-Scapegoat*. Glendale, Calif.: Arthur H. Clark.

Brough, Charles Hillman (1898): *Irrigation in Utah*. John Hopkins University Studies in Historical and Political Science, Extra Volume XIX. Baltimore: Johns Hopkins Press.

Bryce, James (1922): "The Scenery of North America." *National Geographic Magazine*, XLI (April), 339–89.

Bulger, Harold A. (1961): "First Man Through the Grand Canyon." *Bulletin of the Missouri Historical Society*, XVII (July), 321–31.

Butcher, Devereux (1954): *Exploring Our National Parks and Monuments*. Fourth edition. Boston: Houghton Mifflin.

Butler, B. S., G. F. Loughlin, V. C. Heikes, and others (1920): *The Ore Deposits of Utah*. U.S. Geological Survey Professional Paper 111. Washington, D.C.: Government Printing Office.

Campbell, Marius R. (1922): *Guidebook of the Western United States: Part E, The Denver & Rio Grande Western Route*. U. S. Geological Survey Bulletin 707. Washington, D. C.: Government Printing Office.

Carroll, Elsie Chamberlain, comp. (1960): *History of Kane County . . .* Salt Lake City: Utah Printing Company.

Chalfant, James M., ed. (1932): *Colorado River Controversies . . .*, by Robert Brewster Stanton. Foreword by Julius F. Stone. New York: Dodd, Mead.

Chidester, Ida, and Eleanor Bruhn (1949): *Golden Nuggets of Pioneer Days: A History of Garfield County*. Panguitch, Utah: Garfield County News.

Chittenden, G. B. (1877): "Topographical Report on the Grand River District [and] On the San Juan District." *Ninth Annual Report of the United States Geological and Geographical Survey of the Territories . . . 1875*. Washington, D.C.: Government Printing Office. Pp. 335–68.

Chittenden, Hiram M. (1902): *The American Fur Trade of the Far West*. 3 vols. New York: F. P. Harper.

Cleland, Robert Glass (1952): *This Reckless Breed of Men: The Trappers and Fur Traders of the Southwest*. New York: Alfred A. Knopf.

Cleland, Robert Glass, and Juanita Brooks, eds. (1955): *A Mormon Chronicle: The Diaries of John D. Lee, 1848–1876*. 2 vols. San Marino, Calif.: Huntington Library.

Cline, Gloria Griffin (1963): *Exploring the Great Basin*. Norman: University of Oklahoma Press.

Clyde, George D. (1959): "History of Irrigation in Utah." *Utah Historical Quarterly*, XXVII (January), 26–36.

Coffin, R. C. (1921): *Radium, Uranium and Vanadium Deposits of Southwestern Colorado*. Colorado Geological Survey Bulletin 16. Denver: Eames Brothers.

"Colossal Natural Bridges of Utah" (1904): *National Geographic Magazine*, XV (September), 367–9.

Colton, Ray C. (1959): *The Civil War in the Western Territories, Arizona, Colorado, New Mexico, and Utah*. Norman: University of Oklahoma Press.

Corbett, Pearson H. (1952): *Jacob Hamblin the Peacemaker*. Salt Lake City: Deseret Book Company.

Crampton, C. Gregory (1952): "The Discovery of the Green River." *Utah Historical Quarterly*, XX (October), 299–312.

—— (1958): "Humboldt's Utah, 1811." *Utah Historical Quarterly*, XXVI (July), 268–81.

—— (1959): *Outline History of the Glen Canyon Region, 1776–1922.* University of Utah Anthropological Papers No. 42. Glen Canyon Series No. 9 (September).

—— (1960): *Historical Sites in Glen Canyon: Mouth of San Juan River to Lee's Ferry.* University of Utah Anthropological Papers No. 46, Glen Canyon Series No. 12 (June).

—— (1962): *Historical Sites in Glen Canyon: Mouth of Hansen Creek to Mouth of San Juan River.* University of Utah Anthropological Papers No. 61, Glen Canyon Series No. 17 (December).

—— (1963): "Historical Archaeology on the Colorado River." In *The American West: An Appraisal*, edited by Robert G. Ferris. Santa Fe: Museum of New Mexico Press. Pp. 213–18.

Crampton, C. Gregory, and Gloria Griffin (Cline) (1956): "The San Buenaventura, Mythical River of the West." *Pacific Historical Review*, XXV (May), 163–71.

Crampton, C. Gregory, and David E. Miller, eds. (1961): "Journal of Two Campaigns by Utah Territorial Militia Against the Navajo Indians, 1869." *Utah Historical Quarterly*, XXIX (April), 148–76.

Crampton, C. Gregory, and Dwight L. Smith, eds. (1961): *The Hoskaninni Papers: Mining in Glen Canyon, 1897–1902*, by Robert B. Stanton. University of Utah Anthropological Papers No. 54, Glen Canyon Series No. 15 (November).

Creer, Leland H. (1929): *Utah and the Nation.* Seattle: University of Washington Press.

——, ed. (1940): *History of Utah, 1847–1869*, by Andrew Love Neff. Salt Lake City: Deseret News Press.

—— (1947): *The Founding of an Empire: The Exploration and Colonization of Utah, 1776–1856.* Salt Lake City: Bookcraft.

—— (1949): "Spanish-American Slave Trade in the Great Basin, 1800–1853." *New Mexico Historical Review*, XXIV (July), 171–83.

—— (1958a): *Mormon Towns in the Region of the Colorado.* University of Utah Anthropological Papers No. 32, Glen Canyon Series No. 3 (May).

—— (1958b): *The Activities of Jacob Hamblin in the Region of the Colorado.* University of Utah Anthropological Papers No. 33, Glen Canyon Series No. 4 (May).

Culmer, H. L. A. (1892): "Mountain Scenery of Utah." *Contributor*, XIII (Salt Lake City, February–April), 173–8, 201–7, 265–70.

—— (1894): "Mountain Art." *Overland Monthly*, New Series, XXIV (October), 341–52.

—— (1909): "The Scenic Glories of Utah." *Western Monthly*, X (August), 35–41.

—— (1937): "Personal Diary of H. L. A. Culmer 1905." *Southwestern Monuments* (National Park Service, June).

Cummings, Byron (1910a): "The Great Natural Bridges of Utah." *National Geographic Magazine*, XXI (February), 157–66.

—— (1910b): "The Great Natural Bridges of Utah." *Bulletin of the University of Utah*, III, First Archeological Number (November). Reprinted in Cummings Publication Council, *Bulletin 1* (Tucson 1959), 23–42.

—— (1910c): "The Ancient Inhabitants of the San Juan Valley." *Bulletin of the University of Utah*, III, Second Archeological Number (November).

—— (1952): *Indians I Have Known.* Tucson: Arizona Silhouettes.

Cummings, Malcolm B. (1940): "I Finished Last in the Race to Rainbow Bridge." *Desert Magazine*, III (May), 22–5.

—— (1959): "Recollections of Discovery of Rainbow Bridge." Cummings Publication Council, *Bulletin 1* (Tucson 1959), 15–16.

Cunningham, James L. (1943): *Our Family History Subsequent to 1870.* Pittsburgh: Herald Press.

Dale, Edward Everett (1949): *The Indians of the Southwest: A Century of Development under the United States.* Norman: University of Oklahoma Press in co-operation with the Huntington Library.

Dana, Marshall N. (1959): "Reclamation, Its Influence and Impact on the History of the West." *Utah Historical Quarterly*, XXVII (January), 38–49.

Dane, C. H. (1935): *Geology of the Salt Valley Anticline and Adjacent Areas, Grand County, Utah.* U.S. Geological Survey Bulletin 863. Washington, D.C.: Government Printing Office.

Darrah, William C., ed. (1947): "The Exploration of the Colorado River in 1869. [Including the Journals of J. W. Powell, George Y. Bradley, and J. C. Sumner, Together with other Original Documents, Including Biographical Sketches and Preparations for a Second Expedition.] *Utah Historical Quarterly*, XV, 1–153.

—— (1948–9): "Journal of John F. Steward, May 22–November 3, 1871 [with sketches of] Beaman, Fennemore, Hillers, Dellenbaugh, Johnson, and Hattan [and] Three Letters by Andrew Hall." *Utah Historical Quarterly*, XVI–XVII, 175–251, 491–508.

—— (1951): *Powell of the Colorado.* Princeton: Princeton University Press.

Darton, Nelson H. (1916): *Guidebook of the Western United States: Part C, The Santa Fe Route with a Side Trip to the Grand Canyon of the Colorado.* U.S. Geological Survey Bulletin 613. Washington, D.C.: Government Printing Office.

"De Julien, an Unknown Explorer" (1905): *Outing*, XLVI (August), 601–5.

Dellenbaugh, Frederick S. (1902): *The Romance of the Colorado River: The Story of Its Discovery in 1540, With an Account of the Later Explorations, and with Special Reference to the Voyages of Powell Through the Line of the Great Canyons.* New York and London: G. P. Putnam's Sons.

—— (1908, 1926): *A Canyon Voyage: The Narrative of the Second Powell Expedition Down the Green-Colorado River from Wyoming, and the Explorations on Land, in the Years 1871 and 1872.* Second edition, New Haven: Yale University Press; 1926. First edition, New York and London: G. P. Putnam's Sons; 1908.

Deseret News (Salt Lake City), December 28, 1854; August 1, 22, October 10, 31, November 7, 1855.

De Terra, Helmut (1955): *Humboldt: The Life and Times of Alexander von Humboldt, 1769–1859.* New York: Alfred A. Knopf.

DeVoto, Bernard (1952): *The Course of Empire.* Boston: Houghton Mifflin.

Dutton, C. E. (1880): *Report on the Geology of the High Plateaus of Utah, with Atlas.* U.S. Geographical and Geological Survey of the Rocky Mountain Region. Washington, D.C.: Government Printing Office.

—— (1882): *Tertiary History of the Grand Cañon District, with Atlas.* U.S. Geological Survey. Monographs, II. Washington, D.C.: Government Printing Office.

Dyar, W. W. (1904): "The Colossal Bridges of Utah: A Recent Discovery of Natural Wonders." *Century Magazine*, LXVIII (August), 505–11.

Dyer, Francis John (1911): "Adventures in a Land of Wonders." *Overland*, New Series, 58 (October), 343–9.

Emmitt, Robert (1954): *The Last War Trail: The Utes and the Settlement of Colorado*. Norman: University of Oklahoma Press.

Emory, William H. (1857): *Reprot on the United States and Mexican Boundary Survey, Made under the Direction of the Secretary of Interior*, Vol. I. U.S. 34th Cong., 1st Sess., House Ex. Doc. 135. Washington, D.C.: Cornelius Wendell.

Epinosa, José Manuel (1934): "The Legend of Sierra Azul." *New Mexico Historical Review*, IX (April), 113–58.

Euler, Robert C. (1956): *Southern Paiute Ethnohistory*. Flagstaff, Arizona: mimeographed.

Farquhar, Francis P., ed. (1950): *The Colorado River*, by J. B. Kipp. Los Angeles: Muir Dawson.

———— (1953): *The Books of the Colorado River & the Grand Canyon: A Selective Bibliography*. Los Angeles: Glen Dawson.

Fewkes, Jesse Walter (1911): *Preliminary Report on a Visit to the Navaho National Monument, Arizona*. Bureau of American Ethnology Bulletin 50. Washington, D.C.: Government Printing Office.

Fife, Austin, and Alta Fife (1956): *Saints of Sage and Saddle: Folklore Among the Mormons*. Bloomington: Indiana University Press.

Fischer, Richard P. (1942): *Vanadium Deposts of Colorado and Utah: A Preliminary Report*. U.S. Geological Survey Bulletin 936-P. Washington, D.C.: Government Printing Office.

Fisher, D. Jerome (1936): *The Book Cliffs Coal Field in Emery and Grand Counties, Utah*. U.S. Geological Survey Bulletin 852. Washington, D.C.: Government Printing Office.

Fisher, D. Jerome, Charles E. Erdmann, and John B. Reeside, Jr. (1960): *Cretaceous and Tertiary Formations of the Book Cliffs, Carbon, Emery, and Grand Counties, Utah, and Garfield and Mesa Counties, Colorado*. U.S. Geological Survey Professional Paper 332. Washington, D.C.: Government Printing Office.

Follansbee, Robert (1929): *Upper Colorado River and Its Utilization*. U.S. Geological Survey Water-Supply Paper 617. Washington, D.C.: Government Printing Office.

Force, Edwin Truesdell (1936): The Use of the Colorado River in the United States, 1850–1933. MS, Ph.D. dissertation, University of California, Berkeley.

Foreman, Grant, ed. (1941): *A Pathfinder in the Southwest: The Itinery of Lieutenant A. W. Whipple During his Exploration for a Railway Route from Fort Smith to Los Angeles in the Years 1853 & 1854*. Norman: University of Oklahoma Press.

Four Corners Geological Society (1955): *Geology of Parts of Paradox, Black Mesa & San Juan Basins*. Four Corners Field Conference. Durango, Colorado: Four Corners Geological Society.

Franciscan Fathers (1910): *An Ethnologic Dictionary of the Navaho Language*. St. Michaels, Arizona: Franciscan Fathers.

Freeman, Ira S. (1958): *A History of Montezuma County, Colorado*. Boulder: Johnson Publishing Company.

Freeman, Lewis R. (1923): *The Colorado River: Yesterday, Today and Tomorrow*. New York: Dodd, Mead.

———— (1924): *Down the Grand Canyon*. London: William Heinemann.

Freeman, W. B., and R. H. Bolster (1910): *Surface Water Supply of the United States, 1907–8, IX, Colorado River Basin*. U.S. Geological Survey Water-Supply Paper 249. Washington, D.C.: Government Printing Office.

Frémont, John Charles (1845): *Report of the Exploring Expedition to the Rocky Mountains in the Year 1842, and to Oregon and North California in the Years 1843–44*. U.S. 28th Cong., 2nd Sess., House Ex. Doc. 166. Washington, D.C.: Blair & Rives.

———— (1849): *Geographical Memoir upon Upper California, in Illustration of his Map of Oregon and California . . . Addressed to the Senate of the United States*. U.S. 30th Cong., 2nd Sess., House Misc. Doc. No. 5. Washington, D.C.: Tippin & Streeper.

———— (1854): "Letter." *National Intelligencer* (Washington, D.C., June 15).

Frink, Maurice, W. Turrentine Jackson, and Agnes Wright Spring (1956): *When Grass Was King: Contributions to the Western Range Cattle Industry Study*. Boulder: University of Colorado Press.

Fryxell, Fritiof, ed. (1958): *Thomas Moran: Explorer in Search of Beauty*. East Hampton, New York: East Hampton Free Library.

Gannett, Henry (1900): *A Gazetteer of Utah*. U.S. Geological Survey Bulletin 166. Washington, D.C.: Government Printing Office.

Garfield County, Utah (1885–97): Records of the White Canyon Mining District, Garfield and San Juan Counties, Utah Territory, Cass Hite, Recorder. [Entries also by John P. Hite, Ben R. Hite, Homer J. Hite, George L. Gillham, and others.] MS, 2 vols., Recorder's Office, Panguitch.

———— (1883–4): Deeds, A. MS, Recorder's Office, Panguitch.

Gilbert, G. K. (1877): *Report on the Geology of the Henry Mountains*. U.S. Geographical and Geological Survey of the Rocky Mountain Region. Washington, D.C.: Government Printing Office.

Gillmor, Frances, and Louisa Wade Wetherill (1953): *Trader to the Navajos: The Story of the Wetherills of Kayenta*. Second edition. Albuquerque: University of New Mexico Press.

Gilluly, James (1929): *Geology and Oil and Gas Prospects of Part of the San Rafael Swell, Utah*. U.S. Geological Survey Bulletin 806-C. Washington, D.C.: Government Printing Office.

Goetzmann, William H. (1959): *Army Exploration in the American West, 1803–1863*. New Haven: Yale University Press.

Golzé, Alfred R. (1952): *Reclamation in the United States*. New York: McGraw-Hill.

Gordon, Clarence (1883): "Report of Cattle, Sheep, and Swine Supplementary to Enumeration of Live Stock on Farms in 1880." *In* U. S. Department of the Interior, Census Office. Tenth Census (1880). *Report on the Production of Agriculture as Returned at the Tenth Census (June 1, 1880), Embracing General Statistics and Monographs . . .* Washington, D.C.: Government Printing Office. 162 pp.

Gottfredson, Peter (1919): *History of Indian Depredations in Utah*. Salt Lake City: Skelton Publishing Company.

Gray, Ralph (1957): "Three Roads to Rainbow." *National Geographic Magazine*, CXI (April), 547–61.

Greever, William S. (1954): *Arid Domain: The Santa Fe Railway and Its Western Land Grant*. Stanford: Stanford University Press.

Gregory, Herbert E. (1911): "The San Juan Oil Field," U.S. Geological Survey Bulletin 431. Washington, D.C.: Government Printing Office. Pp. 11–25.

———— (1916): *The Navajo Country: A Geographic and Hydrographic Reconnaissance of Parts of Arizona, New Mexico, and Utah*. U.S. Geological Survey Water-Supply Paper 380. Washington, D.C.: Government Printing Office.

———— (1917): *Geology of the Navajo Country: A Reconnaissance of Parts of Arizona, New Mexico, and Utah*. U.S. Geological

Survey Professional Paper 93. Washington, D.C.: Government Printing Office.

——— (1938): *The San Juan Country: A Geographic and Geologic Reconnaissance of Southeastern Utah with Contributions by Malcolm R. Thorpe.* U.S. Geological Survey Professional Paper 188. Washington, D.C.: Government Printing Office.

———, ed. (1939): "Diary of Almon Harris Thompson, Geographer, Explorations of the Colorado River of the West and its Tributaries, 1871–1875." *Utah Historical Quarterly,* VII (January–July), 3–138.

——— (1945a): "Population of Southern Utah." *Economic Geography,* XXI (January), 29–57.

——— (1945b): "Scientific Explorations in Southern Utah." *American Journal of Science,* 243 (October), 527–49.

———, ed. (1948–9): "Journal of Stephen Vandiver Jones, April 21, 1871–December 14, 1872." *Utah Historical Quarterly,* XVI–XVII, 11–174.

——— (1950): *Geology and Geography of the Zion Park Region Utah and Arizona: A Comprehensive Report on a Scenic and Historic Region of the Southwest.* U.S. Geological Survey Professional Paper 220. Washington, D.C.: Government Printing Office.

——— (1951): *The Geology and Geography of the Paunsaugunt Region Utah: A Survey of Parts of Garfield and Kane Counties.* U.S. Geological Survey Professional Paper 276. Washington, D.C.: Government Printing Office.

Gregory, Herbert E., and J. C. Anderson (1939): "Geographic and Geologic Sketch of the Capitol Reef Region, Utah." *Bulletin of the Geological Society of America,* 50 (December), 1827–50.

Gregory, Herbert E., and Raymond C. Moore (1931): *The Kaiparowits Region: A Geographic and Geologic Reconnaissance of Parts of Utah and Arizona.* U.S. Geological Survey Professional Paper 164. Washington, D.C.: Government Printing Office.

Grey, Zane (1922): *Tales of Lonely Trails.* New York and London: Harper & Brothers.

——— (1928): "What the Desert Means to Me." In *Zane Grey, the Man and His Work: An Autobiographical Sketch, Critical Appreciations & Bibliography.* New York and London: Harper & Brothers.

Gudde, Erwin G., and Elisabeth K. Gudde, trans. and eds. (1958): *Charles Preuss: Exploring with Frémont. The Private Diaries of Charles Preuss, Cartographer for John C. Frémont on His First, Second, and Fourth Expeditions to the Far West.* Norman: University of Oklahoma Press.

Hafen, LeRoy R., and Ann W. Hafen (1954): *Old Spanish Trail Santa Fe to Los Angeles With Extracts from Contemporary Records and Including Diaries of Antonio Armijo and Orville Pratt.* Glendale, Calif.: Arthur H. Clark.

———, eds. (1957): *Central Route to the Pacific,* by Gwinn Harris Heap; *With Related Material on Railroad Explorations and Indian Affairs,* by Edward F. Beale, Thomas H. Benton, Kit Carson, and Col. E. A. Hitchcock, *And In Other Documents, 1853–54.* With an Introduction and Notes. Glendale, Calif.: Arthur H. Clark.

———, eds. (1959): *The Diaries of William Henry Jackson, Frontier Photographer to California and Return, 1866–1867; and with the Hayden Survey to the Central Rockies, 1873, and to the Utes and Cliff Dwellings, 1874.* With Introduction and Notes. Glendale, Calif.: Arthur H. Clark.

Hall, Ansel Franklin (1934): *General Report Rainbow Bridge-Monument Valley Expedition of 1933.* Berkeley: University of California Press.

Hall, Frank (1889–95): *History of the State of Colorado . . .* 4 vols. Chicago: Blakely Printing Company.

Hammond, George P. (1956): "The Search for the Fabulous in the Settlement of the Southwest." *Utah Historical Quarterly,* XXIV (January), 1–19.

Hansen, George H., and Mendell M. Bell, comps. (1949): *. . . The Oil and Gas Possibilities of Utah.* Salt Lake City: Utah Geological and Mineralogical Survey.

Hargrave, Lyndon Lane (1935): *Report on Archeological Reconnaissance in the Rainbow Plateau Area of Northern Arizona and Southern Utah Based upon Field Work by the Rainbow Bridge-Monument Valley Expedition of 1933.* Foreword by Ansel F. Hall. Berkeley: University of California Press.

Harris, W. R. (1909): *The Catholic Church in Utah, Including an Exposition of Catholic Faith by Bishop Scanlan; a Review of Spanish and Missionary Exploration; Tribal Divisions; . . . The Journal of the Franciscan Explorers and Discoverers of Utah Lake; the Trailing of the Priests from Santa Fe . . . With a Map of the Route, Illustrations and Delimitations of the Great Basin.* Salt Lake City: Intermountain Catholic Press.

Harshbarger, J. W., C. A. Repenning, and J. H. Irwin (1957): *Stratigraphy of the Uppermost Triassic and the Jurassic Rocks of the Navajo Country.* U.S. Geological Survey Professional Paper 291. Washington, D.C.: Government Printing Office.

Hayden, F. V. (1876): *The Yellowstone National Park and the Mountain Regions of Portions of Idaho, Nevada, Colorado and Utah . . . Illustrated by Chromolithographic Reproductions of Water-Color Sketches by Thomas Moran, Artist to the Expedition of 1871.* Boston: L. Prang and Company.

——— (1877): *. . . Geological and Geographical Atlas of Colorado and Portions of Adjacent Territory . . .* N.p.: Julius Bien.

Heald, Weldon F. (1955): "Who Discovered Rainbow Bridge?" *Sierra Club Bulletin,* XL (October), 24–8.

Herron, W. H. (1917): *Profile Surveys in the Colorado River Basin in Wyoming, Utah, Colorado, and New Mexico.* U.S. Geological Survey Water-Supply Paper 396. Washington, D.C.: Government Printing Office.

Hester, James J. (1962): *Early Navajo Migrations and Acculturation in the Southwest.* Museum of New Mexico Papers in Anthropology No. 6. Santa Fe: Museum of New Mexico.

Hill, Joseph J. (1921): "The Old Spanish Trail: A Study of Spanish and Mexican Trade and Exploration Northwest from New Mexico to the Great Basin and California." *Hispanic American Historical Review,* IV (August), 444–73.

——— (1930): "Spanish and Mexican Exploration and Trade Northwest from New Mexico Into the Great Basin." *Utah Historical Quarterly,* III (January), 3–23.

Hine, Robert V. (1962): *Edward Kern and American Expansion.* New Haven and London: Yale University Press.

Hodge, Frederick W., ed. (1907–10): *Handbook of American Indians North of Mexico.* 2 vols. Bureau of American Ethnology Bulletin 30. Washington, D.C.: Government Printing Office.

Holmes, Edwin F. (1907): "The Great Natural Bridges of Utah." *National Geographic Magazine,* XVIII (March), 199–204.

Holmes, William H. (1877): "Geological Report on the San Juan District." *Ninth Annual Report of the United States Geological and Geographical Survey of the Territories . . . 1875.* Washington, D.C.: Government Printing Office. Pp. 237–76.

——— (1878a): "Report on Ancient Ruins of Southwestern Colorado, Examined During the Summers of 1875 and 1876 . . ." *Tenth Annual Report of the United States Geolog-*

ical and Geographical Survey of the Territories . . . 1876. Washington, D.C.: Government Printing Office.

—— (1878b): "Report on the Geology of the Sierra Abajo and West San Miguel Mountains." *Tenth Annual Report of the United States Geological and Geographical Survey of the Territories . . . 1876.* Washington, D.C.: Government Printing Office.

Humboldt, Alexander von (1811): *Political Essay on the Kingdom of New Spain. Containing Researches Relative to the Geography of Mexico, the Extent of its Surface and its Political Division into Intendancies, the Physical Aspect of the Country, the Population, the State of Agriculture and Manufacturing and Commercial Industry, the Canals Projected between the South Sea and the Atlantic Ocean, The Crown Revenues, the Quantity of Precious Metals Which have Flowed from Mexico into Europe and Asia since the Discovery of the New Continent, and the Military Defence of New Spain. With Physical Sections and Maps, founded on Astronomical Observations, and Trigonometrical and Barometrical Measurements.* 4 vols. Translated from the original French by John Black. London: Longman, Hurst, Rees, Orme & Brown.

—— (1850): *Views of Nature: Or Contemplations on the Sublime Phenomena of Creation; with Scientific Illustrations.* Translated by E. C. Otté and Henry G. Bohn. London: Henry G. Bohn.

Hunt, Charles, assisted by Paul Averitt, and Ralph L. Miller (1953): *Geology and Geography of the Henry Mountains Region Utah: A Survey and Restudy of One of the Classic Areas in Geology.* U.S. Geological Survey Professional Paper 228. Washington, D.C.: Government Printing Office.

Hunt, Charles B. (1956): *Cenozoic Geology of the Colorado Plateau.* U.S. Geological Survey Professional Paper 279. Washington, D.C.: Government Printing Office.

—— (1958): *Structural and Igneous Geology of the La Sal Mountains, Utah.* U.S. Geological Survey Professional Paper 294-I. Washington, D.C.: Government Printing Office.

Hunter, Milton R. (1940): *Brigham Young the Colonizer.* Salt Lake City: Deseret News Press.

Huth, Hans (1957): *Nature and the American: Three Centuries of Changing Attitudes.* Berkeley and Los Angeles: University of California Press.

Intermountain Association of Petroleum Geologists (1954): *Geology of Portions of the High Plateaus and Adjacent Canyon Lands Central and South-Central Utah.* Fifth Annual Field Conference. Salt Lake City: Quality Press.

Ives, Joseph C. (1861): *Report upon the Colorado River of the West Explored in 1857 and 1858 . . .* U.S. 36th Cong., 1st Sess., House Ex. Doc. 90. Washington, D.C.: Government Printing Office.

Jackson, Clarence S. (1947): *Picture Maker of the Old West, William H. Jackson.* New York and London: Charles Scribner's Sons.

Jackson, William Henry (1876): "Report on Ancient Ruins in Southwestern Colorado." *Annual Report of the United States Geological and Geographical Survey of the Territories . . . 1874.* Washington, D.C.: Government Printing Office.

—— (1878): "Report on the Ancient Ruins Examined in 1875 and 1877." *Tenth Annual Report of the United States Geological and Geographical Survey of the Territories . . . 1876.* Washington, D.C.: Government Printing Office. Pp. 409-50.

—— (1924): "First Official Visit to the Cliff Dwellings." *Colorado Magazine,* I (May), 151-9.

—— (1940): *Time Exposure: The Autobiography of William Henry Jackson.* New York: G. P. Putnam's Sons.

James, George Wharton (1900): *In & Around the Grand Canyon: The Grand Canyon of the Colorado River in Arizona.* Boston: Little Brown.

—— (1910): *The Grand Canyon of Arizona, How to See It.* Boston: Little Brown.

—— (1917a): *Arizona the Wonderland . . .* Boston: Page.

—— (1917b): *Reclaiming the Arid West: The Story of the United States Reclamation Service.* New York: Dodd Mead.

—— (1922): *Utah, the Land of Blossoming Valleys . . .* Boston: Page.

Jennings, Jesse D. (1957): *Danger Cave.* University of Utah Anthropological Papers No. 27 (October).

—— (1960): "The Aboriginal Peoples." *Utah Historical Quarterly,* XXVIII (July), 211-21.

Jenson, Andrew, comp. (1914): *Church Chronology: A Record of Important Events Pertaining to the History of the Church of Jesus Christ of Latter-day Saints.* Second edition. Salt Lake City: Deseret News.

—— (1919-22): "Origin of Western Geographic Names Associated with the History of the 'Mormon' People." *Utah Genealogical and Historical Magazine,* X-XIII.

Jenson, Andrew (1938): *Autobiography of Andrew Jenson, Assistant Historian of the Church of Jesus Christ of Latter-day Saints . . .* Salt Lake City: Deseret News Press.

—— (1941): *Encyclopedic History of the Church of Jesus Christ of Latter-day Saints.* Salt Lake City: Deseret News Publishing Company.

Jones, Albert H. (1960): Spencer Mining Operations on the San Juan River and in Glen Canyon, 1908-1911. MS, copy in possession of C. G. Crampton.

Jones, Daniel W. (1890): *Forty Years Among the Indians: A True Yet Thrilling Narrative of the Author's Experience Among the Natives.* Salt Lake City: Juvenile Instruction Office.

Jones, Kumen (1929): "First Settlement of San Juan County, Utah." *Utah Historical Quarterly,* II (January), 8-11.

—— (n.d.): Fifty-Eight Years. Typescript, Utah State Historical Society.

—— (n.d.: The San Juan Mission to the Indians [and autobiographical and miscellaneous writings]. Typescript, Utah State Historical Society, 235 pp.

Jones, Paul (1959): "Reclamation and the Indian." *Utah Historical Quarterly,* XXVII (January), 50-6.

Judd, Neil Morton (1924): "Beyond the Clay Hills: An Account of the National Geographic Society's Reconnaissance of a Previously Unexplored Section in Utah." *National Geographic Magazine,* XLV (March), 275-302.

—— (1927): "The Discovery of Rainbow Bridge." *National Parks Bulletin,* IX (November), 6-16.

—— (1930): "The Excavation and Repair of Betatakin." *Proceedings of the U.S. National Museum,* Vol. 77, Publication 2828. Washington, D.C.: Government Printing Office.

—— (1950): "Pioneering in Southwestern Archeology." In *For the Dean . . .* , edited by Erik K. Reed and Dale S. King. Santa Fe. Pp. 11-27.

Kelly, Charles (1933a): "The Mysterious 'D. Julien.' " *Utah Historical Quarterly,* VI (July), 83-8.

—— (1933b): "Antoine Roubidoux." *Utah Historical Quarterly,* VI (October), 114-16.

—— (1939): "At Eighty-Three, He Is an Explorer." *Saturday Evening Post,* Vol. 211, No. 45 (May 6), 20-1, 77-83.

—— (1940): "Lost Silver of Pish-la-ki." *Desert Magazine,* IV (December), 5-8.

———— (1941): "Proposed Escalante National Monument." *Desert Magazine*, IV (February), 20–2.

————, ed. (1947a): "Captain Francis Marion Bishop's Journal, August 15, 1870–June 3, 1872." *Utah Historical Quarterly*, XV, 159–240.

———— (1947b): "Mormon Crossing at Hole-in-the-Rock." *Desert Magazine*, X (May), 10–14.

————, ed. (1948–9): "Journal of W. C. Powell, April 21, 1871–December 7, 1872." *Utah Historical Quarterly*, XVI–XVII, 253–478.

———— (1953): "Chief Hoskaninni." *Utah Historical Quarterly*, XXI (July), 219–26.

———— (1959): *The Outlaw Trail: A History of Butch Cassidy and His Wild Bunch*. Second edition. New York: Devin-Adair.

Kelly, Charles, and Charlotte Martin (1947): "Zeke Johnson's Natural Bridges." *Desert Magazine*, XI (November), 12–15.

Kelly, Isabel T. (1934): "Southern Paiute Bands." *American Anthropologist*, XXXVI, 548–61.

Kerr, Walter A. (1955): "Byron Cummings: Classic Scholar and Father of University Athletics." *Utah Historical Quarterly*, XXIII (April), 145–50.

Kidder, A. V. (1940): "Exploration in Southeastern Utah in 1908." *American Journal of Archeology*, XIV, 337–59.

King, Murray E. (1940): *Last of the Bandit Riders*, by Matt Warner, as told to Murray E. King. Caldwell, Idaho: Caxton Printers.

Kleinsorge, Paul L. (1941): *The Boulder Canyon Project Historical and Economic Aspects*. With a Foreword by Eliot Jones. Stanford University Press.

Klinck, Richard E. (1953): *Land of Room Enough and Time Enough*. Albuquerque: University of New Mexico Press.

Kluckhohn, Clyde (1927): *To the Foot of the Rainbow: A Tale of Twenty-Five Hundred Miles of Wandering on Horseback Through the Southwest Enchanted Land*. New York, London: Century Company.

———— (1933): *Beyond the Rainbow*. Boston: Christopher Publishing Company.

Kluckhohn, Clyde, and Dorothea Leighton (1958): *The Navaho*. Cambridge: Harvard University Press.

Kolb, E. L. (1914): *Through the Grand Canyon from Wyoming to Mexico*. With a Foreword by Owen Wister. New York: Macmillan.

Korn, Bertram Wallace, ed. (1954): . . . *Incidents of Travel and Adventure in the Far West*, by Solomon Nunes Carvalho. Edited with an Introduction. Philadelphia: Jewish Publication Society.

Lakes, Arthur (1907): "The Natural Bridges of Utah." *Mining World*, XXVI (May), 595.

Larson, Andrew Karl (1961): *"I Was Called to Dixie": The Virgin River Basin: Unique Experiences in Mormon Pioneering*. Salt Lake City: Deseret News Press.

Larson, Gustive O. (1947): *Prelude to the Kingdom: Mormon Desert Conquest: A Chapter in American Cooperative Experience*. Francestown, New Hampshire: Marshall Jones Company.

———— (1958): *Outline History of Utah and the Mormons*. Salt Lake City: Deseret Book Company.

LaRue, E. C. (1916): *Colorado River and Its Utilization*. U.S. Geological Survey Water-Supply Paper 395. Washington, D.C.: Government Printing Office.

———— (1925): *Water Power and Flood Control of Colorado River Below Green River, Utah*. U.S. Geological Survey Water-Supply Paper 556. Washington, D.C.: Government Printing Office.

Lavender, David (1940): "Mormon Cowboy." *Desert Magazine*, III (October), 4–8.

———— (1956): *One Man's West*. Garden City: Doubleday.

Lee, Weston, and Jeanne Lee (1962): *Torrent in the Desert*. Endpapers and Maps by Don Perceval. Flagstaff, Arizona: Northland Press.

Leigh, Rufus Wood (1961): *Five Hundred Utah Place Names: Their Origin and Significance*. Salt Lake City: Deseret News Press.

Lever, W. H., publisher (1898): *History of Sanpete and Emery Counties, Utah* . . . Ogden: W. H. Lever.

Lewis, Robert S., and Thomas Varley (1919): "The Mineral Industry of Utah." *Bulletin of the University of Utah*, X (December).

Lingenfelter, R. E. (1958): *First Through the Grand Canyon*. Foreword by Otis Marston. Los Angeles: Glen Dawson.

Lister, Robert H. (1963): "Salvage Archaeology Today and the Glen Canyon Project." In *The American West: An Appraisal*, edited by Robert G. Ferris. Santa Fe: Museum of New Mexico Press. Pp. 219–25.

Little, James A. (1881): *Jacob Hamblin: A Narrative of his Personal Experience, as a Frontiersman, Missionary to the Indians and Explorer* . . . Salt Lake City: Juvenile Instructor Office.

Look, Al (1956): *U Boom: Uranium on the Colorado Plateau*. Denver: Bell Press.

Lupton, C. T. (1916): *Geology and Coal Resources of Castle Valley in Carbon, Emery, and Sevier Counties, Utah*. U.S. Geological Survey Bulletin 628. Washington, D.C.: Government Printing Office.

Lyman, Albert R. (1909): "The Land of Pagahrit." *Improvement Era*, XII (October), 934–8.

———— (1939): Platte De Alton Lyman. Typescript, Utah State Historical Society, 115 pp.

———— (1948–50): "The Fort on the Firing Line." *Improvement Era*, 51–3 (October 1948–March 1950).

———— (1955?): *History of Blanding, 1905–1955* . . . (Blanding?)

———— (1962): *Indians and Outlaws: Settling of the San Juan Frontier*. Salt Lake City: Bookcraft.

Lyman, Platte D. (1876–1901): Journal, November 12, 1876–March 10, 1901. Typescript, Utah State Historical Society, 102 pp. +165 pp.

McBride, W. C. (1907): "The Cliff Dwellers and the Mormon Theory." *Pacific Monthly*, XVII (June), 697–713.

McClintock, James H. (1921): *Mormon Settlement in Arizona: A Record of Peaceful Conquest of the Desert*. Phoenix: Manufacturing Stationers.

McElprang, Stella, comp. (1949): *Castle Valley: A History of Emery County*. N.p.: Emery County Company of the Daughters of Utah Pioneers.

McKnight, E. T. (1940): *Geology of Area between Green and Colorado Rivers, Grand and San Juan Counties, Utah*. U.S. Geological Survey Bulletin 908. Washington, D.C.: Government Printing Office.

McNitt, Frank (1957): *Richard Wetherill: Anasazi*. Albuquerque: University of New Mexico Press.

———— (1962): *The Indian Traders*. Norman: University of Oklahoma Press.

Macomb, J. N. (1876): *Report of the Exploring Expedition from Santa Fé, New Mexico, to the Junction of the Grand and Green Rivers of the Great Colorado of the West, in 1859, Under the Command of Capt. J. N. Macomb; with a Geological Report by Prof. J. S. Newberry*. Washington, D.C.: Government Printing Office.

Maguire, Don (1899): . . . *Outline History of Utah's Great Mining Districts, Their Past, Present and Future as Producers of the*

Precious Metals. Utah Mining Series No. 4. Chicago, Rio Grande Western Railroad.

Marston, Otis R., comp. (1949–51): Colorado River Journals and Diaries, 1889–1951. Typescript, 2 vols., Reference Library, Grand Canyon National Park.

Marston, Otis R. (1955): "Fast Water." In *This is Dinosaur,* edited by Wallace Stegner. New York: Alfred A. Knopf. Pp. 58–70.

—— (1960): "River Runners: Fast Water Navigation." *Utah Historical Quarterly,* XXVIII (July), 291–308.

Mead, Elwood (1903): *Report of Irrigation Investigations in Utah* . . . U.S. Department of Agriculture, Office of Experiment Stations, Bulletin No. 124. Washington, D.C.: Government Printing Office.

Miller, David E. (1958): "Discovery of Glen Canyon." *Utah Historical Quarterly,* XXVI (July), 220–37.

—— (1959): *Hole-in-the-Rock: An Epic in the Colonization of the Great American West.* Salt Lake City: University of Utah Press.

Miser, Hugh D. (1924): *The San Juan Canyon, South-eastern Utah: A Geographic and Hydrographic Reconnaissance.* U.S. Geological Survey Water-Supply Paper 538. Washington, D.C.: Government Printing Office.

Miser, H. D., K. W. Trimble, and Sidney Paige (1923): "The Rainbow Bridge, Utah." *Geographical Review,* XIII (October), 518–31.

Moore, W. Robert (1955): "Escalante: Utah's River of Arches." *National Geographic Magazine,* CVIII (September), 399–425.

—— (1912): "Cities of Stone in Utah's Canyonland." *National Geographic Magazine,* CXXI (May), 653–76.

Moorehead, Max L., ed. (1954): *Commerce of the Prairies,* by Josiah Gregg. Norman: University of Oklahoma Press.

Morgan, Dale L. (1947–9): "Introduction [to the] Exploration of the Colorado River in 1869 [and to] the Exploration of the Colorado River and the High Plateau of Utah in 1871–72." [Original journals and documents of the Powell Survey.] *Utah Historical Quarterly,* XV–XVII.

—— (1953): *Jedediah Smith and the Opening of the West.* Indianapolis and New York: Bobbs-Merrill.

Morris, Earl H. (1922): "An Unexplored Area of the Southwest." *Natural History,* XXII (November–December), 498–515.

Mortensen, A. R., ed. (1955): "A Journal of John A. Widtsoe, Colorado River Party, September 3–19, 1922, Preliminary to the Santa Fe Conference which Framed the Colorado River Compact." With a Foreword by G. Homer Duhram. *Utah Historical Quarterly,* XXIII (July), 195–231.

Museum of Northern Arizona, Glen Canyon Project (1959–61): [Reports of archeological site inventory, survey and investigation, and archeological history.] In *Bulletins,* Glen Canyon Series Nos. 1–3.

National Intelligencer (Washington, D.C.), June 15, 1854.

Nelson, Lowry (1952): *The Mormon Village: A Pattern and Technique of Land Settlement.* Salt Lake City: University of Utah Press.

Olson, Reuel Olson (1926): *The Colorado River Compact* . . . Thesis . . . Doctor of Philosophy . . . Harvard University . . . 1926. Los Angeles: published by author.

Palmer, William R. (1933): "Paiute Indian Homelands." *Utah Historical Quarterly,* VI (July), 88–102.

Parkhill, Forbes (1961): *The Last of the Indian Wars.* New York: Collier Books.

Peake, Ora Brooks (1937): *The Colorado Range Cattle Industry.* Glendale, Calif.: Arthur H. Clark Company.

Peale, A. C. (1877): "Geological Report on the Grand River District." *Ninth Annual Report of the United States Geological and Geographical Survey of the Territories . . . 1875.* Washington, D.C.: Government Printing Office. Pp. 33–101.

Peattie, Roderick, ed. (1948): *The Inverted Mountains: Canyons of the West.* Contributors, Weldon F. Heald, Edwin D. McKee, Harold S. Colton. New York: Vanguard.

Perkins, Cornelia Adams, Marian Gardner Nielson, and Lenora Butt (1957): *Saga of San Juan.* Salt Lake City: San Juan County Daughters of Utah Pioneers.

Pogue, Joseph E. (1911): "The Great Rainbow Natural Bridge of Southern Utah." *National Geographic Magazine,* XXII (November), 1048–56.

Porter, Eliot (1963): *The Place No One Knew: Glen Canyon on the Colorado.* San Francisco: Sierra Club.

Powell, J. W. (1874): *Report of the Explorations in 1873 of the Colorado of the West and Its Tributaries . . . Under the Direction of the Smithsonian Institution.* Washington, D.C.: Government Printing Office.

—— (1875a): *Exploration of the Colorado River of the West and Its Tributaries. Explored in 1869, 1870, 1871, and 1872, Under the Direction of the Secretary of the Smithsonian Institution.* Washington, D.C.: Government Printing Office.

—— (1875b): "An Overland Trip to the Grand Cañon." *Scribner's Monthly,* X (October), 659–78.

—— (1875c): "The Ancient Province of Tusayan." *Scribner's Monthly,* XI (December), 193–213.

—— (1876): *Report on the Geology of the Eastern Portion of the Uinta Mountains and a Region of Country Adjacent Thereto.* U.S. Geographical and Geological Survey of the Territories. Washington, D.C.: Government Printing Office.

—— (1879): *Report on the Arid Lands of the United States, with a More Detailed Account of the Lands of Utah.* Second edition. Washington, D.C.: Government Printing Office.

—— (1895): *Canyons of the Colorado.* Meadville, Penn.: Flood and Vincent.

Powell, J. W., and G. W. Ingalls (1874): "Report of . . . Special Commissioners to Enumerate Indians in Nevada and Adjacent Places." *Annual Report of the Commissioner of Indian Affairs . . . 1873.* Washington, D.C.: Government Printing Office.

Prudden, T. Mitchell (1903): "The Prehistoric Ruins of the San Juan Watershed in Utah, Arizona, Colorado, and New Mexico." *American Anthropologist,* New Series, V (April–June), 224–88.

—— (1906): *On the Great American Plateau, Wanderings Among Canyons and Buttes, in the Land of the Cliff-Dweller, and the Indian of To-day.* New York and London: G. P. Putnam's Sons.

Redd, Charles E. (1950): "Short Cut to the San Juan." *Brand Book Denver Posse of Westerners 1949.* Denver: Golden Press. Pp. 3–24.

Reed, Erik K., and Dale S. King (1950): *For the Dean, Essays in Anthropology in Honor of Byron Cummings on His Eighty-Ninth Birthday, September 20, 1950.* Santa Fe: Hohokam Museum Association, and Southwestern Monuments Association.

Reynolds, Thursey Jessen (1948): *Centennial Echos from Carbon County.* N.p.: Daughters of Utah Pioneers of Carbon County.

Richardson, Sullivan C. (1940a): "Hole-in-the-Rock." *Improvement Era,* XL (January), 18–21, 54–6.

—— (1940b): "Retracing the Trek Through the Hole-in-the-Rock." *Travel,* LXXV (June), 24–8, 47–8.

Rickard, T. A. (1932): *A History of American Mining.* New York and London: McGraw-Hill.

Roberts, B. H. (1930): *A Comprehensive History of the Church of Jesus Christ of Latter-day Saints, Century I.* 6 vols. Salt Lake City: Deseret News Press.

Roberts, Frank H. H., Jr. (1936): "Survey of Southwestern Archeology." *Annual Report of the Smithsonian Institution . . . 1935.* Washington, D.C.: Government Printing Office. Pp. 507–33.

Rockwell, Wilson (1956): *The Utes: A Forgotten People.* Denver: Sage Books.

Rocky Mountain News (Denver), March 16, 1880; April 14, May 23, 1882.

Roosevelt, Theodore (1913): "Across the Navajo Desert." *Outlook*, CV (October), 308–17.

Rouse, Irving (1962): "Summary of Southwestern Archeology Today." In *An Introduction to the Study of Southwestern Archeology with a Preliminary Account of Excavations at Pecos*, by Alfred Vincent Kidder. New Haven and London: Yale University Press.

Royce, Charles C., comp. (1889): *Indian Land Cessions in the United States.* With an Introduction by Cyrus Thomas. Bureau of American Ethnology Eighteenth Annual Report, Part 2. Washington, D.C.: Government Printing Office.

Ruess, Everett (1950): *On Desert Trails with Everett Ruess.* With Introduction by Hugh Lacy, and Foreword by Randall Henderson. Palm Desert, Calif.: Desert Magazine Press.

Rust, David D. (1901): "Boating on the Colorado." *Improvement Era*, IV (May), 507–12.

San Juan County, Utah (1884–1906): Miscellaneous Record B. MS, Recorder's Office, Monticello.

——— (1891): Mining Claims, C. MS, Recorder's Office, Monticello.

Schmeckebier, L. F. (1904): *Catalogue and Index of the Publications of the Hayden, King, Powell, and Wheeler Surveys . . .* U.S. Geological Survey Bulletin 222. Washington, D.C.: Government Printing Office.

Scorup, Stena (1944): *J. S. Scorup: A Utah Cattleman.* Privately printed.

Shankland, Robert (1951): *Steve Mather of the National Parks.* Introduction by Gilbert Grosvenor. New York: Alfred A. Knopf.

Silvey, Frank (n.d.): *History and Settlement of Northern San Juan County.* Foreword by Becky Walker. N.p.

Simpson, James H. (1850): *Journal of a Military Reconnaissance from Santa Fe, New Mexico, to the Navajo Country, Made with Troops under the Command of Brevet Lieutenant Colonel John M. Washington, Chief of the 9th Military Department, and Governor of New Mexico, in 1849.* U.S. 31st Cong., 1st Sess., Sen. Ex. Doc. 64. Washington, D.C.: Union Office.

——— (1876): *. . . Report of Explorations Across the Great Basin of the Territory of Utah . . . in 1859.* Washington, D.C.: Government Printing Office.

Sitgreaves, L. (1853): *Report of an Expedition Down the Zuni and Colorado Rivers . . .* U.S. 32nd Cong., 1st Sess., Sen. Ex. Doc. 59. Washington, D.C.: Robert Armstrong.

Smith, Dwight L. (1960): "The Engineer and the Canyon." *Utah Historical Quarterly*, XXVIII (July), 262–73.

Smith, J. Fred, Jr., and Lyman C. Huff, E. Neal Hinrichs, and Robert G. Luedke (1963): *Geology of the Capitol Reef Area, Wayne and Garfield Counties, Utah.* U.S. Geological Survey Professional Paper 363. Washington, D.C.: Government Printing Office.

Snow, Anne (1953): *Rainbow Views: A History of Wayne County . . .* Springville, Utah: Art City Publishing Company.

Snow, William J. (1929): "Utah Indians and Spanish Slave Trade." *Utah Historical Quarterly*, II (July), 67–73.

Spieker, E. M. (1931): *The Wasatch Plateau Coal Field, Utah.* U.S. Geological Survey Bulletin 819. Washington, D.C.: Government Printing Office.

Sprague, Marshall (1957): *Massacre: The Tragedy at White River.* Boston and Toronto: Little Brown.

Stanton, Robert Brewster (1890): "Through the Grand Cañon of the Colorado," *Scribner's Magazine*, VIII (November), 591–613.

——— (1892): "Availability of the Cañons of the Colorado River of the West for Railway Purposes." *American Society of Civil Engineers Transactions*, XXVI (April), 283–332.

——— (1893): "Engineering with a Camera in the Cañons of the Colorado." *Cosmopolitan*, XV (July), 292–303.

Stegner, Wallace (1942): *Mormon Country.* New York: Duell, Sloan & Pearce.

——— (1954): *Beyond the Hundredth Meridian: John Wesley Powell and the Second Opening of the West . . .* With an Introduction by Bernard DeVoto. Boston: Houghton Mifflin.

———, ed. (1955): *This Is Dinosaur: Echo Park Country and Its Magic Rivers.* New York: Alfred A. Knopf.

Steward, Julian H. (1938): *Basin-Plateau Aboriginal Sociopolitical Groups.* Bureau of American Ethnology Bulletin 120. Washington, D.C.: Government Printing Office.

Stokes, William Lee, ed. (1954): *Guidebook to the Geology of Utah: Number 9, Uranium Deposits and General Geology of Southeastern Utah.* Salt Lake City: Utah Geological Society.

Stone, Julius F. (1909): [Album of photographs taken during his Green River-Colorado River voyage in 1909. Coverage of the 552 black and white photographs is from Green River, Wyoming, to a point above Lee's Ferry in Arizona.] Reference Library, Grand Canyon National Park, Arizona.

——— (1932): *Canyon Country: The Romance of a Drop of Water and a Grain of Sand.* Foreword by Henry Fairfield Osborn. New York and London: G. P. Putnam's Sons.

Sutton, Wain, ed., and others (1949): *Utah: A Centennial History.* 3 vols. New York: Lewis Publishing Company.

Swanton, John R. (1953): *The Indian Tribes of North America.* Bureau of American Ethnology Bulletin 153. Washington, D.C.: Government Printing Office.

Taft, Robert (1938): *Photography and the American Scene: A Social History, 1839–1889.* New York: Macmillan.

——— (1953): *Artists and Illustrators of the Old West, 1850–1900.* New York and London: Charles Scribner's Sons.

Tanner, Faun McConkie (1937): *A History of Moab, Utah.* Moab: Times-Independent.

Taylor, Eli F. (1931): "Indian Reservations in Utah." *Utah Historical Quarterly*, IV (January), 29–31.

Taylor, Philip A. M. (1962): "Early Mormon Loyalty and the Leadership of Brigham Young." *Utah Historical Quarterly*, XXX (Spring), 103–32.

Thomas, George (1920): *The Development of Institutions Under Irrigation, with Special Reference to Early Utah Conditions.* New York: Macmillan.

——— (1948): *Early Irrigation in the Western States.* Salt Lake City: University of Utah.

Thompson, A. H. (1875): "Report on a Trip to the Mouth of the Dirty Devil [in 1872]." In J. W. Powell, *Exploration of the Colorado River of the West and Its Tributaries Explored in 1869, 1870, 1871, and 1872 . . .* Washington, D.C.: Government Printing Office. Pp. 133–45.

Thwaites, Reuben G., ed. (1905): *The Personal Narrative of James O. Pattie of Kentucky . . .* Early Western Travels, 1748–1846, XVIII. Cleveland: A. H. Clark.

Tribune (Salt Lake City), July 1, 1892–January 11, 1893; January 10, 1960.

Tyler, S. Lyman (1951a): "The Yuta Indians Before 1680." *Western Humanities Review*, V (Spring), 153–63.

———— (1951b): Before Escalante: An Early History of the Yuta Indians and the Area North of New Mexico. Unpublished Ph.D. dissertation, University of Utah, Salt Lake City.

———— (1952): "The Myth of the Lake of Copala and Land of Teguayo." *Utah Historical Quarterly*, XX (October), 313–29.

———— (1954): "The Spaniard and the Ute." *Utah Historical Quarterly*, XXII (October), 343–61.

Underhill, Ruth M. (1956): *The Navaho*. Norman: University of Oklahoma Press.

U.S. Bureau of Reclamation (1903 to date): . . . *Annual Report, 1902+*. Washington, D.C.: Government Printing Office.

———— (1946–7): *The Colorado River . . . A Comprehensive Report on the Development of the Water Resources of the Colorado River Basin for Navigation, Power Productions, and other Beneficial Uses in Arizona, California, Colorado, Nevada, New Mexico, Utah, and Wyoming . . . March, 1946* [to be Preceded by] . . . *Interim Report on the Status of Investigation Authorized to be Made by the Boulder Canyon Project Act and the Boulder Canyon Project Adjustment Act . . . July, 1947.* 2 parts. U.S. 80th Cong., 1st Sess., House Doc. 419. Washington, D.C.: Government Printing Office.

U.S. Geological Survey (1883 to date): *Mineral Resources of the United States, Calendar Year, 1882+*. Washington, D.C.: Government Printing Office.

U.S. National Park Service (1950): *A Survey of the Recreational Resources of the Colorado River Basin . . . , 1946*. Washington, D.C.: Government Printing Office.

United States vs. Utah (Supreme Court of the United States, Number 14, October Term, 1929) (1929): Testimony before Charles Warren, Special Master, September–December, 1929 at Washington, D.C., Denver, Los Angeles, and Salt Lake City. 32 vols. Typescript, Utah State Historical Society, Salt Lake City, 5536 pp.

United States vs. Utah (Supreme Court of the United States, Number 14, October Term, 1929) (1930): *Report of the Special Master . . .* Washington, D.C.: Judd & Detweiler.

United States vs. Utah (Supreme Court of the United States, Number 14, October Term, 1929) (1931): *Abstract in Narrative Form of the Testimony Taken Before the Special Master . . .* 2 vols. Washington, D.C.: Government Printing Office.

U.S. War Department, Bureau of Topographical Engineers (1858): *Map of Utah Territory Showing the Routes Connecting It with California and the East . . . From the Latest and Most Reliable Data.* Richmond, Virginia: Ritchie and Dunnavant.

———— (1860?): [Map of the] *Territory and Military Department of Utah Compiled in the Bureau of Topograph*l. *Eng*rs . . . *Chiefly for Military Purposes . . . 1860.* Washington, D.C.?

U.S. War Department, Corps of Topographical Engineers (1855–61): *Reports of Explorations and Surveys to Ascertain the Most Practicable and Economical Route for a Railroad from the Mississippi River to the Pacific Ocean, Made under Direction of the Secretary of War, in 1853–56, According to Acts of Congress of March 3, 1853, May 31, 1854, and August 5, 1854.* 12 vols. Washington, D.C.: Beverley Tucker and George W. Bowman.

U.S. Work Projects Administration (1940a): *Inventory of the County Archives of Utah: No. 4, Carbon County (Price).* Ogden: Historical Records Survey Project.

———— (1940b): *Origin of Utah Place Names.* Third edition. Salt Lake City: State Department of Public Instruction.

———— (1941): *Utah: A Guide to the State.* New York: Hastings House.

University of Utah, Glen Canyon Project (1958–63): [Reports on archeological surveys and excavations, biological studies, historical papers, and related matters, edited by the Department of Anthropology.] *In* Anthropological Papers, Glen Canyon Series, 1–20.

Utah Historical Quarterly, XXVI (July 1958); XXVIII (July 1960). Special issues on Utah's parks and scenic wonders, and on the Colorado, River of the West.

Van Valkenburgh, Richard (1941): *Diné Bikéyah*, edited by May Wilcox Adams and John C. McPhee. Window Rock, Arizona: Office of Indian Affairs.

Vélez de Escalante, Silvestre de (1854): "Diario y Derrotero de . . . Francisco Antanasio Domínguez y Silvestre Vélez de Escalante." *Documentos para la historia de Mexico*, Segunda Serie, I. Mexico: F. Escalante. Pp. 375–558.

Vinton, Stallo, ed. (1930): *Overland with Kit Carson: A Narrative of the Old Spanish Trail in '48*, by George Douglas Brewerton. New York: Coward-McCann.

Walker, Don D. (1962): "Longhorns Come to Utah." *Utah Historical Quarterly*, XXX (Spring), 135–47.

Warman, Cy (1898): *Frontier Stories.* New York: Charles Scribner's Sons.

———— (c. 1911): *Songs.* Boston: Rand Avery Co.

Warren, Gouverneur K. (1861): ". . . Memoir to Accompany the Map of the Territory of the United States from the Mississippi River to the Pacific Ocean, Giving a Brief Account of Each of the Exploring Expeditions Since A.D. 1800, with a Detailed Description of the Methods Adopted in Compiling the General Map . . . 1859." In *Reports of Explorations and Surveys to Ascertain the Most Practicable and Economical Route for a Railroad from the Mississippi River to the Pacific Ocean, Made Under the Direction of the Secretary of War, in 1853–56*, Vol. XI. Washington, D.C.: George W. Bowman.

Warrum, Noble, ed., and others (1919–20): *Utah Since Statehood: Historical and Biographical.* 4 vols. Chicago–Salt Lake City: S. J. Clarke.

Waters, Frank (1946): *The Colorado.* New York and Toronto: Rinehart.

———— (1963): *Book of the Hopi.* Drawings and source material recorded by Oswald White Bear Fredericks. New York: Viking Press.

Wentworth, Edward Norris (1948): *America's Sheep Trails: History, Personalities.* Ames: Iowa State College Press.

Wheat, Carl I. (1957–63): *1540–1861: Mapping the Transmississippi West.* Vol. I (1957): *The Spanish Entrada to the Louisiana Purchase, 1540–1804*; Vol. II (1958): *From Lewis and Clark to Frémont, 1804–1845*; Vol. III (1959): *From the Mexican War to the Boundary Surveys, 1846–1854*; Vol. IV (1960): *From the Pacific Railroad Surveys to the Onset of the Civil War, 1855–1860*; Vol. V (1963): *From the Civil War to the Geological Survey.* 5 vols., Vol. V in 2 parts. San Francisco: Institute of Historical Cartography.

Wheeler, George M. (1875): *Report upon United States Geographical Surveys West of the One Hundredth Meridian . . . Geology.* Washington, D.C.: Government Printing Office.

———— (1889): *Report upon United States Geographical Surveys West of the One Hundredth Meridian . . . Vol. I: Geographical Report . . .* Washington, D.C.: Government Printing Office.

Whipple, A. W. (1855): "Report of Explorations for a Railway Route, Near the 35th Parallel of North Latitude, From the

Mississippi River to the Pacific Ocean." In *Reports of Explorations and Surveys to Ascertain the Most Practical and Economical Route for a Railroad from the Mississippi to the Pacific Ocean*, Vol. III. Washington, D.C.: Beverley Tucker, Printer.

Whitney, Orson F. (1892–1904): *History of Utah . . .* 4 vols. Salt Lake City: George Q. Cannon.

Wilkins, James H., ed. (1913): *The Great Diamond Hoax and Other Stirring Incidents in the Life of Asbury Harpending*. San Francisco: James H. Barry Company; 1913. Another edition, with a Foreword by Glen Dawson, Norman: University of Oklahoma Press; 1958.

Wilkins, Thurman (1958): *Clarence King: A Biography*. New York: Macmillan.

Woodbury, Angus M. (1950): *A History of Southern Utah and Its National Parks*. Second edition. Salt Lake City: Utah State Historical Society; 1950. Originally published in Vol. XII, *Utah Historical Quarterly* (1944).

—— (1960): "The Colorado River: The Physical and Biological Setting." *Utah Historical Quarterly*, XXVIII (July), 199–208.

Woodbury, Angus M., and others (1959): *Ecological Studies of the Flora and Fauna in Glen Canyon*. University of Utah Anthropological Papers No. 40, Glen Canyon Series No. 7.

Woodruff, E. G. (1912): *Geology of the San Juan Oil Field*, U.S. Geological Survey Bulletin 471. Washington, D.C.: Government Printing Office. Pp. 76–104.

Woodward, Arthur (1946): *A Brief History of Navajo Silversmithing*. With Field Notes by Richard Van Valkenburgh. Museum of Northern Arizona Bulletin No. 14. Second edition, Flagstaff: Northern Arizona Society of Science and Art.

Woolley, Ralf R. (1930): *The Green River and Its Utilization*. U.S. Geological Survey Water-Supply Paper 618. Washington, D.C.: Government Printing Office.

Wormington, H. M. (1955): *A Reappraisal of the Fremont Culture*. Denver Museum of Natural History Proceedings Number 1 (Denver).

—— (1956): *Prehistoric Indians of the Southwest*. Third edition. Denver: Denver Museum of National History.

Yost, Billie Williams (1958): *Bread Upon the Sands*. Foreword by Merle Armitage. Caldwell, Idaho: Caxton Printers.

Young, Stuart M. (1959): "Statement . . . Concerning the Discovery of Rainbow Bridge." Cummings Publication Council, *Bulletin 1* (Tucson), 14.

Index

BLACK AND WHITE ILLUSTRATIONS ARE INDEXED BY SUBJECT AND ARE INDICATED BY AN ASTERISK. A LISTING OF COLOR PLATES APPEARS AT THE FRONT OF THE VOLUME.

Abajo Mountains, 20, 26; description of, 28; gold in, 133
*Abajo Mountains, 80
Agathla Peak, 32
*Anasazi Canyon, slick-rock trail, 13
Anasazi culture, description of, 86, 88
Andrus, Captain James, pursuit of Navajo Indians, 92, 94
Aneth oil field, 144
*Angel Arch, Needles country, 76–7
Animal life, 84
Aquarius Plateau, 19; description of, 149; features first sketched, 71; see also Boulder Mountain
Arch Canyon, 31
Arches National Monument, 24; description of, 26
*Arches National Monument, Court House Towers section, 30
*Arches National Monument, Landscape Arch, 41
Arid lands, Powell's report on, 71
Arizona Strip, 19
Armijo, Antonio, expedition of, 48
Armstrong Canyon, 31
Artists and photographers, of Great Surveys, 149, 150
Averett, Elijah, killed, 94
Aztec Creek, 32
*Aztec Creek in Forbidding Canyon, 115

Baker, Charles, 121
*Baker Ranch, Hall's Creek, 81
Beale, E. F., route survey, 56
Beaman, E. O., photographer for Powell Survey, 71
Bear's Ears, description of, 28
Bear's Ears Plateau, see Elk Ridge
Beckwith, E. G., with J. W. Gunnison, 56
Begashibito Wash, 32
Benton, Thomas Hart, 56
Bernheimer, Charles L., expeditions and writings, 164
Berry family, killed, 92
Betatakin, 32, 86; discovery of, 154

*Big Ruin, Salt Creek, Needles country, 83
Billings, Alfred N., 79
*Bishop, F. M., map by, 69
Black Hawk War, 92–5
Black Mesa, 32
Black Rim, 23
Blanding, founding of, 114
Blue Mountains, see Abajo Mountains
Blue Notch, 31
Bluff, 40; founding of, 107
Bluff Pool, 114
Book Cliffs, 39; description of, 24
*Book Cliffs, 54
Boot Mesa, 32
Boston Bar, 144
Boulder Canyon Project Act, 146
Boulder Mountain, 19, 20; view from, 1866, 94–5
Bowdie Canyon, 39
Bowknot, The, 39
Bridge Creek, 32
Bromide Basin, 128
Brown, Frank M., 131
Brown, Lewis P., 125
Bryce, Ebenezer, 116
Bryce Canyon, description of, 94–5
Bryce Canyon National Park, 16, 19, 158
Buckskin Gulch, 19
Bullfrog Creek, 40
Butler, Jack, prospector, 128
Butler Wash, 26, 39

*Caineville, Utah, 99
California Bar, 126, 144
California gold rush, 56, 120
Camp Stone, gold dredge assembled at, 141
Canyon country, boundaries, 3, 23; general description, 3–40
Canyon de Chelly, visited by Simpson, 56
Canyon de Chelly National Monument, 160
*Capitol Gorge, columns at head of, 87
Capitol Reef National Monument, 20, 158
Caravan trade, between New Mexico and California, 50
Carbon County, organization of, 144

Carlisle, Harold and Edmund, 114
Carpenter, William, 144
Carrizo Mountains, 28, 31; gold in, 133
Cassidy, Butch, 116
Castle Creek, 31
Castle Gate, 24
Castle Valley, 20, 26
Cataract Canyon, 15, 28; description of, 39; named by Powell, 66
*Cataract Canyon, 67
*Cataract Canyon, "Big Drop," 70
*Cataract Canyon, near the head of, 47
Cathedral Valley, 20
Cattlemen, discoveries of, 152
Cattle raising, 114, 116
Cedar Canyon, 31
Cerro Azul, Spanish name for Navajo Mountain, 120
Chaco Canyon, visited by Simpson, 56
Chaol Canyon, 32
Charles H. Spencer, 142
*Charles H. Spencer, at Lee's Ferry, 146
*Chesler Park, Needles country, 28–9
Chinle Creek, 40
Chinle Valley, 31
Chinle Wash, 32, 40
Chittenden, G. B., of Hayden Survey, 72
Christmas Canyon Dome, see Upheaval Dome
Church of Jesus Christ of Latter-day Saints, see Mormons
Circle Cliffs, 20
*Circle Cliffs, The Diadem, 122–3
Clay Hill Crossing, 40, 118–19
*Clay Hill Crossing, 133
Clay Hill Pass, Hole-in-the-Rock trail, 107
Clay Hills, 31
Climate, 81–2
Coal mining, 144
Cockscomb, 19
Collett, Reuben, 104
Colorado gold rush, 120–1
Colorado National Monument, 160
Colorado Plateau, description of, 15
Colorado River, 15; naming of, 16; passage

through canyon country, 34; Powell's voyages through, 65–71
Colorado River Compact, 146
Comb Ridge, 31, 40, 107
Comb Wash, 40
Confluence of Green and Colorado rivers, 39; determined by Macomb, 60
Copper Canyon, 31; mines in, 124
Copper mining, 144
Coronado, 43
Corps of Topographical Engineers, see Topographical Engineers
Cowles, Henry N., 145
Cross Canyon, 39
Crossing of the Fathers, 40; Domínguez and Escalante at, 44; Hamblin at, 90; inscriptions at, 50; Navajo Indians escape across, 92; route used during Mexican era, 48
*Crossing of the Fathers, inscriptions at, 45
Culmer, H. L. A., artist, 153
*Culmer, H. L. A., 158
Cummings, Byron, explorations and writings, 153–4, 158
Cummings Mesa, 32, 40
*Cummings Mesa, 14

Dance Hall Rock, 106
*Dance Hall Rock, 103
Dandy Crossing, 134; named by Cass Hite, 124
*Dandy Crossing, ferry at, 161
Dandy Crossing Bar, 126
Dark Canyon, 28, 39
*Dark Canyon Rapids, Cataract Canyon, 130
Davis, Jefferson, authorizes search for routes, 56
Dead Horse Point, 34, 116; description of, 26
*Dead Horse Point, view of the Colorado from, 36–7
Decker, Elizabeth, 107, 150
Dellenbaugh, Frederick S., 149; writings, 165
Denver, Colorado Canyon, and Pacific Railroad Company, 131
*Denver, Colorado Canyon, and Pacific Railroad Company, inscriptions left by surveyors at Mystery Canyon, 133
Denver & Rio Grande Western Railroad, 26, 112, 134, 164; crosses Green River at Spanish Trail, 56
Desert culture, 86
Diamond hoax, 121
Digger Indians, see Paiute Indians
Dirty Devil River, 20, 23, 39; drainage described, 71; named by Powell, 66
*Dirty Devil enters the Colorado, 72–3
Dixie, in southern Utah, 89
Dolores River, 34
Domínguez, Francisco Atanasio, exploration by, 43–5
Domínguez and Escalante, achievements of, 45–6
Domínguez and Escalante route, plotted by Philip Harry, 59, 64
Douglass, W. B., 154
*Druid Arch, 11

Dunn, William, killed by Indians, 66
Dutton, C. E., character of reports, 149–50; description of Aquarius Plateau, 149; quote, 19; reports on High Plateaus and Grand Canyon, 71
*Dutton, Clarence E., 152
Dyar, W. W., 152

East Kaibab Monocline, 19
Echo Cliffs, 32, 40
Eddy, Clyde, voyage, 142
*Eddy expedition, inscriptions in Cataract Canyon, 159
Egloffstein, F. W., 149; maps for Macomb and Ives, 64
El Capitan, see Agathla Peak
Elk Mountain Mission, 79, 85, 88
Elk Ridge, 26, 39; description of, 28
Emory, W. H., 55
Escalante, Francisco Vélez de, 149; exploration by 43–5
Escalante Mountain, 19; see also Boulder Mountain
Escalante River, 20, 40; drainage described, 71
*Escalante River, slick-rock wilderness, 105

*Factory Butte, 50
Fennemore, James, photographer for Powell Survey, 71
Fewkes, Jesse Walter, 154
Fifty-Mile Mountain, 19; see also Kaiparowits Plateau
*Fifty-Mile Mountain, Soda Cabin at, 104
"fins," 15
Fisher Towers, 26
Forbidding Canyon, 32
Fort Moqui, prehistoric ruins at Hite, 125
*Fort Moqui, Glen Canyon, 74
Forty Mile Spring, rendezvous point, 106
Four Corners area, 28, 119
Frémont, John C., explorations by, 55; route survey, 56
Fremont culture, 86, 88
Fremont River, 20, 23
*Fremont River, at Hanksville, 17
Fur trade, 50–3
Fur traders, geographical contributions, 53; routes of, 48–53

Gabel Mining District, 142
Galloway, Nathaniel, 164
Gannett, Henry, of Hayden Survey, 72
Gilbert, Grove K., report on Henry Mountains, 71; theory of gold in Henry Mountains, 126; on Wheeler Survey, 71
*Gilbert, Grove K., 23
Gilpin, William, 121
Glen Canyon, gold dredge in, 138, 141; gold rush, 124–8, 134–5; named by Powell, 39, 66
*Glen Canyon and Grand Bench, 96–7
*Glen Canyon of the Colorado, 126–7
Glen Canyon Dam, 3, 39, 40

*Glen Canyon Tributary, 61
Goblin Valley, 15, 23
*Goblin Valley, 157
Gold dredge, in Glen Canyon, 138, 141
Gold rush, in California, 56, 120; in Colorado, 120–1; in Glen Canyon, 124–8, 134–5; in San Juan River, 133–4, 142
*Gold rush to canyon country, map of, 1892, 132
Good Hope Bar, 126, 144; water wheels at, 135
Goodridge, E. L., 144
Gooseneck, The, of the Colorado, 34
Goosenecks, of the San Juan, 40
*Goosenecks of the San Juan River, 108–9
Government exploration, 8
Grand Bench, 40
Grand Canyon, Spanish discovery of, 44
Grand Canyon National Park, 160
Grand Gulch Plateau, 31
Grand Mesa, 24
Grand View Point, 26
*Grand View Point toward the Abajo Mountains, 57
Gray Canyon, 39
Gray's Pasture, 26
Great Basin, Spanish exploration of, 44; explored and named by Frémont, 55
Green River, 15, 23; named San Buenaventura by Spaniards, 46; passage through canyon country, 39
*Green River joins the Colorado, 35
Green River, town of, 39, 134
Green River Desert, 23
Gregory, Herbert E., 16, 31, 158
*Gregory, Herbert E., 34
Gretchen Bar, 144
Grey, Zane, Rainbow Bridge visited by, writings of, 160
Grey Mesa, 31; on Hole-in-the-Rock trail, 106
Gunnison, John W., route survey, 56
*Gunsight Pass, 10
Gypsum Canyon, 28, 39
*Gypsum Canyon, mouth of, 38
Gypsum Creek, 31

Hall, Charles, 111; ferryboat assembled by, 106
*Hall, Charles, 112
Hall, Joseph T., 145
Hall's Creek, 40
Hall's Crossing, 40; description of, 111, 112; route to, 111
Hamblin, Jacob, 89–92, 95, 98, 149; supplies Powell expedition, 68
Hanksville, 20, 23, 116
Happy Canyon, 23
Harry, Philip, plots Domínguez and Escalante route, 59, 64
Hatch Point Mesa, 34
*Hawkeye Bridge, Navajo Mountain, 33
Hayden Survey, 65, 72, 149–50, results of, 74, 76
Heap, Gwinn Harris, 56

Henry, Joseph, Henry Mountains named after, 68
Henry Mountains, 20, 40, 72; described, 1866, 95; features first sketched, 71; Gilbert's report on, 71; gold discovered in, 128; named by Powell, 68
Henry Mountains Mining District, 125
*Hidden Passage, Glen Canyon, 75
High Plateaus, description of, 16–24; Dutton's report on, 71
Hillers, J. K., photographer for Powell Survey, 71
Hite, Ben R., 133
Hite, Cass, and Henry Mountains Mining District, 125; biographical sketch, 124; finds copper, 144; discovers gold in Glen Canyon, 125; mining at Ticaboo, 131; names mine after Merrick and Mitchell, 123; sees natural bridges, 152
*Hite, Cass, 125
Hite, Homer J., 133
Hite, John, 133, 141
Hite, town of, 144; post office at, 134; settlement, 40; in 1883, 124–5
*Hite, pioneer cabin at, 129
*Hite settlement in Glen Canyon, 136–7
Hobbs, George, 121
Hole-in-the-Rock, description of, 106; expedition, 103–7; Stanton's crews at, 141; trading post at, 145
*Hole-in-the-Rock, 100
Hole-in-the-Rock Crossing, 40
Holmes, E. F., 153
Holmes, W. H., 150; artist for Powell Survey, 71; of Hayden Survey, 72
Hopi Indians, Mormon mission to, 89–92
Hoskaninni Company, 152; gold dredge operation in Glen Canyon, 138, 141
*Hoskaninni Company gold dredge, 138
*Hoskaninni Company gold dredge, remains of, 139
Hoskininni, Navajo chief, 124
Hoskininni Mesa, 31
*Hoskininni Mesa, view from, 90–1
Hosteen Pish-la-ki, 124; see also Hite, Cass
Hovenweep National Monument, 31, 160; description of ruins, 1855, 85–6; ruins in, 88
*Hovenweep National Monument, prehistoric ruins, 5
Howell, Edwin E., of Wheeler Survey, 71
Howland, O. G., and Seneca, killed by Indians, 66
Hudson, Spud, 114
Humboldt, Alexander von, works of, 45–6
*Humboldt, Alexander von, "Carte Générale," 1811, 49
Humboldt River, named by Frémont, 55
Huntington, W. D., 85

Indian Creek, 26, 34
Inscription House, 32, 86; discovery of, 154
Island Mining District, 142
"Island mountains," see Laccolithic mountains
Ives, Joseph C., travels up the Colorado, 59

Jackson, W. H., 149; of Hayden Survey, 72
Janin, Henry, 121
*Jeeping in the canyon country, 162–3
Jenson, Andrew, Hole-in-the-Rock visited by, 106
Johnson, Ezekiel (Zeke), 160
*Johnson, Ezekiel (Zeke), 160
Jones, Kumen, 119
Julien, Denis, inscriptions of, 53
*Julien, D., inscription, 53
Junction Butte, 26

Kaibito Creek, 32
Kaibito Plateau, 32
Kaiparowits Plateau, 19, 40; features first sketched, 71
Kane Springs Canyon, 34
Kansas and New Mexico Land and Cattle Company, 114
Kayenta, 32; Wetherill trading post at, 160
Kayenta culture, 86, 88
Keam, Thomas V., 144
Keet Seel, 32, 86, 154
*Kelly, Charles, 163
Kern, Richard, 149
Kigalia, Navajo Chief, 119
King, Clarence, exposes diamond hoax, 121; survey of, 65
Kingdom of God, 101
*Kishpaugh Butte, San Rafael Swell, 58
*Kitchen House, Kitchen Canyon, 80
Klethla Valley, 32
Klondike Bar, 144
*Klondike Bar, trail to, 129
Kolb, Emery and Ellsworth, 141; voyage, 165
*Kolb brothers inscription in Cataract Canyon, 161

Labyrinth Canyon, 39
Laccolithic mountains, 16; see also Henry, Abajo, La Sal, Carrizo mountains, Navajo Mountain, and Ute Mountain
Lacey, Widow, 114
Laguna Creek, 32
Lake Canyon, 31
Lake Pagahrit, 107
Lake Powell, 39; floods mining field, 144; greatest width, 40
*Lake Powell and Gunsight Butte, 166–7
Land of Standing Rocks, 15, 23, 28
*Land of Standing Rocks, 70
Land's End Plateau, description of, 23
Larson, Olivia, gives birth in desert, 107
La Rue, E. C., 146, 165
La Sal Mountains, 20, 26; gold in, 133
*Last Chance Canyon, 42
Last Chance Creek, 40
Leche-e Rock, 32
Lee, John D., 95, 97–8; opens trade with Navajo Indians, 118
Lee's Ferry, 19, 32, 40; Domínguez and Escalante at, 44; history of, 95, 97–8; mining at, 142; post office at, 135
*Lee's Ferry in operation, 1910, 99
Lime Creek amphitheater, 40

Little-Hole-in-the-Rock, 106
"Little Rockies," 20; see also Henry Mountains
*Little Rockies, Mount Ellsworth and Mount Holmes and Glen Canyon, 18–19
Lockhart Canyon, 34
Lodore Canyon, 39
Long, Horace J., 152
Loper, Bert, 141, 164
Lyman, Platte D., 106

Macomb, John N., description of canyons, 48; expedition of 1859, 60
Macomb expedition, results of, 64
Marble Canyon, 34
Marsh Pass, 32
Mason, Charles, 153
Maze, The, 23
McElmo Creek, 31
McEwan, John, 79
McIntyre, Robert, killed, 92
Meeker massacre, 145
Merrick, James, killed, 119; prospector, 121
Merrick-Mitchell mine, 123; prospectors look for, 123–4
Mesa Verde, 31; ruins found at, 145
Mesa Verde culture, 86, 88
Mesa Verde National Park, 88, 153
Mexican Bend, 48
Mexican Hat, 31, 40; oil at, 144
Mexican Seep, 48
Miera, Bernardo de, cartographer for Domínguez-Escalante expedition, 45–6; names Navajo Mountain "Cerro Azul," 120
Millard Canyon, 23, 39
Miller, George M., 124
*Miller, G., inscription, 125
Miners, first to explore canyons, 150, 152
Mining, general, 8
Mitchell, Ernest, killed, 119; prospector, 121
Moab, 26, 34; mining near, 145
Moenkopi Wash, 32
Monett, E. R., 164
Monitor Mesa, 32
Montezuma Canyon, 31
Montezuma Creek, proposed settlement at, 104
Monticello, 114
Monumental Mining District, 142
Monument Upwarp, 40; description of, 31
Monument Valley, 31, 32; described by Newberry, 60, 64; Merrick and Mitchell killed in, 123; prospecting in, 123–4
*Monument Valley, 6–7
*Monument Valley, touring in a Maxwell, 159
Moqui Canyon, 31
Moran, Thomas, 149–50; artist for Powell Survey, 71
Mormons, colonization, 8, 101–3; expansion, 89–92; missions, 101
Mormon village, 101, 150
Moss Backs, 31
Mound Canyon, named by Powell, 66
Mountain Meadows massacre, 97

Mountain men, 50, 53
Muddy River, 20
Muley Twist Canyon, 111
*Muley Twist Canyon, 110
Music Temple, visited by Powell, 66
Mystery Canyon, Stanton Survey at, 131

Nakai Canyon, 31
Nakai Dome, 31
Nakai Mesa, 31
Names, left by U. S. Government explorers, 4; of Indian origin, 4; imaginative and picturesque, 7–8; of Mormon pioneer origin, 4; of outlaw origin, 7; of religious origin, 7; of Spanish origin, 4; typical of the West, 7
Narrow Canyon, 39
*Narrow Canyon and Henry Mountains, 62
Nasja-begay, Paiute guide, 154
National Reclamation Act, 165
Natural bridges, publicized, 152–4
Natural Bridges National Monument, 31, 152; creation of, 153
*Natural Bridges National Monument, Sipapu Natural Bridge, 156
Navajo Canyon, 32
Navajo Indians, life of, 145; Mormon war with, 92–5; move into canyon country and relations with other Indians, 118–19; silver work, 121; wars with the United States, 118
*Navajo Indians near Goulding's Trading Post, 52
Navajo Mountain, 20, 31, 40, 120; description of, 32
Navajo National Monument, 32; creation of, 154; ruins in, 86
Navajo Reservation, 31
Needles, The, 15, 39; description of, 28; described by Bradley, 65; described by Newberry, 60
Nevills, Norman D., 165
*Nevills, Norman D., 160
Newberry, J. S., of Macomb expedition, 60; descriptions of, 149
New Mexico, naming of, 43
No Man's Mesa, 31
North Wash, 39
Notch, The, 28

O'Donel, Pat, 114
Oil fields, 144
Ojo Verde, visited by Macomb, 60
Oljeto, Wetherill trading post at, 145
Oljeto Mesa, 32
*Oljeto Trading Post, 157
Oljeto Wash, 31
Olympia Bar, 144; water wheels at, 135
Oñate, Juan de, 43
Orange Cliffs, 23
Ouray and Uintah Indian Reservation, 24
Outlaws, 8, 116

Paiute Indians, 88; sold as slaves, 48; on San Juan River, 118–19

Paria River, 19; visited by Domínguez and Escalante, 44; drainage described, 71
Paunsaugunt Plateau, 16
Peale, A. C., of Hayden Survey, 72
People, The, see Navajo Indians
Petroleum, 144
Pipe Spring National Monument, 160
Pish-la-ki, Hosteen, 124; see also Hite, Cass
Pish-la-ki mine, see Merrick-Mitchell mine
Piute Creek, 31, 32
*Piute Creek, prehistoric petroglyphs, 168
Piute Farms, 40
Piute Mesa, 31
*Piute Mesa, Pottery Pueblo, 62
Placer mining, methods, 134–5
Plant life, 82, 84
Polk-Posey War, see Ute War
Polygamy, 145
Portal, The, 34
Pot-se-nip Mountains, see Henry Mountains
Powell, J. W., canyon voyages and survey of, 65–71; and Hamblin, make peace with Navajo Indians, 95; irrigation survey and reclamation, 145; report on arid lands, 76; reports on Colorado River, Uinta Mountains, and arid lands, 71; scientific work of, 76
*Powell, J. W., inscription of second expedition, 74
Powell Survey, 65–71, 149; results of, 74, 76
*Prehistoric irrigation ditch, Cha Creek, 82
Prehistoric ruins, speculation about, first descriptions, 86
Preuss, Charles, cartographer for Frémont, 55
Price River, 16, 20
Promontory, Utah, last spike driven, 56
Prospectors, open the West, 120
Prudden, T. Mitchell, 158
Pueblo, prehistoric people, 86
Pueblo Revolt, 43

Radium mining, 144
Railroads, to be built through canyons, 131; coming of, 114
Rainbow Bridge, 32; discovery of, 154; tourist attraction, 160
*Rainbow Bridge, 150–1
*Rainbow Bridge and Navajo Mountain, 148
Rainbow Bridge National Monument, creation of, 154
Rainbow Plateau, 32
Reclamation, 8, 145–6
Recreational use of canyon country, 164
Red Canyon, 31, 39
Red House Cliffs, 31
Red Lake Canyon, 39
Red Rim, 23, 39; see also Orange Cliffs
Red Rock Plateau, see San Juan Triangle
Richardson Amphitheater, 26
Richmond, William, 164
Rincon, 40
Rio de Nabajoó, Spanish name for San Juan River, 46
Rio Santa Teresa, see Paria River
*Ripgut Fence, Boulder, Utah, 98

Roan Plateau, see Book Cliffs
Robber's Roost, 23, 116
*Robber's Roost Headquarters, 119
Roosevelt, Theodore, visits Rainbow Bridge, 160
Roubidoux, Antoine, 53
Russell, Charles, S., 164
Rust, David E., 165
Rustlers, 116

Sage Plain, 31
Salt Creek, 26, 34
San Buenaventura River, looked for by Frémont, 55; Spanish name for Green River, 4, 46
San Juan Hill, Hole-in-the-Rock trail, 107
San Juan Mountains, 31
San Juan River, 31, 40; course determined by Macomb, 60; gold rush, 133–4, 142; passage through canyon country, 40
*San Juan River, junction with the Colorado, 9
San Juan Triangle, description of, 31
San Rafael Desert, see Green River Desert
San Rafael Reef, 20
*San Rafael Reef, 21
San Rafael River, 20, 23, 39
San Rafael Swell, description of, 20
Santa Fe Railroad, 112, 134
Schock Bar, 144
Schow, Andrew P., 104
Scorup, J. A. (Al), 116; at natural bridges, 152
Scorup-Somerville Cattle Company, 116
Segi Canyon, 32
Sheep Canyon, 39
Sheep raising, 114
Shivwits Indians, kill Powell's men, 66, 95
Shonto, 32
Shonto Canyon, 32
Shonto Wash, 32
Shurtz, Peter, 102, 104
Sierra Azul, myth of, 120
Simpson, James H., explorations in 1849, 56; exploration in 1859, 59
Sinbad, origin in Arabian Nights, 20
*Sinbad, San Rafael Swell, 22
Sitgreaves, Lorenzo, survey, 59
Skeleton Mesa, 32
Slave trade, 48
*Slickhorn Gulch, San Juan River, oil drilling equipment, 12
Soil, 84–5
Smith, George Albert, Jr., killed, 92
Smith, Silas S., 104, 106
Southern California Edison Company, maps canyons, 160
Southern Ute Indians, 145
Spanish explorations, 8, 43
Spanish Trail, 48–50; mapped with accuracy, 64
Spencer, Charles H., mining operations, 142
Spencer Camp, 142
*Spencer Camp, oxen-drawn freight wagons en route to, 143
Split Mountain Canyon, 39

*Spur, The, view from, 24–5
Standing Rock Basin, description of, 26
Stanton, Robert Brewster, 131; gold mining in Glen Canyon, 138, 141; railroad survey, 8
*Stanton, Robert Brewster, 135
Stanton Railroad Survey, 131, 133
Stillwater Canyon, 39
Stone, Julius, 141; voyage, 165
*Storm over the desert, 93
Straight Cliffs, 19
Summer, Jack, 131; in Glen Canyon, 128; with Powell, 68

Table Cliff Plateau, 19; see also Boulder Mountain
Tavaputs Plateau, 24; see also Book Cliffs
Thompson, A. H., cartographer for Powell Survey, 71
Thousand Lake Mountain, 20
Ticaboo, 144
Ticaboo Bar, 126
Topographical Engineers, contributions, 64; surveys, 55–9
Tower Butte, 32
Trachyte Creek, 39, 40
*Trachyte Ranch and Mount Hillers, 94
*Trails to Glen Canyon, prehistoric and historic, 117
Train Rock, 32
Trimble, K. W., 160

Uinta Basin, 24, 44
Uinta Mountains, 39
U.S. Geographical and Geological Survey of the Rocky Mountain Region, 68; see also Powell Survey
U.S. Geographical Survey West of the One Hundredth Meridian, see Wheeler Survey

U.S. Geological and Geographical Survey of the Territories, see Hayden Survey
U.S. Geological Survey, maps canyons, 160
Upheaval Dome, description of, 26
*Upheaval Dome, 27
Upper Colorado River Storage Act, 145
Uranium mining, 144
Utah Lake, 44
Utah's Grand Canyon, description of, 34
Utah State Route 95, 3
Utah War, 59
Ute Ford, 90; see also Crossing of the Fathers
Ute Indians, 88; Four Corners area, 118–19; relations with Spanish, 43
Ute Mountain, 28, 31
Ute War, 145

Valley of the Gods, 40
*Valley of the Gods, Lime Creek Basin, 63
Vanadium mining, 144
Vargas, Diego de, 43
Vélez de Escalante, Francisco, see Escalante, Francisco Vélez de
Verdure, 114
Vermilion Cliffs, 19
Virgin River culture, 86, 88

Walker War, 88
Warman, Cy, 164
Warm Creek, Spencer mining operations, 142
*Warm Creek, ruins of Spencer headquarters at, 147
Warren, G. K., map of 1857, 59
Wasatch Plateau, 20
Water courses, description of, 15
Waterpocket Fold, 20, 40, 111, 112; features sketched, 71
West Canyon, 40
Wetherill, John, 153; at Mesa Verde, 145; and Louisa Wade, 160; and Richard, 153

*Wetherill, John, 158
Weyss, John E., 149
Wheeler, George M., 71; survey of, 65
Wheeler Survey, 149; final report, 71; results of, 74, 76
Whipple, A. M., 59
Whirlpool Canyon, 39
White, James, 121
White Canyon, 39; description of, 31
White Canyon Mining District, 126
White Cliffs, 19
White Mesa, description of, 32
*White Mesa, Cathedral Arch, 51
*White Mesa, Inaccessible Ruin, 155
*White Mesa, monolith, 2
*White Mesa, mushroom, 113
*White Mesa, Natural Arch, 78
White Rim, 23, 26, 39
White Rocks, trading post at, 53
Whitmore, J. M., killed, 92
Widtsoe, John A., description by, 165
Wild Bunch, 116
Wilderness, man's reaction to, 8, 12, 149–65
Williams, W. F., 154
Williams Mining District, 142

Young, Brigham, 101, 103
Young, J. S., 149
Young, Stuart M., 158

Zaguaganas, Rio de las, Spanish name for Colorado River, 46
Zahn, Hector and Otto, 142
*Zahn, Otto J., 140
Zahn Mining Company, 142
Zahn's Camp, 142
*Zahn's Camp, steam boiler at, 140
Zilnez Mesa, 31
Zion National Park, 158

A Note on the Types

THE TEXT of this book has been set on the Monotype in a typeface named *Bembo*. The roman is a copy of a letter cut by Francesco Griffo of Bologna for the celebrated Venetian printer Aldus Manutius in 1495. It was first used to print a small tract, *De Aetna*, written by Pietro Bembo (later Cardinal and secretary to Pope Leo X). Although Aldus was responsible for the first italic types (also cut by Griffo) in 1501, the companion italic for the present Bembo was based upon chancery types used by Giovanniantonio Tagliente, a great writing master who practiced in Venice during the 1520's. The Monotype Bembo was cut under the direction of Stanley Morison, and first issued in 1929.

THE DISPLAY type in this book has been set on the Monotype in a face named *Bell*. Monotype Bell is a facsimile version of the letter cut in 1788 by Richard Austin for John Bell's British Letter Foundry. Some fonts of Bell, the first British modern face, were purchased in 1864 by Henry O. Houghton for his Riverside Press in Cambridge, Massachusetts, and these types were listed as "English Copperface" in the 1887 specimen book of the Press. Some books and pamphlets were printed from these types for Martin Brimmer of Boston, but afterwards the types lay dormant for many years until they were "rediscovered" by Bruce Rogers in 1898 and, under the name Brimmer, used in many distinguished books designed by him. Some fonts of Bell were acquired in 1903 by Daniel Berkeley Updike for his Merrymount Press and used there under the name Mountjoye. Since that time, researches by Stanley Morison have shown that Brimmer, Mountjoye, and Bell are one and the same. This monotype cutting was done in 1931 from punches now in the Stephenson, Blake foundry.